D1594839

Learn Chinese

A Comprehensive Guide to Learning Chinese for Beginners, Including Grammar, Short Stories and Popular Phrases

Contents

Part 1: Chinese

Learn Mandarin Chinese for Beginners: A Simple Guide That Will Help You on Your Language Learning Journey

Introduction

Welcome to *Chinese: Learn Mandarin Chinese for Beginners: A Simple Guide That Will Help You on Your Language Learning Journey*! This will be your first step toward success during the process of Chinese study.

There are only 10 chapters in this book. However, after learning these chapters, a solid foundation will be established both in pronunciation and basic knowledge of the Chinese language. In addition, you will also master some words and expressions for daily communication.

If you want to impress a future audience with your "perfect" spoken Chinese, a lot of time and effort while studying this book will need to be invested. Not only will you need to master the 3 basic elements of pronunciation (i.e. initials, vowels, and most importantly, tones), but you will also have to understand the sound change in certain circumstances.

Perhaps you may have heard people complaining that Chinese is difficult to learn. However, after studying this book, you will find that it is indeed not true. After finishing this book, you will easily master some Chinese expressions. A solid foundation is thus laid for advanced study in the future.

In addition to Chinese pronunciation, this book will also familiarize you with dialogue commonly used in daily communication.

Examples include greeting, how to introduce yourself and other people, educational background, work, family, and friends, likes and dislikes, food and drink, and other common topics. You will have a sense of accomplishment after finishing these 10 chapters, because you will be able to speak quite a few idiomatic sentences which will enable you to have basic communications with native speakers. If you find that some translations in this book feel unnatural in English, we want you to note that we've used the literal method on purpose so that differences between the language systems can be stressed.
Chinese: Learn Mandarin Chinese for Beginners: A Simple Guide That Will Help You on Your Language Learning Journey is the key to entering the world of the Chinese language. We hope you find it fun and wish you success!

Chapter 1: Learning Chinese Tones

Among the components of a Chinese syllable, there is a tone besides the initial and the final. Generally speaking, one Chinese character corresponds to one syllable. A Chinese syllable can have no initials, but must have a final and a tone. Syllables with the same initials and finals but in different tones usually have different meanings.

Chinese has four main tones, as follows:

The main vocal characteristic of the first tone is high and flat. When it is articulated, the vocal cords are tightened up and the pitch is kept at a relatively higher level for a while. Let's see some examples so you can understand it better:

参加, cān jiā, to take part in/to join

今天, jīn tiān, today

沙发, shā fā, sofa

香蕉, xiāng jiāo, banana

司机, sī jī, driver

分钟, fēn zhōng, minute

应该, yīng gāi, should

西餐, xī cān, western food.

关系, guān xì, relationship/in relation to

春天, chūn tiān, spring

抒发, shū fā, to express

通知, tōng zhī, notice/to inform

The second tone is a rising tone. It rises from the middle to a higher level while the vocal cords are gradually tightened up. Let's see some examples so you can understand it better:

回答, huí dá, to answer

集合, jí hé, assemblage/to gather

明年, míng nián, next year.

篮球, lán qiú, basketball

年级, nián jí, grade

同学, tóng xué, classmate

厨房, chúfáng, kitchen

从前, cóng qián, in the past

留学, liú xué, to study abroad

邮局, yóu jú, post office

原来, yuán lái, turn out to be

儿童, ér tóng, small child

The third tone is a dipping tone. The pitch goes from middle to low, then to high. Let's see some examples so you can understand it better:

辅导, fǔ dǎo, to coach

可以, kě yǐ, should/sure

了解, liǎo jiě, to understand

手表, shǒu biǎo, watch

所以. suǒ yǐ, therefore/so

洗澡, xǐ zǎo, take a shower

小姐, xiǎo jiě, Ms.

语法, yǔ fǎ, grammar

也许, yě xǔ, maybe/perhaps

只好, zhǐ hǎo, have to

When the fourth tone is pronounced, the vocal cords are first tightened and then relaxed. The voice hence rapidly falls from the higher to the lower level. It is relatively easy to pronounce for most people. Let's see some examples so you can understand it better:

毕业, bì yè, to graduate

宿舍, sù shè, dormitory

大概, dà gài, probably

锻炼, duàn liàn, to exercise

运动, yùn dòng, sport

介绍, jiè shào, to introduce

画报, huà bào, pictorial

教授, jiào shòu, professor

庆祝, qìng zhù, to celebrate

继续, jì xù, continue

饭店, fàn diàn, restaurant

过去, guò qù, in the past/to come over

Intensive Practice

Now, let's practice with more vocabulary mixed by different tones.

1. First tone and second tone.

当然, dāng rán, of course

科学, kē xué, science

非常, fēi cháng, extremely/very

刚才, gāng cái, just now/a moment ago

欢迎, huān yíng, welcome

生词, shēng cí, new vocabulary

中文, zhōng wén, Chinese

私人, sī rén, personal/ private

家庭, jiātíng, home

青年, qīng nián, youth

将来, jiāng lái, future

要求, yāo qiú, requirement/to ask

房间, fáng jiān, room

国家, guó jiā, country

离开, lí kāi, to leave

明天, míng tiān, tomorrow

同屋, tóng wū, roommate

毛衣, máo yī, sweater

结婚, jié hūn, to get married

时间, shí jiān, time

邻居, lín jū, neighbor

昨天, zuó tiān, yesterday

提高, tí gāo, to improve

毛巾, máo jīn, towel

2. First tone and third tone.

方法, fāng fǎ, method

身体, shēn tǐ, body

听写, tīng xiě, dictation

英语, yīng yǔ, English

班长, bān zhǎng, monitor

东北, dōng běi, northeast

黑板, hēi bǎn, blackboard

风景, fēng jǐng, landscape

宾馆, bīn guǎn, hotel

中午, zhōng wǔ, noon

出版, chū bǎn, to publish

开始, kāi shǐ, to start

火车, huǒ chē, train

好吃, hǎo chī, delicious

紧张, jǐn zhāng, nervous

简单, jiǎn dān,simple

老师, lǎo shī, teacher

母亲, mǔ qīn, mother

首都, shǒu dū, capital

许多, xǔ duō, many

已经, yǐ jīng, already

语音, yǔ yīn, voice

3. First tone and fourth tone.

帮助, bāng zhù, to help,

车站, chē zhàn, station,

方便, fāng biàn, convenient

高兴, gāo xìng, happy

鸡蛋, jī dàn, egg

天气, tiān qì, weather

温度, wēn dù, temperature

相信, xiāng xìn, to believe

因为, yīn wéi, because

通过, tōng guò, to pass

干净, gàn jìng, clean

丰富, fēng fù, colorful

汽车, qì chē, automobile

教师, jiào shī, teacher

上班, shàng bān, to go to work

大约, dà yuē, roughly/probably

电梯, diàn tī, elevator/ lifter

放心, fàng xīn, to relax

健康, jiàn kāng, health

日期, rì qī, date

外教, wài jiào, foreign teacher

后天, hòu tiān, the day after tomorrow

对方, duì fāng, the other side

进修, jìn xiū, to get trained

4. Second tone and third tone.

词典, cí diǎn, dictionary

而且, ér qiě, and

牛奶, niú nǎi, milk

没有, méi yǒu, no

门口, mén kǒu, doorway

苹果, píng guǒ, apple

球场, qiú chǎng, field

游泳, yóu yǒng, swimming

人口, rén kǒu, population

从此, cóng cǐ, from then on

传统, chuán tǒng, tradition

厘米, lí mǐ, centimeter

解决, jiě jué, to solve

旅行, lǚ xing, to travel

起床, qǐ chuáng, to get up

请求, qǐng qiú, to ask/requirement

水平, shuǐ ping, level

小时, xiǎo shí, hour

选择, xuǎn zé, to choose/choice

以为, yǐ wéi, to think

语言, yǔ yán, language

主人, zhǔ rén, master/host

5. Second tone and fourth tone.

不错, bú cuò, not bad

迟到, chí dào, late

合适, hé shì, suitable

劳驾, láo jià, excuse me

邮票, yóu piào, stamp

服务, fú wù, service/to serve

年纪, nián jì, age

皮带, pí dài, belt

然后, rán hòu, then

节日, jié rì, festival

成绩, chéng jì, grade

伯父, bó fù, uncle

不行, búxíng, no way

联系, lián xì, to contact

认为, rèn wéi, to think

上学, shàng xué, to go to school

太阳, tài yáng, sun

预习, yù xí, to preview

季节, jìjié, season

电池, diàn chí, battery

绿茶, lǜ chá, green tea

气球, qì qiú, balloon

后年, hòu nián, the year after next year

外国, wài guó, foreign country

6. Third tone and fourth tone.

比较, bǐ jiào, to compare

感谢, gǎn xiè, to thank

好看, hǎo kàn, good looking

考试, kǎo shì, exam

礼物, lǐ wù, gift

满意, mǎn yì, satisfying

米饭, mǐ fàn, rice

讨论, tǎo lùn, to discuss

晚会, wǎn huì, banquet

早饭, zǎo fàn, breakfast

办法, bàn fǎ, method

剧场, jù chǎng, theater

记者, jì zhě, journalist

大小, dà xiǎo, size

刻苦, kè kǔ, hardworking

要紧, yào jǐn, important

政府, zhèng fǔ, government

课本, kè běn, textbook

道理, dào lǐ, principle

电子, diàn zǐ, electron / electronic

不久, bú jiǔ, soon after/ shortly

号码, hào mǎ, number

It's highly recommended to hear the tones demonstrated by a native speaker since it's hard to get an idea of what they sound like purely through text.

Additional Knowledge

Generally speaking, the tone of each syllable in Chinese is fixed. However, when two or more than two syllables are pronounced together, there is sometimes a tonal modulation which is called “Tone Sandhi". Here are some tips for you to pronounce much more accurately in accordance with Tone Sandhi. These might be too hard for beginners, so just read and try if you are interested.

1. When two adjacent syllables both carry third tones, the first syllable must be pronounced as the second tone. For example: **你好** (nǐ hǎo) must be pronounced as ní hǎo and **可以** (kě yǐ) must be pronounced as ké yǐ.

2. When a third tone syllable is followed by syllables of the other three tones, and most syllables are with a neutral tone, only the first half of the third tone is pronounced.

3. Some syllables in Chinese are pronounced both short and lightly. This is called the neutral tone. The neutral tone always appears after

another syllable or between other syllables. It cannot appear as the first syllable of a word or a sentence. In a disyllabic word with reduplicated syllables, the second syllable is usually read in the neutral tone. Apart from that, there is no simple or easy way to learn neutral tones. They must be learned, memorized, and mastered one by one.

4. The pitch of a neutral tone varies according to the tone of the syllable that comes before it. Normally, when it comes after a first, second, or fourth tone, its pitch is relatively low. Only when it comes after a third tone does its pitch become relatively higher.

5. There is a retroflex final "er" in the finals of Chinese. It is not used to combine with other initials, but forms a syllable on its own. For example, 儿(ér) is often used as a suffix. After a long time of liaison, its pronunciation is transformed in such a way that it is pronounced together with the syllable that comes before it as a single unit. This phenomenon is called retro-flexion.

6. When it is read independently or is at the end of a word, 一 is pronounced as yī; when it precedes a 1st, 2nd, or a 3rd tone, 一 is pronounced as yì ; when it precedes a 4th tone, 一 is pronounced as yí.

7. The tone of 不 does not change when it stands by itself or precedes a 1st, 2nd or a 3rd tone, pronounced as bù, but it is pronounced as bú when it precedes a 4th tone.

If you can master these, you will become an excellent Chinese speaker.

Warm up

Memorizing vocabulary is important to every learner, but accuracy is even more important. When you learn a character, you're expected to pronounce it correctly by using the right tone because different pronunciations could have entirely different meanings.

Once you have a basic grasp of vocabulary and pronunciation, you can move on to basic conversational phrases which are used in everyday Chinese speech. Starting with practicing basic conversational Chinese will allow you to get familiar with the language. Now let's practice; we will analyze the phrases afterwards.

你好（nǐ hǎo）。Hello/How are you?

早上好（zǎo shang hǎo）。Good morning.

下午好（xià wǔ hǎo）。Good afternoon.

晚上好（wǎn shang hǎo）。Good evening.

晚安（wǎn ān）。Good night.

你叫什么名字（nǐ jiào shén me míng zì）？What is your name?

是的（shì de）。Yes.

不是（bú shì）。No.

谢谢你（xiè xie nǐ）。Thank you.

不用谢（bú yòng xiè）。You're welcome./My pleasure.

对不起（duì bù qǐ）。Excuse me/sorry.

我不懂（wǒ bù dǒng）。I don't understand.

再见（zài jiàn）。Goodbye.

没关系（méi guān xi）。It's okay.

明天见（míng tiān jiàn）。See you tomorrow.

请进（qǐng jìn）。Come in please.

认识你很高兴（rèn shi nǐ hěn gāo xìng）。It's nice to meet you.

How do you feel so far? Do you have a feeling that you have already mastered a little bit Chinese? Well, if you can speak the above sentences fluently with correct tones, your Chinese listeners will besurprised.

Chapter 2: Learning Basic Chinese Grammar

It's easy to get a headache and be bored when talking about grammar. Chinese grammar is especially hard even for native speakers. But in this book, no attempt has been made to give a comprehensive or systematic account of Chinese grammar; only essential points will be introduced. So don't dread this part too much. Learning some basic grammar is really helpful for you to further your study in the Chinese language.

To ease the task for our dear learner, brief notes have been given for the more difficult expressions in the texts to facilitate your understanding of the Chinese language. The classification of Chinese sentence patterns is a rather complicated question. The patterns listed in this book are solely for reference.

Nouns, adjectives, pronouns

Nouns are words that denote people or things. Those nouns that are the names of people, places, and organizations are called proper nouns. In Chinese sentences, nouns normally function as subjects, objects, or attributes. We will analyze some special classes of nouns later.

Adjectives are the words that describe the shape, quality, or state of a person or a thing. In Chinese sentences, adjectives normally function as predicates, attributes, adverbials, or complements.

Nouns and adjectives are very easy. What you need to do is when you hear a word in English, think about how you would say it in Chinese. If you don't know how to say it, write it down and look it up later. It's handy to keep a little notebook with you for this purpose. Attach little Chinese labels (with the character, the pinyin and the pronunciation) to items around your house, such as the mirror, the TV, and chairs. You'll see the words so often that you'll learn them without realizing it.

Pronouns are the words that stand for nouns, verbs, and adjectives. Chinese pronouns are classified as personal pronouns, demonstrative pronouns, and interrogative pronouns. In Chinese sentences, pronouns normally function as subjects, objects, or attributes. Now, let’s talk about the three different kinds of pronouns one by one.

1. Personal pronoun

你/您（nǐ/nín), you

Both of them are second person singular pronouns. **你**（nǐ） is the usual form while **您**（nín） is the honorific or polite form. The plural of **你** （nǐ） is formed by the suffix 们 （men） . The plural of **您** （nín） is formed by using a numeral. Occasionally **您**们 （nín men） appears in writing, but it is never used in spoken Chinese.

我们/**咱**们（wǒ men/zán men), we/us

Both of them are first person plural pronouns. However, **咱**们（zán men） includes the speaker and the person spoken to, while **我**们 （wǒ men） may be inclusive or exclusive, i.e. the person spoken to may be included or excluded. Please pay attention here, **我**（wǒ）is a first person singular pronoun, but **咱**（zán） can seldom be used as a singular pronoun. Without 们（men）, 咱（zán）, in most occasions, is still a plural pronoun.

他/她/它（tā), him (he)/ her (she)/ it

All of them pronounced as tā, 他/她（tā）are third person singular pronouns, while 它（tā）refers to things. Their plural forms are 他们/她们/它们（tā）respectively.

Note here, 们（men）is a plural suffix. When added to a singular pronoun or singular personal noun, it makes it plural. However, 们（men） is never added to noun modified by a numeral.

2. Demonstrative pronouns

这/那（zhè/ nà）

They stand for either a person or thing. 这（zhè） refers to what is nearer to the speaker, and 那（nà）to what is farther off. For example:

这是我的车，那是他的车（zhè shì wǒ de chē, nà shì tā de chē）。

This is my car, and that's his car.

一切（yí qiè）

It is often used as an attribute to modify a noun. It denotes the whole amount or quantity of the thing or things referred to by the noun. It is often used together with 都（dōu）which occurs after 一切（yí qiè）. For example:

他的一切行李都准备好了（tā de yí qiè xíng lidōu zhǔnbèi hǎo le）。

(All of) his luggage has been prepared.

家里一切都好，不用牵挂（jiā lǐyí qièdōu hǎo, bú yòng qiān guà）。

Everything is fine at home; don't worry.

另外（lìng wài）

It is often used as an attribute to modify a noun or a quantity word. It indicates that the thing or quantity referred to is outside the range of what has been previously mentioned. Often **的**（de）occurs between **另外**（lìng wài）and the noun or quantity word it modifies. For example:

今天一部分时间工作，另外的时间玩电脑游戏（jīn tiān yí bù fèn shí jiān gōng zuò, lìng wài de shí jiān wán diàn nǎo yóu xì）。

Part of today's time will be used for work; the other part will be used for computer games.

一些人喜欢你，另外一些人不喜欢你（yìxiē rén xǐ huān nǐ, lìng wài yìxiē rén bù xǐ huān nǐ）。

Some people like you but others don't.

3. Interrogative pronouns

什么（shén me）

It is used in interrogative sentences, serving as an object by itself or together with a nominal element following it. For example:

你叫什么名字（nǐ jiào shén me míng zì）？

What is your name?

这是什么（zhè shì shén me）？

What's this?

谁（shuí）

The interrogative pronoun 谁（shuí）is used to ask about the name or identity of a person. For example:

他是谁（tā shì shuí）？

Who is he?

谁是王先生（shuí shì wáng xiān shēng）？

Who is Mr. Wang?

哪（nǎ）

When the interrogative pronoun **哪**（nǎ） is used in a question, the structure is **哪**（nǎ）+ measure word/noun + noun. For example,

哪本书（nǎ běn shū）？

Which book?

哪个国家（nǎ gè guó jiā）？

Which country?

几（jǐ）

It is used to ask about a number, usually less than ten. For example:

你女儿几岁了（nǐ nǚ ér jǐ suì le）？

How old is your daughter?

你来过**中国几次**（nǐ lái guò zhōng guó jǐ cì）？

How many times have you been in China?

多少（duō shǎo）

It is used to ask about numbers larger than ten. The measure word following it can be omitted. **多少**（duō shǎo） can also be used to inquire about prices, usually in the sentence pattern "……**多少**钱（duō shǎo qián）". The basic unit of **人民**币（rén mín bì）/ RMB is **元**（yuán）, usually replaced by 块（kuài） in spoken Chinese. For example:

你们大学有多少学生（nǐ men dà xué yǒu duō shǎo xué shēng）？

How many students are in your university?

这个杯子多少钱（zhè gè bēi zǐ duō shǎo qián）？

How much isthis cup?

怎么（zěn me）

It is used before a verb to ask about the manner or an action. For example:

这个地方怎么走（zhè gè dì fāng zěn me zǒu）？

How do I get to this place?

他怎么还不来（tā zěn me hái bú lái）？

Why is he still not coming?

哪儿（nǎ ér）

It is used to ask about the location of somebody or something. For example:

你去哪儿了（nǐ qù nǎ ér le）？

Where have you been?

我的外套在哪儿（wǒ de wài tào zài nǎ ér）？

Where is my coat?

怎么样（zěn me yàng）

It is used to ask about the condition/opinion of something or someone. For example:

明天我来接你怎么样（míng tiān wǒ lái jiē nǐ zěn me yàng）？

How about I come to pick you up tomorrow?

你的中文怎么样（nǐ de zhōng wén zěn me yàng）？

How is your Chinese?

Verb, modal verb, and adverb

Verbs are the words that express the action, behavior, or change of a person or a thing. In Chinese sentences they normally function as predicates. Chinese verbs do not need to change according to the tense. Tenses are expressed by the use of particles, some adverbs, and nouns denoting time. So verbs tend to be easier for learners compared to English. Let's discuss several verbs that appear with high frequency in daily communication.

有（yǒu）

It can be used in an existential sentence to indicate a person or thing exists somewhere. For example:

桌子上有一本书（zhuō zǐ shàng yǒu yìběn shū）。

There is a book on the table.

床底下有一只猫（chuáng dǐ xià yǒu yìzhī māo）。

There is a cat under the bed.
In the negative form of a **有**（yǒu）sentence, **没有**（méi yǒu）is used without a numeral classifier before the object. For example:

桌子上没有书（zhuō zǐ shàng méi yǒu shū）。

There is no book on the table.

床底下没有猫（chuáng dǐ xià méi yǒu māo）。

There is no cat under the bed.

有（yǒu）is sometimes used before a quantity word to indicate that a certain number has been reached. For example:

我认识他有十年了（wǒ rèn shí tā yǒu shí nián le）。

I've known him for like ten years.

中国的历史已经有五千**年了**（zhōng guó de lì shǐ yǐ jīng yǒu wǔ qiān nián le）。

China's history has reached five thousand years.

要（yào）

When used alone as a predicate, it means want/would like. It takes a noun as its object. The negative form is **不要**（bú yào）. For example:

你要什么（nǐ yào shénme）？

What do you want?

我要这个，还要那个（wǒ yào zhè gè, hái yào nà gè）。

I want this, and I want that.

我要一个面包（wǒ yào yígè miàn bāo ）。

I want a piece of bread.

在（zài）

It means "to be, to exist, to be living," indicating where a person or thing is. It is often followed by an object expressing place or position. The negative form is **不在**（búzài）. For example:

我在图书馆，不在公园（wǒ zài tú shū guǎn, bú zài gōng yuán）。

I'm inthe library, not inthe park.

The sentence pattern "noun + 在（zài）+ noun" is widely used in Chinese to express location; it is equal to English "subject + linking verb + prepositional phrase".

Like Chinese sentences with adjectives as predicates, normally no linking verb is needed between the subject and 在（zài）……. The word 是（shì）would make the sentence rather emphatic and is used only when the speaker intends to emphasize an assertion, as if to refute a contrary statement. In such cases 是（shì）is spoken with a stress, for example:

我是在图书馆，不是在公园（wǒ shì zài tú shū guǎn, bú shì zài gōng yuán）。

I'm inthe library, not in the park.

When it is followed by a word of locality and acts as the predicate of a sentence, it indicates the location of somebody or something. For example:

我的行李在房间里（wǒ de xínglǐ zài fáng jiān lǐ）。

My luggage is in the room.

我妹妹在车上（wǒ mèi mei zài chē shàng）。

My sister is in the car.

了（liǎo）

It often occurs after another verb or an adjective as a complement. It shows that an action is likely to take place or a quality or a state of things is likely to change. 了（liǎo）is usually preceded by the structural particle 得（de）. The negative form is 不了（bù liǎo）without 得（de）. For example:

这点儿工作我一个人做得了（zhè diǎn ér gōng zuò wǒyígè rén zuòdeliǎo）。

It is possible for me to manage this bit of work.

行李太多，一个人拿不了（xínglǐ tài duō, yígè rén ná bù liǎo）。

There will be too much luggage for one man to carry.

A "verb/ adjective + 得了（liǎo）" is similar in meaning to the English pattern "It is possible/likely to do..." while the negative form "verb/ adjective + 不了（bù liǎo）" is often used to mean "It is impossible /unlikely to do..."

请（qǐng）

When the verb 请（qǐng） is used before another verb, an imperative sentence is formed, indicating a polite suggestion or hope. For example:

请坐（qǐng zuò）。

Please sit down.

请听我说（qǐng tīng wǒ shuō）。

Please listen to me.

还（huán）

It is placed before a noun or a pronoun. It means to return something to somebody or somewhere. For example:

明天把书还我（míng tiān bǎ shū huán wǒ）。

Return my book to me tomorrow.

他没还我钱（tā méi huán wǒ qián）。

He didn't pay me back.完（wán）

When used after another verb, it plays a complementary role, expressing the idea that the action has been finished. It is often used in conjunction with adverbs like 已经（yǐ jīng）. For example:

我已经干完工作了（wǒ yǐ jīng gàn wán gōng zuò le）。

I've finished working.

他已经写完作业了（tā yǐ jīng xiě wán zuò yè le）。

He has finished writing his homework.

"Verb + 完（wán）" in Chinese may be compared to English "to finish + verb + ing." For example:

他已经复习完语法了（tā yǐ jīng fù xí wán yǔ fǎ le）。

He has finished reviewing his grammar.

她已经听完录音了（tā yǐ jīng tīng wán lù yīn le）。

She has finished listening to the recording.

While "to finish" is mainly a transitive verb, 完（wán） usually does not take an object. To express the idea "finish doing something", we must say "verb + 完（wán） + object".

There is a group of verbs in Chinese that indicate thought or emotion such as 关心/喜欢/思念（guān xīn/ xǐ huān/ sī niàn）. Their meaning is rather abstract, and their usage is not quite the same as that of verbs in general. They may be modified by adverbs of degree such as 太/很/非常（tài/ hěn/ fēi cháng ）. For example:

他太关心政治了（tā tài guān xīn zhèng zhì le）。

He cares too much about politics.

我很喜欢你（wǒ hěn xǐ huān nǐ）。

I'm very fond of you.

她非常思念你（tā fēi cháng sī niàn nǐ）。

She missed you so much.

Modal verbs express a desire, necessity, or possibility. They are often used together with verbs or adjectives to serve as predicates of sentences. When used alone, they act as other verbs. Let's learn some verbs and modal verbs those often appear in the sentences.

要（yào）

As a modal verb, it precedes a verb, indicating the wish and will to do something. For example:

我要买一辆自行车（wǒ yào mǎi yī liàng zì xíngchē）。

I'm going to buy a bike.

她要学游泳（tā yào xué yóu yǒng）。

She's going to learn swimming.

想（xiǎng）

It is usually used before a verb to express a hope or plan. For example:

我想买本书（wǒ xiǎng mǎi běn shū）。

I want to buy a book.

他想去爬山（tā xiǎng qù pá shān）。

He wants to go mountain climbing.

能（néng）

It is usually used before a verb to form the predicate indicating a skill or a possibility. The interrogative sentence structure "能……吗（néng...ma）?" is often used to indicate a request or hope for permission. For example:

我能进来吗（wǒ néng jìn lái ma）?

May I come in?

明天下午我能过去（míng tiān xià wǔ wǒ néng guò qù）。

I can go there tomorrow in the afternoon.

会（huì）

It is used before a verb, indicating acquiring a skill through learning. Its negative form is 不会（bú huì）. For example:

他会说中文（tā huì shuō zhōng wén）。

He can speak Chinese.

我不会游泳（wǒ bú huì yóu yǒng）。

I cannot swim.

It also indicates the possibility of the situation mentioned. For example:

你会拉小提琴吗（nǐ huì lā xiǎo tí qín ma）? 会（huì）。

Can you play the violin? –Yes, I can.

明天她会来吗（míng tiān tā huì lái ma）? 她会来（tā huì lái）。

Will she come tomorrow? – Yes, she will.

Chinese modal verbs are similar to English modal verbs both in their function and meaning. They are usually not used by themselves but are joined by other verbs to function as predicates except in short answers. Semantically it is not difficult to find their English equivalents or approximations.

Adverbs are the words that modify verbs or adjectives by expressing time, scope, quality, state, or degree. For example: 不（bù）, 都（dōu）, 很（hěn）, 太（tài）, etc. Adverbs do not modify nouns. Now, let's learn some adverbs together because they are really helpful for forming sentences.

才（cái）

It modifies a verb, giving the idea that some action or something has just happened. For example:

我才到（wǒ cái dào）。

I've just arrived.

他才离开（tā cái lí kāi）。

He has just left.

比较（bǐ jiào）

It may be used either as a verb or an adverb. When used as an adverb, it modifies adjectives or certain verbs, indicating that a quality or state of things has attained a certain degree. For example:

今天比较冷（jīn tiān bǐ jiào lěng）。

Today is much colder.

我比较喜欢动作片（wǒ bǐ jiào xǐ huān dòng zuò piàn）。

I prefer action movies.

都（dōu）

It is an adverb of scope. It means "all, in all cases", "with no exception." What is modified by it must be in the plural and placed before it. For example:

他们都是中国人（tā men dōu shì zhōng guó rén）。

They are all Chinese.

我们都喜欢喝茶（wǒ men dōu xǐ huān hē chá）。

We all like to drink tea.

很（hěn）

It is often used before an adjective or a verb expressing thought or emotion to denote degree. The usual pattern is "很（hěn）+ adjective/verb". Negation is achieved by adding 不（bù）before or after 很（hěn）, but different positions imply different degrees in negation. For example: 很不好（hěn bùhǎo）means very bad while 不很好（bú hěn hǎo）means not very good. For example:

他是一个很友好的人（tā shìyígè hěn yǒu hǎo de rén）。

He's a very friendly guy.

她的脾气很不好（tā de pí qì hěn bùhǎo）。

She has a very bad temper.

这家旅馆的环境不是很好（zhè jiā lǚ guǎn de huán jìng bú shì hěn hǎo）。

The environment of this hotel is not good.

When used in an affirmative sentence, it has only a weak sense, much weaker than the English adverb "very", which expresses a high degree of quality. Indeed, 很（hěn）is sometimes used for the sake of euphony, for without it the sentence may sound awkward. For example:

你的身体好（nǐ de shēn tǐ hǎo）。

你的身体很好（nǐ de shēn tǐ hěn hǎo）。

Both of the sentences mean "You are in good health." But the first sentence sounds strange and awkward to a native speaker.

可能（kě néng）

It expresses supposition or estimation. Occurring before a verb, an adjective, or the subject, it indicates that an action is likely to take place, an event or state of things is likely to happen or be in existence. The usual pattern is "……可能（kě néng） + verb

/adjective……”. The negative form is **不可能**（bú kě néng）, which usually does not appear before the subject. For example:

他可能去图书馆了（tā kě néng qù tú shū guǎn le）。

He may have gone to the library.

我可能要出差（wǒ kě néng yào chū chāi）。

I may have a business trip.

非常（fēi cháng）

It modifies adjectives or certain verbs, indicating that a quality or state of things has attained a very high degree. For example:

今天非常热（jīn tiān fēi cháng rè）。Today is very hot.

我非常高兴（wǒ fēi cháng gāo xìng）。I'm very happy.

太（tài）

It indicates a high degree. **了**（le） is often used at the end of the sentences with **太**（tài）, but not in negative sentences. For example:

天太热了（tiān tài rè le）。The weather is too hot.

我听不太懂（wǒ tīng bú tài dǒng）。 I don't quite understand.

还（hái）

Used as an adverbial, it modifies a verb or an adjective. It expresses the repetition of an action, continuity of a state, the further development of an event, or it's reaching a higher degree. For example:

我下周还要出差（wǒ xià zhōu hái yào chū chāi）。

I still have a business trip next week.

冰箱里还有两个苹果（bīng xiāng lǐ hái yǒu liǎng gè píng guǒ）。

There are still two apples in the fridge.

没有/没（méi yǒu/ méi）

When occurring before a verb or an adjective, **没有/没**（méi yǒu/ méi）denies that an action has already begun or a state of things has come into being. The usual pattern is "……没有/没（méi yǒu/ méi） + verb/ adjective……" For example:

我没回家（wǒ méi huí jiā）。

I didn't go home.

昨天没有下雨（zuó tiān méi yǒu xià yǔ）。

Yesterday didn't rain.

经常/常常（jīng cháng/ cháng cháng）

It modifies verbs, indicating a high frequency of an action. The negative form is 不常（bùcháng）.

我经常去图书馆（wǒ jīng cháng qù tú shū guǎn）。

I often go to the library.

他不常出门（tābùcháng chū mén）。

He seldom goes out.

随时（suí shí）

It is often used as an adverbial to modify a verb, indicating that the action may take place at any time, or regardless of time. For example:

我随时有空（wǒ suí shí yǒu kòng）。

I'm free at any time.

欢迎随时来找我（huān yíng suí shí lái zhǎo wǒ）。

(You're) welcome to visit me at any time.

在/正在（zài/ zhèng zài）

When used before a verb, 在/正在（zài / zhèng zài） are adverbs of time, denoting that an action is in progress. The usual pattern is "……在/正在（zài / zhèng zài） + verb ……". If 不（bù） occurs before 在（zài）, it is a negation. If 不（bù） is placed before 正在（zhèng zài）, it forms a rhetorical question, making the meaning of the sentence affirmative. For example:

他在听歌，他不在学习（tā zài tīng gē, tā bú zài xué xí ）。

He's listening to the music; he's not studying.

她不正在唱歌（tā bú zhèng zài chàng gē）？

Isn't she singing?

Generally speaking, the 在/不在（zài / bú zài）sentence pattern is approximate to the English progressive aspect. It may refer to the past, the present, or the future, the specific time being brought out by time-words or the context.

已经（yǐ jīng）

It is used to modify a verb or an adjective. It shows the completion of an action or that quality or state of things has reached a certain degree. For example:

我已经到了（wǒ yǐ jīng dào le）。

I've arrived.

演出已经开始了（yǎn chū yǐ jīng kāi shǐ le）。

The show has begun.

挺（tǐng）

It is often used as an adverbial to modify an adjective or a verb of thought or emotion, indicating that a quality or state of things has attained a high degree. This word is quite common in colloquial speech. For example:

我挺想你（wǒ tǐng xiǎng nǐ）。

I miss you very much.

这里的天挺蓝（zhè lǐ de tiān tǐng lán）。

The sky here is quite blue.

一直（yìzhí）

It often modifies a verb or an adjective as an adverbial. It indicates the continuity of an action or a state. For example:

他一直喜欢你（tāyìzhí xǐ huān nǐ）。

He always liked you.

商店一直营业到晚上十点（shāng diàn yìzhí yíng yè dào wǎn shàng shí diǎn）。

The store is open until 10 pm.

一定（yídìng）

When used before a verb or an adjective, it is an adverb. When in first person, 一定（yídìng）expresses a firm will on the part of the speaker. In second or third person, 一定（yídìng）denotes an urgent request by the speaker or a strong probability. There are usually 要（yào）, 会（huì）, 能（néng）, etc. between 一定（yídìng）and a verb or adjective. For example:

我们一定会来接你（wǒ men yídìng huì lái jiē nǐ）。

We will surely come to pick you up.

你一定要听老师讲话（nǐyídìng yào tīng lǎo shī jiǎng huà）。

You have to listen to your teacher.

一共（yígòng）

It expresses totality. It often modifies a verb or an adverbial to indicate a total sum. It is also sometimes joined directly with a quantity word. For example:

我一共买了三个苹果（wǒyígòng mǎi le sān gè píng guǒ）。

I bought three apples in total.

四个苹果一共一千克（sì gè píng guǒyígòng yī qiān kè）。

Four apples weigh 1kg in total.

一共多少钱（yígòng duō shǎo qián）?

How much in total?

The subject, the predicate, and the object

The subject in a Chinese sentence is the topic to talk about and the predicate tells how it is or what it is. The subject is usually a noun or a pronoun and the predicate, a verb or an adjective. The sentence element that is governed by a verb and denotes a person or thing affected by the action expressed by the verb is called an object. In Chinese sentences, an object is usually placed after a verb. Objects are often nouns or pronouns. Let's take an example and analyze it:

我们学习中文（wǒ men xué xí zhōng wén）。

We learn Chinese.

我们（wǒ men）, a pronoun, is the subject; **学习**（xué xí）, a verb, is the predicate; **中文**（zhōng wén）, a noun, is the object. Pretty easy, right?

A sentence with a verb as its predicate is one in which a verb plays the part of the predicate. In such a sentence, the predicate expresses the action or behavior of the subject. A verb may or may not take an object. A sentence with a verb as its predicate is negated by using the negative adverb **不**（bù）before the predicate verb. For example:

我们学习游泳（wǒ men xué xí yóu yǒng）。

We learn to swim.

我们不学习游泳（wǒ men bù xué xí yóu yǒng）。

We don't learn to swim.

我们（wǒ men）, a pronoun, is the subject; **学习**（xué xí）, a verb, is the predicate; **游泳**（yóu yǒng）, a verb, is the object. Not hard, right?

Prepositions and the adverbial

Prepositions are words that are placed before nouns or pronouns and are used together with them to express the direction, object, time, place, etc. of an action. Prepositions and the nouns or pronouns following them form prepositional constructions. For example:

在（zài）

It combines with a noun or a phrase denoting time, place, or direction to form a prepositional construction which is used as an adverbial to express the time or place of an action. Negation is achieved by adding **不**（bù）before **在**（zài). For example:

我在图书馆看书（wǒ zài tú shū guǎn kàn shū）。

I'm in the library reading a book.

我在医院工作（wǒ zài yī yuàn gōng zuò）。

I'm working in a hospital.

往（wǎng）

It is used with a noun or pronoun to form a prepositional construction which modifies a verb, showing the direction of an action. A prepositional construction with 往（wǎng）either precedes it as an adverbial or follows it as a complement. For example:

你再往前走五分钟就到了（nǐ zài wǎng qián zǒu wǔ fēn zhōng jiù dào le）。

You will arrive there by walking forward for another five minutes.

前往北京的航班将在五分钟后起飞（qián wǎng běi jīng de háng bān jiāng zài wǔ fēn zhōng hòu qǐ fēi）。

The flight to Beijing will depart in five minutes.

从（cóng）

It indicates a starting point. It is usually combined with a noun or nominal phrase that denotes time or place to form a prepositional construction. It is used as an adverbial modifying a verb by telling when or where the action starts. For example:

我从公园回来（wǒ cóng gōng yuán huí lái）。

I came back from the park.

她从去年开始学中文（tā cóng qù nián kāi shǐ xué zhōng wén）。

She's been learning Chinese since last year.

由（yóu）

It is usually combined with a noun or pronoun to form a prepositional construction. It is used as an adverbial modifying a verb showing the doer of the action. In a sentence with 由（yóu）introducing the doer, the subject is the receiver of the action. When the verb takes an object, there is a certain semantic relationship between the subject and the object. The usual pattern is "……由（yóu）+ noun/pronoun + verb…… ". It may be compared with the English preposition "by" and implies the passive voice. For example:

中文由我来教（zhōng wén yóu wǒ lái jiāo）。

I'll be teaching Chinese.

这项活动由我负责（zhè xiàng huó dòng yóu wǒ fù zé）。

This activity will be my responsibility.

向（xiàng）

The preposition **向**（xiàng）and the noun or pronoun following it forms a prepositional construction that modifies a verb. It shows the direction in which an action goes. It may be used before a verb and acts as an adverbial, or after a verb and functions as a complement. For example:

图书馆向这边走，公园向那边走（tú shū guǎn xiàng zhè biān zǒu, gōng yuán xiàng nà biān zǒu）。

Go this way to the library and that way to the park.

Prepositional constructions with **向**（xiàng）may also denote the object of an action, for example:

我向服务员要了发票（wǒ xiàng fú wù yuán yào le fā piào）。

I asked for the invoice from the waiter.

他向我借了一本书（tā xiàng wǒ jiè le yìběn shū）。

He borrowed a book from me.

When it denotes the direction in which an action goes, it is more or less equivalent to the English preposition "to" or "toward". However, when **向**（xiàng）refers to the object of an action, it is often equivalent to "from" in English.

和/跟（hé /gēn）

When used as prepositions, they are combined with a noun or pronoun to form prepositional constructions, which are as adverbials modifying verbs. The prepositional constructions indicate the object of an action. **和**（hé）and **跟**（gēn）are similar in use. For example:

我已经和他说了这件事（wǒ yǐ jīng hé tā shuō le zhè jiàn shì）。

I've told him this thing.

她跟我说她喜欢我（tā gēn wǒ shuō tā xǐ huān wǒ）。

She told me that she liked me.

Adverbials are usually adverbs, adjectives, prepositional constructions, or some nouns denoting time or place. In Chinese, adverbials normally occur before the verbs or adjectives they modify. Adverbials expressing time, place, or scope are sometimes placed before subjects. For example:

我们都学中文（wǒ men dōu xué zhōng wén）。

We're all learning Chinese.

昨天下午，他在教室学习（zuó tiān xià wǔ, tā zài jiào shì xué xí）。

Yesterday afternoon, he was studying in the classroom.

In general, when speaking Chinese, we can divide different adverbials into time, place, degree, starting point, manner, direction, and object. Now, let's discuss them one by one.

When a time word serves as an adverbial modifier in a sentence, it expresses the time at which an action takes place or a state of things comes into existence. It may be an adverb, a noun denoting time, or a time-phrase. It often follows the subject. Sometimes it can be used before the subject, a verb, or an adjective. For example:

我下周去中国（wǒ xià zhōu qù zhōng guó）。

I will go to China next week.

他下午两点来接你（tā xià wǔ liǎng diǎn lái jiē nǐ）。

He will pick you up at 2pm.

上个月我请假了（shàng gè yuè wǒ qǐng jiǎ le）。

I asked for days off last month.

An adverbial of place shows where an action takes place. It is often a prepositional construction or a noun denoting place. For example:

我在公园散步（wǒ zài gōng yuán sàn bù）。

I'm in the park walking.

我在床上看书（wǒ zài chuáng shàng kàn shū）。

I'm on the bed reading.

An adverbial of degree indicates the degree that a quality or state of things has attained. It is usually an adverb and modifies an adjective or a verb of thought or emotion. For example:

他最喜欢踢足球（tā zuì xǐ huān tī zú qiú）。

He likes to play soccer the most.

她很热情（tā hěn rè qíng）。

She is really welcoming.

An adverbial of starting point expresses the beginning of an action in time, space, or number. It is usually a prepositional construction. For example:

他从美国来（tā cóng měi guó lái）。

He comes from America.

电影从晚上七点开始（diàn yǐng cóng wǎn shàng qī diǎn kāi shǐ）。

The movie starts at seven in the evening

An adverbial of manner shows the way in which an action is carried out. It is usually an adjective or adverb. For example:

我们一起学习中文（wǒ men yìqǐ xué xí zhōng wén）。

We're learning Chinese together.

他们都推荐你（tā men dōu tuī jiàn nǐ）。

They all recommend you.

An adverbial of direction tells the direction in which an action progresses. It is usually a construction with a preposition. For example:

往前走就是机场（wǎng qián zǒu jiù shì jī chǎng）。

Keep going forward, and there will be the airport.

由北京前来的航班将在五分钟抵达（yóu běi jīng qián lái de háng bān jiāng zài wǔ fèn zhōng dǐ dá）。

The flight from Beijing will arrive in five minutes.

An adverbial of object tells the object of an action or the doer of an action. It is usually a prepositional construction with prepositions such as 向（xiàng） and 由（yóu). For example:

他不停向我挥手（tābùtíng xiàng wǒ huī shǒu）。

He constantly waves to me.

最后一个节目由她出演（zuì hòu yígèjiémù yóu tā chū yǎn）。

She'll be performing in the last show.

Conjunction, particle, and the attribute

Conjunctions are the words that connect words, phrases, or clauses and by doing so, express the relationships between them. Let's learn some words here.

和/跟/与（hé/ gēn/ yǔ）

They are used to connect two or more elements, indicating a parallel relationship. When more than two items are connected, they can be used only between the last two items. For example:

桌子上有一本书和一杯水（zhuō zǐ shàng yǒu yì běn shū héyì bēi shuǐ）。

There is a book and a cup of water on the table.

我喜欢吃香蕉、苹果和西瓜（wǒ xǐ huān chī xiāng jiāo, píng guǒ hé xī guā ）。

I like to eat banana, apple, and watermelon.

我与他相处不好（wǒ yǔ tāxiāng chǔ bùhǎo）。

I'm not getting along well with him.

Particles are words that are added to words, phrases, or sentences to express additional meaning. Chinese particles fall into three groups: structural particles, aspect particles, and modal particles. Let's take some examples.

吗（ma）

The particle 吗（ma）indicates an interrogative mood. When 吗（ma）is added at the end of a declarative sentence, the sentence turns into a question. For example:

你是美国人吗（nǐ shì měi guó rén ma）？

Are you an American?

你喜欢这首歌吗（nǐ xǐ huān zhè shǒu gē ma）？

Do you like this song?

的/地/得（de）

When the structural particle **的**（de）is attached to a noun, a verb, an adjective, or a word of other parts of speech, they enter into what is called "a construction with **的**（de）". Such a construction is equivalent to a noun both in nature and function. For example:

他是我的老师（tā shì wǒ de lǎo shī）。

He's my teacher.

这是她的书（zhè shì tā de shū）。

This is her book.

There are similar constructions in English. When the **的**（de）construction is made up of a noun and **的**（de）, it is like the independent genitive（the genitive without a headword）in English. For example:

这本书是我的（zhè běn shū shì wǒ de）。

This book is mine.

这只铅笔不是你的（zhè zhī qiān bǐ bú shì nǐ de）。

This pencil is not yours.

When the construction is made up of an adjective and **的**（de）, it is like an adjective plus the prop-word "one." For example:

他的外套是新的（tā de wài tào shì xīn de）。

His coat is a new one.

When a verb enters into a **的**（de）construction, though comparable with a non-finite verb modifying the prop-word "one", it is better to turn the Chinese sentence into an English sentence with the predicate verb in the passive voice. For example:

那本小说是从图书馆借来的（nà běn xiǎo shuō shì cóng tú shū guǎn jiè lái de）。

That novel was borrowed from the library.

When **的**（de）is at the end of a sentence, it expresses affirmation. For example:

你会好起来的（nǐ huì hǎo qǐ lái de）。

You will recover.

我会来接你的（wǒ huì lái jiē nǐ de）。

I will pick you up.

地（de）is used before a verb or an adjective to show that what precedes it is an adverbial modifying the verb or the adjective. As a rule, a disyllabic adjective or a monosyllabic adjective with an adverb of degree before it calls for the use of the particle **地**（de）.

飞机安全地着陆了（fēi jī ān quán de zhuólù le）。

The plane landed safely.

她开心地走了（tā kāi xīn dezǒu le）。

She left happily.

得（de）is used after a verb or an adjective to show that the following element is a complement to the verb or the adjective. Complements of degree or result are usually preceded by **得**（de). For example:

他跑得很快（tā pǎo de hěn kuài）。

He runs fast.

我的中文说得很流利（wǒ de zhōng wén shuō de hěn liú lì）。

I can speak Chinese fluently.

……**的**话（de huà）

It is a modal particle of assumption. Occurring at the end of a clause, 的话（de huà）indicates that what is said is an assumption. For example:

他还不来的话我就走（tā hái bù lái de huà wǒ jiù zǒu）。

I'll leave if he still doesn't show up.

不出意外的话我们马上就到了（bù chū yì wài de huà wǒ men mǎ shàng jiù dào le）。

We'll be there shortly unless something unexpected happens.

呢（ne）

It is used after a noun or pronoun, forming a question about the situation mentioned previously. The commonly used sentence pattern is A…B 呢（ne）? For example:

我今天很好，你呢（wǒ jīn tiān hěn hǎo, nǐ ne ）?

I'm fine today; how about you?

你呢（nǐ ne） means 你今天好吗（nǐ jīn tiān hǎo ma） in this context.

It can also ask about the location of somebody or something. For example:

我的钱包呢（wǒ de qián bāo ne）?

Where is my wallet?

她在哪儿呢（tā zài nǎ ér ne）?

Where is she?

When placed after a declarative sentence, it means that the action is just going on. It is often used in conjunction with adverbs like 在/正在（zài / zhèng zài). For example:

她在跳舞呢（tā zài tiào wǔ ne）。

She's dancing right now.

我在睡觉呢（wǒ zài shuì jiào ne）。

I'm sleeping.

吧（ba）

When used at the end of an imperative sentence, it indicates suggestion or command with a softened mood. For example:

我们在这家餐厅吃饭吧（wǒ men zài zhè jiā cān tīng chī fàn ba）。

Let's eat at this restaurant.

他不在这，你等会再来吧（tā bú zài zhè, nǐ děng huì zài lái ba）。

He's not here; you can come back later.

When used at the end of an interrogative sentence, it indicates supposition. Questions with **吧**（ba）at the end are similar to English disjunctive questions spoken with a falling tone.

For example:

这本书是你的吧（zhè běn shū shì nǐ de ba）？

This book is yours, isn't it?

啊（ā）

It is used at the end of a declarative sentence to set the mood. The pronunciations of **啊**（ā）varies with the finals of the syllables before it, and in written Chinese, the variants are represented by different characters sometimes. For example:

这里真美啊（zhè lǐ zhēn měi ā）！

What a beautiful place!

这座山真高啊（zhè zuò shān zhēn gāo ā）！

This mountain is so tall!

了（le）

了（le） is used at the end of a sentence to indicate a change or the occurrence of a new situation or completion. For example:

你的朋友来了（nǐ de péng yǒu lái le）。

Your friend has arrived.

他一会就要走了（tā yī huì jiù yào zǒu le）。

He will leave soon.

了（le）can be also be used between a verb and its object. There is usually a modifier before the object of the verb such as a numeral classifier, an adjective, or a pronoun, etc, For example:

她买了几个苹果（tā mǎi le jǐ gè píng guǒ）。

She bought a few apples.

你看见了几个人（nǐ kàn jiàn le jǐ gè rén）？

How many people have you seen?

The negative form of 了（le）in both cases above is 没（méi）+ verb + object. In the negative form, 了（le）should be omitted. For example:

你的朋友没来（nǐ de péng yǒu méi lái）。

Your friend hasn't come.

她没买苹果（tā méi mǎi píng guǒ）。

She didn't buy the apple.

过（guò）

Used after a verb, the aspect particle 过（guò）indicates that the action took place in the past and ended before the present time or that there was such an experience. The usual pattern is "...verb + 过（guò）..." Negation is achieved by adding 没（méi） or 没有（méi yǒu）before the verb, For example:

我吃过饭了（wǒ chī guò fàn le）。

I've eaten already.

我没去过美国（wǒ méi qù guò měi guó）。

I've never been to America.

Both aspect particles, 过（guò）and 了 （le） indicate an action which takes place before a certain moment. 过（guò）emphasizes the completion of an action and often implies a reference to that moment whereas 了 （le） only indicates a prior experience.

Therefore, in most cases, a verb with 过（guò）is comparable with English perfect tense and verbs with 了（le） are comparable with simple past tense.

着（zhe）

When used after a verb, 着（zhe）indicates that the action is in progress or remains unchanged. No word can be inserted between the verb and 着（zhe). For example:

他正在看着一本漫画书（tā zhèng zài kàn zhe yì běn màn huà shū）。

He is currently reading a comic book.

他们在热烈的讨论着什么东西（tā men zài rè liè de tǎo lùn zhe shén me dōng xī）。

They're fiercely discussing something.

The attribute is usually a noun, a pronoun, an adjective, a numeral, or a measure word. In Chinese, an attribute is as a rule placed before a noun which it modifies. Such a noun is called the "headword". The structural particle 的（de）is often used between a noun and its headword. For example:

我的朋友是老师（wǒ de péng yǒu shì lǎo shī ）。

My friend is a teacher. "我的（wǒ de）" is the attribute here.

她是一个好学生（tā shìyí gè hǎo xué shēng）。

She's a good student. "一个（yí gè）" is the attribute here.

Note here, attributes in Chinese sentences, whether they are words, phrases or clauses, are almost invariable placed before headwords. The particle 的（de）is a sign of an attribute. It may be used after a word, phrase, or clause to make it an attribute, but numerals and demonstrative pronouns do not need 的（de）when they function as attributes. When a noun is modified by a series of attributes, 的（de） can be used after each attribute.

Restrictive attributes express the time, number, possession, etc. of the persons or things spoken of, telling whose, when, where, how many, how much they are. For example:

这是我的钢笔，那是他的钢笔（zhè shì wǒ de gāng bǐ, nà shì tā de gāng bǐ）。

This is my pen, and that is his pen.

她没去看昨天的电影（tā méi qù kàn zuó tiān de diàn yǐng）。

She didn't go see yesterday's movie.

Position words and construction with position words

Position words are the words that indicate direction or position. They are a subclass of noun. There are two types of them: simple position words such as **上**（shàng），**下**（xià），**里**（lǐ）and compound words such as **上面**（shàng miàn），**下面**（xià miàn），**里面**（lǐ miàn）.

Position words may be attached to other words to form constructions with position words, e.g. **楼上**（lóu shàng），**床下**（chuáng xià），**假期里**（jiǎ qī lǐ），**房**间内（fáng jiān nèi）.

Position words are a special class of nouns in Chinese. They usually express the location（either in time or space）of things. Very often they are equivalent to English prepositions, e.g. **房**间里 （fáng jiān lǐ）— in the room, **桌子下** （zhuō zǐ xià）— under the table, **礼堂外**（lǐ táng wài）— outside of auditorium, 报纸上（bào zhǐ shàng）— on the newspaper. A Chinese position word does not always equal an English preposition. For example, position words may be used alone to serve as a sentence element. Constructions with position words sometimes act like prepositional phrases and sometimes do not; they may perform the function of a subject whereas English prepositional phrases can never be a subject. For example:

楼下有个小卖部（lóu xià yǒu gè xiǎo mài bù）。

There is a small store downstairs.

房间里很热（fáng jiān lǐ hěn rè）。

It's hot in the room.

In the two sentences, "楼上（lóu shàng）" and "房间里（fáng jiān lǐ）" are the constructions with position words acting as the subject but "downstairs" and "in the room" are not.

Now, let's discuss some position words together. They're sure to be very useful.

里（lǐ）and 外（wài）are both both position words but with opposite meanings. 里（lǐ）means in or inside something while 外（wài）means outside something, For example:

商场里东西很多（shāng chǎng lǐ dōng xī hěn duō）。

There are lots of things in the mall.

他的家在城市外（tā de jiā zài chéng shì wài）。

He lives outside the city.

As a position word, 来/以来（lái /yǐ lái）is used a word or expression denoting a period of time. It denotes the duration from a point of time in the past to the time of speaking. For example:

这几年以来，我去过很多地方（zhè jǐ nián yǐ lái, wǒ qù guò hěn duō dì fāng）。

During recent years, I've been to many places.

Compound position words are made up of simple position words and 之（zhī）or 以（yǐ） which precedes them or simple position words and 面（miàn），边（biān），or 头（tóu）which follows them.

Though usually adverbials, constructions with position words may also act as subjects. In sentences with such subjects, the predicates are either adjectives or verbs of existence. For example:

俱乐部里有放映厅（jù lè bù lǐ yǒu fàng yìng tīng）。

There is a projection room in the club.

公园里有很多人（gōng yuán lǐ yǒu hěn duō rén）。

There are a lot of people inthe park.

房间里很整洁（fáng jiān lǐ hěn zhěng jié）。

The room is clean and tidy.

Just to remember: the Chinese sentence which has a position word construction as subject and a verb of existence as predicate is equal in meaning to the English sentence "There + to be + subject + adverbial." When the predicate is an adjective instead of a verb of existence, the sentence is similar to the English SVC verb patterns, the noun in the position word construction functioning as the subject.

The complement and the independent element

The complement is a supplementary or explanatory element which is attached to a verb or an adjective. It indicates how the action is going on, what the result is, how many times or how long it is done, or what degree or extent a quality or state of things reaches. It is usually an adjective, an adverb, or a verb. Now, we'll discuss a complement of result, number, manner, degree, direction, and possibility here.

A complement of result tells the result of an action. It is usually a verb or an adjective. For example:

我们已经看完了电影（wǒ men yǐ jīng kàn wán le diàn yǐng）。

We have finished watching the movie.

你说什么我听不清楚（nǐ shuōshénme wǒ tīng bùqīng chǔ）。

What are you saying? I can't hear you clearly.

The complement of number tells how many times an action takes place or how long it lasts. It is usually a quantity word. For example:

我还想多睡一会儿（wǒ hái xiǎng duō shuìyìhuì ér）。

I still want to sleep for a while.

再等我五分钟（zài děng wǒ wǔ fēn zhōng ）。

Just wait for me for another five minutes.

In many cases, Chinese complements are similar （in meaning） to English adverbials. A complement of numbers functions in Chinese sentences as adverbials of time in English sentences.

The complement of manner tells how an action takes place. For example:

请你讲慢一点（qǐng nǐ jiǎng màn yìdiǎn）。

Please speak slowly.

你能开车开快一点吗?**我要**迟到了（nǐ néng kāi chē kāi kuài yìdiǎn ma? wǒ yào chí dào le ）。

Can you drive faster? I'll be late.

A complement of degree tells the degree that a quality or state of things has reached. It is usually an adverb or adjective. For example:

我身体很好（wǒ shēn tǐ hěn hǎo）。

I'm in good health.

他是一个挺不错的人（tā shìyígè tǐng bú cuò de rén）。

He is quite a nice guy.

The completion of direction tells the direction of an action or a state. In this case, a directional verb often occurs after another verb or an adjective. For example:

她送来了水果和蛋糕（tā sòng lái le shuǐ guǒ hé dàn gāo）。

She bring usfruits and cakes.

他向你走过来了（tā xiàng nǐ zǒu guò lái le）。

He comes over to you.

The complement of possibility tells the possibility of an action taking place or being realized. It is usually a verb or an adjective. Negation is formed by adding **不**（bù）after the predicate verb.

路程不远，我们今天能赶到（lù chéng bù yuǎn, wǒ men jīn tiān néng gǎn dào）。

It's not far; we can make it today.

现在我没空，去不了（xiàn zài wǒ méi kōng, qù bù liǎo）。

I'm not available now; I cannot go there.

An independent element in a sentence is one which has no structural relation with other elements and is rather flexible in word position. It may be a vocative, an echo, an interjection, or a reminder. It may also be used to express supposition, affirmation, emphasis, etc. All in all, it will help your fluency greatly. For example:

看你，又忘了吧，我不喜欢喝可乐（kàn nǐ, yòu wàng le ba, wǒ bù xǐ huān hē kě lè）。

Look at you, you forgot again? I don't like coke.

哎呀，我们好久不见了（ài ya, wǒ men hǎo jiǔ bú jiàn le）。

Ah, we haven't seen each other in such a long time.

A brief introduction to other language points

Chinese has a lot of different kinds of sentence structures. Up to now in this chapter, I think our readers might feel bored from learning the grammar and have so many things to digest already. So, we will only introduce some very basic grammar for sentences here. Frankly speaking, you can even forget all the grammar mentioned in this book. Just remember the examples, keep learning different words, make your own examples, and you will get there finally.

Declarative sentences and interrogative sentences

A declarative sentence is a statement or an assertion. It is spoken with a flat tone. An interrogative sentence is a question. It is spoken with the tail rising. There are several types of Chinese interrogative sentences: yes-no questions, special questions, alternative questions, and affirmative/negative questions.

Chinese yes-no questions are equivalent to English general questions, but their formation is much simpler. Any Chinese declarative sentence can be turned into a yes-no question simply by adding 吗（ma）at its end.

In forming Chinese special questions, no inversion of any kind is required. Interrogative pronouns may be placed either at the head of a sentence, or at its end, or within the sentence, the position depending on the grammatical function of the interrogative pronoun. If it acts as a subject, it occupies the position of a subject; if it is used as an object, it takes the position of an object, etc. So, the word order of a special question is the same as that of a normal declarative sentence. This goes to show that word order in Chinese is sometimes quite rigid.

Elliptical sentence

Some sentence elements may be omitted in certain contexts in Chinese. For example:

谁在唱歌?**她**（shuí zài chàng gē? tā）。

Who's singing? She is.

今天去图书馆了吗?**去了**（jīn tiān qù tú shū guǎn le ma? qù le）。

Have you been to the library today? (I've) been there.

In the above sentence, the words "**在唱歌**（zài chàng gē）" and "图书馆（tú shū guǎn）" are omitted.

Pivotal sentence

In some Chinese sentences, the predicate consists of two verbs（or a verb and an adjective）in succession and the object of the first verb is at the same time the subject of the following verb（or adjective）. Such sentences are called pivotal sentences. The first verb in such a sentence is often a causative verb which calls forth an action indicated by the second verb. For example:

我们请她唱中文歌（wǒ men qǐng tā chàng zhōng wén gē）。

We asked her to sing Chinese songs.

老师要我按时交作业（lǎo shī yào wǒ àn shí jiāo zuò yè）。

The teacher told me to hand in the homework on time.

Like the examples above, the bulk of Chinese pivotal sentences are similar to English sentences with accusative-with-infinitive constructions（e.g. to allow/ask/command /force /order/persuade /request /tell somebody to do something）.

Other pivotal sentences are comparable to English sentences with verb + object + particle/noun/adjective/adverbial, etc. For example:

她辅导我学中文（tā fǔ dǎo wǒ xué zhōng wén）。

She coached me in Chinese.

他们选你当俱乐部主席（tā men xuǎn nǐ dāng jù lè bù zhǔ xí）。

They voted you chairman of the club.

The verb **有**（yǒu）may be used in a pivotal sentence. It is usually placed before the pivotal verb. Many of the pivotal sentences with the verb **有**（yǒu）are without a subject. For example:

有个人来找你（yǒu gè rén lái zhǎo nǐ）。

There's someone looking for you.

周末有很多人去公园（zhōu mò yǒu hěn duō rén qù gōng yuán）。

There are a lot of people going to the park during the weekend.

The verb **祝**（zhù） may be used in a pivotal sentence expressing good wishes. It is used to offer congratulations or when bidding farewell. Sentences with **祝**（zhù）are sometimes without a subject. For example:

祝我好运吧（zhù wǒ hǎo yùn ba）。

Wish me good luck.

祝贺你（zhù hè nǐ）！

Congratulations!

Actions in the past

As mentioned earlier, Chinese verbs need not change according to the tense.

Actions in the past time or past experiences are expressed by using an adverbial of time before the verb or the aspect particle 过（guò）after the verb or both. The pattern is "...adverbial of time + verb + 过（guò）..." For example:

这本书他已经看过了（zhè běn shū tā yǐ jīng kàn guò le）。

He's already read this book.

她去年来过一次中国（tā qù nián lái guòyícì zhōng guó）。

She went to China once last year.

The negative form is "...adverbial of time + 没（méi）+ verb + 过（guò）..." For example:

她昨天没回过家（tā zuó tiān méi huí guò jiā）。

She didn't come back home yesterday.

Completed actions

The aspect particle 了（le）, or a complement of result, or both of them are used to show that an action has been completed or that something has been realized. The pattern is "...verb + complement of result + 了（le）". For example:

她已经写完作业了（tā yǐ jīng xiě wán zuò yè le）。

She's already finished her homework.

他已经回来了（tā yǐ jīng huí lái le）。

He's already come back.

The completion of an action indicates a stage that the action has reached. It has no relevance to time. An action, whether it took place in the past, is taking place now, or will take place in the future, must have its stage of completion. But when translating into English, we don't need to use the corresponding tense. For example:

他昨天去了公园（tā zuó tiān qù le gōng yuán）。

He went to the park yesterday.

明天我们下了班就去看电影（míng tiān wǒ men xià le bān jiù qù kàn diàn yǐng）。

We'll go to the cinema after we get off work tomorrow.

Progressive aspect of an action

A verb may take an adverbial of time before it, or the aspect particle 着（zhe）after it or both, to show that the action referred to is in progress or that an event remains what it has been. For example:

他在练习说中文（tā zài liàn xí shuō zhōng wén）。

He's practicing speaking Chinese.

外面下着大雨（wài miàn xià zhe dà yǔ）。

It's raining heavily outside.

The progressive aspect of an action denotes a state that the action is in. It has no relation with time. Almost any action has a progressive aspect regardless of the time of its happening. For example:

我们明天带着相机去吧（wǒ men míng tiān dài zhe xiàng jī qù ba）。

Let's take a camera there tomorrow.

昨天晚上窗户一直开着（zuó tiān wǎn shàng chuāng hùyìzhí kāi zhe）。

The window was open the whole night yesterday.

Focus here. In English, of course you can say, "He's dying out there," but in Chinese, there is no such expression.

Affirmative + negative question

An affirmative + negative question is one which is formed by placing the affirmation and negation of the predicate verb or adjective side by side. For example:

你有没有学过中文（nǐ yǒu méi yǒu xué guò zhōng wén）?

Have you studied Chinese or not?

你信不信我（nǐ xìn bú xìn wǒ）?

Do you believe me or not?

If the verb takes an object, the object may be placed between the affirmative and negative forms of the verb. This makes you speak much more like a native speaker. The first sentence of the above examples above may be turned to:

你有学过中文没（nǐ yǒu xué guò zhōng wén méi）?

The affirmative + negative questions can be considered as a special kind of yes-no questions. They have the same meaning as yes-no questions but are more colloquial in style.

The apposition

When two words or expressions in a sentence stand for the same person or thing and perform the same grammatical function, with one explaining or denoting the other, then the former is said to be in apposition to the latter. The two words or expressions are sometimes placed side-by-side, and sometimes one is at the head of a sentence whereas the other occurs in the middle of the sentence. The one that occurs in the middle is usually a pronoun. For example:

中国、美国，这两个国家的风景都很美丽（zhōng guó, měi guó, zhè liǎng gè guó jiā de fēng jǐng dōu hěn měi lì）。

China and America, both of them have beautiful landscapes.

香蕉、苹果和橘子，它们都是我爱吃的水果（xiāng jiāo, píng guǒ hé jú zǐ, tā men dōu shì wǒ ài chī de shuǐ guǒ）。

Banana, apple and orange, they are all fruits I love eating.

A special feature of Chinese apposition is that pronouns may be in apposition to nouns. In sentences above, the pronoun 这（zhè）and 它们（tā men）may be omitted; without them, the sentences still stand. The use of pronouns as apposition is often colloquial in style; sometimes it could be emotional as one may find in lyrics.

Sentence with two objects

In some sentences, the predicate verb affects two objects and therefore takes two objects. For example:

他问我一个问题（tā wèn wǒyígè wèn tí）。

He asked me a question.

她教你们中文（tā jiāo nǐ men zhōng wén）。

She teaches you Chinese.

Of the two objects, the first, 我（wǒ），你们（nǐ men） in the above examples, which refers to persons, are called indirect objects, or the near object. The second objects such as 问题（wèn tí），中文（zhōng wén）in the above examples, refers to things and are called the direct object, or the far object.

Sentence with an adjectival predicate

Used in the structure subject + adverb of degree + adjective, the adjective describes the nature or state of somebody or something, usually following the adverb of degree 很（hěn）. The negative form is subject + 不（bù）+ adjective. For example:

我很好（wǒ hěn hǎo）。

I'm very good.

她的中文不好（tā de zhōng wén bù hǎo）。

Her Chinese is not very good.

Sentence with a nominal predicate

It is a sentence whose predicate is a nominal element. It is usually used to indicate age, time, date, etc. For example:

明天星期一（míng tiān xīng qī yī）。

Tomorrow is Monday.

我今年二十五岁（wǒ jīn nián èr shí wǔ suì）。

I'm twenty-five years old this year.

Sentence with a serial verb construction

去/来（qù / lái ）+ place + to do sth

The predicate of a sentence with a serial verb construction consists of two or more verbs. The latter verb can be the purpose of the former. The object of the first verb, i.e. the place, can sometimes be omitted. For example:

我们去中国看大熊猫（wǒ men qù zhōng guó kàn dà xióng māo）。

We're going to China to look at pandas.

她来公园散步（tā lái gōng yuán sàn bù）。

She comes to the park to take a walk.

Sentence with a subject-predicate phrase as the predicate

In Chinese, there is a kind of sentence in which the predicate is a subject predicate phrase. The structure is subject of sentence + predicate of the sentence/subject + predicate. For example:

我身体不太舒服（wǒ shēn tǐ bú tài shū fú）。

I don't feel well.

我牙疼（wǒ yá téng ）。

My tooth aches.

The subject in the subject-predicate phrase is usually part of the subject of the sentence related to it.

Sentence with verbal expressions in series

A sentence with verbal expressions in series is one in which the predicate consists of two or more verbs （with or without an adjective） to tell something about the same subject. In speech, there is no pause between the verbs. There are various relationships between the verbs. Apart form 来 （lái） and 去（qù）; these verbs are usually not used alone, but with some other elements. For example:

我要去饭店吃晚饭（wǒ yào qù fàn diàn chī wǎn fàn）。

I want to go to the restaurant for dinner.

她用中文唱歌（tā yòng zhōng wén chàng gē）。

She uses Chinese to sing.

Verbal expressions in series are a syntactic peculiarity of Chinese sentences. This are possible because Chinese tends to use verbs and Chinese verbs have no non-finite forms.

The verbal expressions in series may have various relationships between them. They may be coordinate (the action referred to by the first verb preceding the others.) They may have a principal-subordinate relationship (one of the verbs denoting purpose, condition, manner, time, place, etc.) Therefore verbal expressions in series are comparable to English coordinate verbs, or a predicate verb with a a non-finite verb, or a predicate verb with an adverbial.

Sentences with 是（shì）

The 是（shì） sentence is a determinable sentence with 是（shì）, indicating what somebody or something equals or belongs to. It is expressed by "noun / pronoun + 是（shì）+ noun / pronoun". The negative sentence is formed by adding the negative adverb 不（bù） before 是（shì）, for example:

我是中国人（wǒ shì zhōng guó rén）。

I am a Chinese.

我不是中国人（wǒ bú shì zhōng guó rén ）。

I am not a Chinese.

The Chinese sentence pattern “noun / pronoun + 是(shì） + noun / pronoun” is equal to the English sentence pattern “subject + link verb + complement”. Negation is achieved by putting 不 （bù） before 是（shì）while in the English sentence the negative particle “not” is placed after the link verb.

The structure 是……的 （shì... de） is used to emphasize time, place, or manner. When the occurrence of something is known, it can be use to emphasize when, where, and in which manner it occurred. 是 （shì）can be omitted in positive and interrogative sentences, but not in negative sentences. For example:

我是昨天来的（wǒ shì zuó tiān lái de）。

I came here yesterday.

这是在图书馆借的（zhè shì zài tú shū guǎn jiè de）。

This was borrowed from the library.

他不是昨天来的（tā bú shì zuó tiān lái de）。

He didn’t arrive yesterday.

Composite sentence

Chinese composite sentences fall into two types: compound and complex. In a compound sentence, the component clauses are equal in importance, and there is no subordination in meaning. A complex sentence is generally made up of two clauses: one of them expresses the main idea of the sentence and is called the principal clause, and the other modifies or restricts the meaning of the principal clause and is called the subordinate clause.

Compound sentences may involve coordination, sequence, progression, alternation, etc. Complex sentences may have clauses of transition, supposition, condition, cause, etc.

The various relations between clauses are often indicated by words that are used to connect clauses. These words are called correlative words, e.g. 是……还是 （shì... hái shì ）, which indicates alternation; **不但……而且**（bú dàn... ér qiě） which indicates progression; **如果……就**（rú guǒ... jiù）, which indicates condition. For example:

你是美国人还是英国人（nǐ shì měi guó rén hái shì yīng guó rén）?

Are you an American or a British?

她不但会唱歌，还会跳舞（tā bú dàn huì chàng gē, hái huì tiào wǔ）。

She can not only sing but also dance.**如果明天下雨**，**我**们就呆在家里（rú guǒ míng tiān xià yǔ, wǒ men jiù dāi zài jiā lǐ）。

If it rains tomorrow, we'll stay at home.

While English complex sentences normally need conjunctions to connect clauses, Chinese complex sentences may go without correlative words. This is true particularly in spoken Chinese. For example:

你不去我去（nǐ bú qù wǒ qù）。

If （or since） you won't go, I'll go.

他昨天病了，**没去上**课（tā zuó tiān bìng le, méi qù shàng kè）。

He was absent from class because he was ill.

Chapter 3: How to Count

Numbers are widely used in Chinese people's daily lives. It will bring inconvenience if they are used and spoken incorrectly. Luckily, the Chinese numerical system is fairly straightforward and logical. Once you have learned the first eleven numbers, you will be able to count from 0 to 99.

Below you will find the numbers zero to ten. Please make sure to practice saying each number using the correct tone.

Zero: 零, líng

One: 一, yī

Two: 二, èr

Three: 三, sān

Four: 四, sì

Five: 五, wǔ

Six: 六, liù

Seven: 七, qī

Eight: 八, bā

Nine: 九, jiǔ

Ten: 十, shí

Once you have mastered the numbers zero to ten, you can continue counting in double digits by saying the number in the tens' position, then the word 十 (shí), followed by the number in the one's position. For example: The number 48 is written and spoken as 四十八 (sì shí bā). The number 30 is written and spoken as 三十 (sān shí), the number 19 is written and spoken as 一十九 (yī shí jiǔ) or just 十九 (shí jiǔ)

The word for hundred in Chinese is 百 (bǎi), so 100 is spoken as 一百 (yìbǎi), 200 is spoken as 二百 (èrbǎi), 300 is spoken as 三百 (sānbǎi), etc.

Once you have mastered the word 百 (bǎi), you can continue counting all triple digits by saying the number in the hundreds' position, then the word 百 (bǎi, followed by saying the number in the tens' position, then the word 十 (shí), followed by the number in the one's position. For example:

The number 148 is written and spoken as 一百四十八 (yìbǎisì shí bā). The number 230 is written and spoken as 二百三十 (èr bǎisān shí), the number 319 is written and spoken as 三百一十九 (sān bǎiyī shí jiǔ). Attention, you cannot omit the 一 (yī) here. Additionally, numbers like 401, 502, etc, are written and spoken as 四百零一 (sìbǎiling yī), 五百零二 (wǔbǎiling èr), etc.

There is also 千 (qiān) for thousand, 万 (wàn) for ten thousand, 亿 (yì) for a hundred million. Just imagine how hard pronouncing 235,442,251 is in English! In Chinese, it’s 二亿三千五百四十四万二千二百五十一 (èr yì sān wǔbǎisì shí sì wàn èr qiān èr bǎiwǔ shí yī).

Another thing that may be of interest, 两 (liǎng) is used for two when counting people and things, it can be also used as the first digit in two hundred (两百), two thousand (两千), etc, but only for the first digit. For example, 222 people can be spoken as 两百二十二人 (liǎng bǎièr shí èr rén) or 二百二十二人 (èr bǎièr shí èr rén).

Ordinal numbers are formed by adding 第 (dì) before the number. For example, 第一 (dì yī) means 1st, 第二 (dì èr) means 2nd, etc. 第 (dì) is sometimes omitted in numbers designating the order in a sequence, e.g. 二楼（èr lóu） equals 第二楼（dì èr lóu）, the second floor.

The names for the twelve months in a year are formed by adding the suffix 月（yuè） after the number: 一月（yī yuè）, 二月（èr yuè）... It is same for expressing the week. By using the prefix 星期（xīng qī） or 周（zhōu） before the number, you then can say all of them. The one exception is for Sunday. In oral Chinese, native speakers use 周天（zhōu tiān）or 星期天（xīng qī tiān）instead of 周七（zhōu qī） or 星期七（xīng qīqī）. You can also express the names for days in a month by adding the suffix 日（rì） or 号（hào） after the number. For year, you can use the suffix 年（nián） after numbers, for example: 2019 年（èr líng yī jiǔ nián）. Compared with English, this is really easy to remember, right? If you're able to memorize the numbers, you should be able to say anything above.

In the telephone numbers, room numbers and bus/car numbers, the numeral 1 is often pronounced as yāo so as to clearly distinguish yī from qī.

In Chinese, a numeral does not modify a noun directly, but is followed by a measure word. Nouns have their proper measure words to go with, e.g. 一个人 （yí gè rén）, 两条狗（liǎng tiáo gǒu）, 三辆车 （sān liàng chē） which means one person, two dogs, and three cars. Frankly speaking, this causes much headache for learners. Measure words have to be learned together with each individual noun. However, there is a general measure word 个（gè） which is applicable to almost every individual noun. In case you are not sure which measure word goes with a certain noun, you may use 个（gè） as a substitute. This way, your Chinese will not be so idiomatic, but it is better than not to use a measure word at all.

Fun facts:

Sometimes in written Chinese, numbers can represent certain phrases because they sound similar. For example:

521. Don’t say “wǔbǎi èr shí yī” here, just “wǔ èr yī”; it sounds similar to 我爱你（wǒ ài nǐ）, which means “I love you”.

518. Don’t say “wǔbǎi yī shí bā” here, just “wǔ yāo bā”; it sounds similar to 我要发（wǒ yào fā）, which means “I’ll be rich”.

1314. Don’t say “yī qiān sān bǎi yī shí sì” here, just “yī sān yī sì”; it sounds similar to 一生一世（yì shēng yí shì）, which means “All life long”.

There are other things to talk about related to numbers, which can be covered in more advanced lessons.

Chapter 4: How to be polite when speaking Chinese?

Native Chinese speakers have a paragraph summarizing the key point to be polite. In this chapter, our main objective is to learn about this paragraph. If you can bear this paragraph in mind and use it accordingly when speaking Chinese, your listeners will surely consider you to be a very polite person. You may keep in mind that you don't really need to use these expressions with someone close to you as they are far too formal. Here is the paragraph.

请人帮忙说劳驾，请给方便说借光。

麻烦别人说打扰，不知适宜用冒昧。

求人解答用请问，请人指点用赐教。

赞人见解用高见，自己意见用拙见。

看望别人用拜访，宾客来到用光临。

陪伴朋友用奉陪，中途先走用失陪。

等候客人用恭候，迎接表歉用失迎。

别人离开用再见，请人不送用留步。

欢迎顾客称光顾，答人问候用托福。

问人年龄用贵庚，老人年龄用高寿。

读人文章用拜读，请人改文用斧正。

对方字画为墨宝，自己字画用拙笔。

邀请别人用屈驾，招待不周说怠慢。

请人收礼用笑纳，辞谢馈赠用心领。

问人姓氏用贵姓，回答询问用免贵。

表演技能用献丑，别人赞扬说过奖。

向人祝贺道恭喜，答人道贺用同喜。

请人担职用屈就，暂时充任说承乏。

对方亲眷多带令，称呼己方常带家。

qǐng rén bāng máng shuō láo jià, qǐng gěi fāng biàn shuō jiè guāng
má fán bié rén shuō dǎ rǎo, bù zhī shì yí yòng mào mèi
qiú rén jiě dá yòng qǐng wèn, qǐng rén zhǐ diǎn yòng cì jiào
zàn rén jiàn jiě yòng gāo jiàn, zì jǐ yì jiàn yòng zhuō jiàn
kàn wàng bié rén yòng bài fǎng, bīn kè lái dào yòng guāng lín
péi bàn péng yǒu yòng fèng péi, zhōng tú xiān zǒu yòng shī péi
děng hòu kè rén yòng gōng hòu, yíng jiē biǎo qiàn yòng shī yíng
bié rén lí kāi yòng zài jiàn, qǐng rén bú sòng yòng liú bù
huān yíng gù kè chēng guāng gù, dá rén wèn hòu yòng tuō fú
wèn rén nián líng yòng guì gēng, lǎo rén nián líng yòng gāo shòu
dú rén wén zhāng yòng bài dú, qǐng rén gǎi wén yòng fǔ zhèng
duì fāng zì huà wéi mò bǎo, zì jǐ zì huà yòng zhuō bǐ
yāo qǐng bié rén yòng qū jià, zhāo dài bùzhōu shuō dài màn
qǐng rén shōu lǐ yòng xiào nà, cí xiè kuì zèng yòng xīn lǐng
wèn rén xìng shì yòng guì xìng, huí dá xún wèn yòng miǎn guì
biǎo yǎn jì néng yòng xiàn chǒu, bié rén zàn yáng shuō guò jiǎng
xiàng rén zhù hè dào gōng xǐ, dá rén dào hè yòng tóng xǐ
qǐng rén dān zhí yòng qū jiù, zàn shí chōng rèn shuō chéng fá
duì fāng qīn juàn duō dài lìng, chēng hū jǐ fāng cháng dài jiā

Don't panic! We will analyze this paragraph sentence by sentence. After we finish this chapter, you will see how easy it is to remember the ways to express yourself politely.

请人帮忙说劳驾，请给方便说借光（qǐng rén bāng máng shuō láo jià, qǐng gěi fāng biàn shuō jiè guāng）。

When asking for a favor, remember to use 劳驾（láo jià）which means please. For example:

劳驾帮我拿一下（láo jià bāng wǒ náyí xià）。

Please help me hold this.

When you want to move some where but someone is blocking your way, remember to say **借光**（jiè guāng）which means excuse me. For example:

借光，我过去（jiè guāng, wǒ guò qù）。

Excuse me, please let me pass.

麻烦别人说打扰，不知适宜用冒昧（má fán bié rén shuō dǎ rǎo, bù zhī shì yí yòng mào mèi）。

When you have some questions to ask a stranger, you can say **打**扰了（dǎ rǎo le）which means sorry to bother you. If you are not sure whether it is OK or when it is appropriate to ask the question, you can use **冒昧**（mào mèi） to start the sentence. For example:

打扰一下，请问机场在哪（dǎ rǎo yí xià, qǐng wèn jī chǎng zài nǎ）？

Sorry to bother you, could you please show me the way to the airport?

冒昧问一句，我能走了吗（mào mèi wèn yí jù, wǒ néng zǒu le ma）**？**

Excuse me, when can I leave?**求人解答用**请问，请人指点用赐教（qiú rén jiě dá yòng qǐng wèn, qǐng rén zhǐ diǎn yòng cì jiào）。

When asking questions, remember to use "请问" （qǐng wèn）.

When you need someone to help you to solve a problem, use 赐教 （cì jiào）to show modesty. For example:

请问你叫什么名字（qǐng wèn nǐ jiào shénme míng zì）？

May I have your name please?

这道题我实在想不出来，不知您能否赐教 （zhè dào tí wǒ shí zài xiǎng bù chū lái, bù zhī nín néng fǒu cì jiào）？

I really can't solve this problem, could you please help me out?

赞人见解用高见，自己意见用拙见（zàn rén jiàn jiě yòng gāo jiàn, zì jǐ yì jiàn yòng zhuō jiàn）。

When complimenting someone's opinions, use 高见（gāo jiàn）.

While mentioning your own opinions, use 拙见 （zhuō jià). For example:

您的这番高见让我获益匪浅（nín de zhè fān gāo jiàn ràng wǒ huò yì fěi qiǎn）。

Your wonderful opinion has benefited me a lot.

小小拙见，让您见笑了（xiǎo xiǎo zhuō jiàn, ràng nín jiàn xiào le）。

Please pardon me with my limited thoughts.

看望别人用拜访，宾客来到用光临（kàn wàng bié rén yòng bài fǎng, bīn kè lái dào yòng guāng lín）。

When visiting a client, supervisor, or a senior, use 拜访（bài fǎng）.

When you are welcoming visitors, use 光临 （guāng lín). For example:

有时间我想拜访一下你的父母（yǒu shí jiān wǒ xiǎng bài fǎng yíxià nǐ de fù mǔ）。

I would like to visit your parents when I have time.

非常感谢您的光临（fēi cháng gǎn xiè nín de guāng lín）。

Thank you for visiting us.

陪伴朋友用奉陪，中途先走用失陪（péi bàn péng yǒu yòng fèng péi, zhōng tú xiān zǒu yòng shī péi）。

When accompanying friends, you can use **奉陪**（fèng péi）. If you need to leave at the middle of an event/activity, don't forget to use **失陪**（shī péi). For example:

大家都是朋友，那我就奉陪到底了（dà jiā dōu shì péng yǒu, nà wǒ jiù fèng péi dào dǐ le）。

We're all friends, so I'll be withyou to the end.

我有点急事需要处理，失陪了（wǒ yǒu diǎn jí shì xū yào chù lǐ, shī péi le）。

I'm sorry for leavng early because of something urgent.**等候客人用恭候，迎接表歉用失迎**（děng hòu kè rén yòng gōng hòu, yíng jiē biǎo qiàn yòng shī yíng）。

When waiting for esteemed guests to arrive, use **恭候**（gōng hòu）. If you've missed your guests or they arrived before you, you can use **失迎**（shī yíng). For example:

我们会在此恭候您的大驾（wǒ men huì zài cǐ gōng hòu nín de dà jià）。

We're honored to await your arrival.

不好意思，失迎了（bù hǎo yì sī, shī yíng le ）。

I'm really sorry for not welcoming you earlier.

别人离开用再见，请人不送用留步（bié rén lí kāi yòng zài jiàn, qǐng rén bú sòng yòng liú bù）。

When parting with someone, don't forget to say **再**见（zài jiàn）. If someone insists on accompaning you to the last minute, you can say **留步**（liú bù）.

非常感谢您的热情招待，请留步（fēi cháng gǎn xiè nín de rè qíng zhāo dài, qǐng liú bù）。
Thank you very much for your warm hospitality; you don’t need to see me out.
欢迎顾客称光顾，答人问候用托福（huān yíng gù kè chēng guāng gù, dá rén wèn hòu yòng tuō fú）。
When expressing your gratitude to your visitors, you can use **光**顾（guāng gù）. When answering someone’s questions related to your current statusor situation, you can use **托福**（tuō fú). For example:
非常感谢您的光顾（fēi cháng gǎn xiè nín de guāng gù）。
Thank you very much for visiting us.
最近怎么样?——**托您的福，一切安好**（zuì jìn zěn me yàng? ——tuō nín de fú， yí qiè ān hǎo）。
How are you lately?——Everything’s fine, thank you for asking.
问人年龄用贵庚，老人年龄用高寿（wèn rén nián líng yòng guì gēng, lǎo rén nián líng yòng gāo shòu）。
When asking someone’s age, you can use the word 贵庚（guì gēng）, but don’t use this word when asking kids. For a senior, you should use the word **高寿**（gāo shòu）.
In traditional Chinese culture, age is not considered to be private. It is a topic often brought up in social occasions. Nevertheless, different ways are employed to ask about the age of different people. For kids younger than ten, people ask “**你今年几**岁了?”（nǐ jīn nián jǐ suì le） For a young person or someone of one’s own age, one may ask “**你今年多大了**?”（nǐ jīn nián duō dà le） or the polite way, “**您**贵庚（nín guì gēng）?”. For an elder person, however, one should use “**您高寿**（nín gāo shòu）?” to show respect.

读人文章用拜读，请人改文用斧正（dú rén wén zhāng yòng bài dú, qǐng rén gǎi wén yòng fǔ zhèng）。

When reading someone's paperwork, use the word **拜读**（bài dú）, when you need someone to proofread your paperwork, use the word **斧正**（fǔ zhèng）. For example:

听说您的论文出版了，能否拜读一下（tīng shuō nín de lùn wén chū bǎn le, néng fǒu bài dú yī xià）?

I heard that your essay has been published; could I read it?

我的稿子写完了，请斧正（wǒ de gǎo zǐ xiě wán le, qǐng fǔ zhèng）。

I've finished writing my paper; please proofread it.

对方字画为墨宝，自己字画用拙笔（duì fāng zì huà wéi mò bǎo, zì jǐ zì huà yòng zhuō bǐ）。

If you want to compliment someone's painting, use the word **墨宝**（mò bǎo）. If you paint, and you would like someone to look at it, use the word **拙笔**（zhuō bǐ). For example:

让我来欣赏一下您的墨宝（ràng wǒ lái xīn shǎng yī xià nín de mò bǎo）。

Please allow me to enjoy your masterpiece.

我这里也有一些拙笔，请您过目（wǒ zhè lǐ yě yǒu yī xiē zhuō bǐ, qǐng nín guò mù）。

I have here some of my paintings; please take a look.

邀请别人用屈驾，招待不周说怠慢（yāo qǐng bié rén yòng qū jià, zhāo dài bú zhōu shuō dài màn）。

If you want to invite someone to go with you, remember to use the word **屈驾**（qū jià）. If you're treating your guests, you can use the word **怠慢**（dài màn). For example:

请问您能屈驾跟我走一趟吗（qǐng wèn nín néng qū jià gēn wǒ zǒu yī tàng ma）？

Are you able to travelwith me?

招待不周，多有怠慢，请见谅 （zhāo dài bú zhōu, duō yǒu dài màn, qǐng jiàn liàng）。

Please forgive me for the oversight.

请人收礼用笑纳，辞谢馈赠用心领（qǐng rén shōu lǐ yòng xiào nà, cí xiè kuì zèng yòng xīn lǐng）。

When you are giving gift to someone, you can use **笑**纳（xiào nà）.

When refusing someone's gift, you can say **心**领（xīn lǐng）. For example:

小小薄礼，请笑纳（xiǎo xiǎo báo lǐ, qǐng xiào nà）。

Please accept this small gift.

您的礼物我心领了（nín de lǐ wù wǒ xīn lǐng le）。

Thank you for the gift. I must reject, but I've taken it to heart.

问人姓氏用贵姓，回答询问用免贵 （wèn rén xìng shì yòng guì xìng, huí dá xún wèn yòng miǎn guì）。

When asking for someone's surname, use the word 贵姓（guì xìng）. To answer the question, start the sentence with **免**贵（miǎn guì）. We'll analyze these in the next chapter.

表演技能用献丑，别人赞扬说过奖（biǎo yǎn jì néng yòng xiàn chǒu, bié rén zàn yáng shuō guò jiǎng）。

When you want to put on a performance, like singing or dancing, you can use **献丑**（xiàn chǒu）. If the audience likes your show and compliments you, you can use 过奖（guò jiǎng）to respond. For example:

既然大家盛情难却，那我就献丑唱上一段（jì rán dà jiā shèng qíng nán què, nà wǒ jiù xiàn chǒu chàng shàng yí duàn ）。
Thank you for your warm invitation. I'll embarrass myself and sing a song.
您唱得真好! ——**您**过奖了（nín chàng dé zhēn hǎo! ——nín guò jiǎng le）。
You sing really well! ——You're far too kind.
向人祝贺道恭喜，答人道贺用同喜（xiàng rén zhù hè dào gōng xǐ, dá rén dào hè yòng tóng xǐ）。
When something good happens to someone, and you are happy forhim, you can use **恭喜**（gōng xǐ）. As a response to **恭喜**（gōng xǐ）, you can use **同喜** （tóng xǐ）.
我成功了（wǒ chéng gōng le）！——**真是恭喜你**（zhēn shì gōng xǐ nǐ le）**了**。——**同喜同喜**（tóng xǐ tóng xǐ）！
I've succeeded! ——Congratulations! ——Thank you.
请人担职用屈就，暂时充任说承乏（qǐng rén dān zhí yòng qū jiù, zàn shí chōng rèn shuō chéng fá）。
If you are trying to offer an important corporate position to someone, you can use the phrase **屈就**（qū jiù）. On the contrary, if someone is offering a position to you, you should use the word **承乏**（chéng fá）.
不知您能否屈就我司总经理一职（bú zhī nín néng fǒu qū jiù wǒ sī zǒng jīng lǐ yī zhí）？
Would you mind accepting the offer of being the general manager of our company?
既然如此，我只好承乏其位了（jì rán rú cǐ， wǒzhíhǎo chéng fá qí wèi le）。
I'll have to take the job if you insist, but if you find someone better, please replace me.

对方亲眷多带令，称呼己方常带家（duì fāng qīn juàn duō dài lìng, chēng hū jǐ fāng cháng dài jiā）。

Just take some examples here:

令尊（lìng zūn）, your father

令堂（lìng táng）, your mother

令爱（lìng ài）, your daughter

令郎（lìng láng）, your son

家父（jiā fù）, my father

家母（jiā mǔ）, my mother

All these mentioned are pronouns, very hard pronouns. So just try to keep them in mind for some additional understnading. We'll have detailed discussions in our advanced books.

All in all, due to cultural differences, many of the polite expressions may be strange for an English speaker. You may be able to tell when reading the translation. Please remember here, many translations are just literally translated from Chinese so as to help your understanding.

Chapter 5: Greeting and Introduction

We'll introduce you a sample paragraph here, then we'll discuss some of the most commonly used sentences and practice speaking them one by one. If you can remember these, you should be able to form your own sentences.

大家早上好，**我叫**张阳，来自中国，很高兴认识大家。五年前，我大学毕业并取得学士学位，我的专业是中国文学。我当时的梦想是成为一名记者，因此毕业后，我到处寻找工作，在不同的报社实习。现在我是一个网络小说作者，我很喜欢我现在的工作，**因**为我有时间可以到处旅行。我去过很多国家，比如日本、韩国、美国和澳大利亚。每个国家都有各自的特色，我特别喜欢美国的现代和繁华。在独自旅行的时候，我结识了很多朋友。因为资金有限，我在每个国家呆的时间都不会太长，虽然停留不了多久，但我每天都很高兴。哦，对了，我还没有结婚，也没有孩子。

我出生于 1992 **年** 3 **月** 1 **日**，**今年** 27 岁。我没有兄弟姐妹，爸爸妈妈就只有我一个孩子，我现在自己住在北京的公寓里。我的爸爸是一名医生，妈妈是一名中学教师，他们住在上海。我的父母养了一条可爱的小狗，名字叫豆豆，每次回家，晚上我都会带它去公园散步。上海有我很多小时候的朋友，他们有的已经结婚生子，有的还在继续上学。我们有时会约好见个面，一同谈谈学习、工作和生活中的事。总之，我对现在很满意。

感谢你来听我的故事，再见。

dà jiā zǎo shàng hǎo, wǒ jiào zhāng yáng, lái zì zhōng guó, hěn gāo xìng rèn shí dà jiā. wǔ nián qián, wǒ dà xué bì yè bìng qǔ dé xué shì xué wèi, wǒ de zhuān yè shì zhōng guó wén xué. wǒ dāng shí de mèng xiǎng shì chéng wéi yìmíng jì zhě, yīn cǐ bì yè hòu, wǒ dào chù xún zhǎo gōng zuò, zài bú tóng de bào shè shí xí. xiàn zài wǒ shìyígè wǎng luò xiǎo shuō zuò zhě, wǒ hěn xǐ huān wǒ xiàn zài de gōng zuò, yīn wéi wǒ yǒu shí jiān kě yǐ dào chù lǚxíng. wǒ qù guò hěn duō guó jiā, bǐ rú rì běn, hán guó, měi guó hé ào dà lì yà. měi gè guó jiā dōu yǒu gè zì de tè sè, wǒ tè bié xǐ huān měi guó de xiàn dài hé fán huá. zài dú zì lǚxíngde shí hòu, wǒ jié shí le hěn duō péng yǒu. yīn wéi zī jīn yǒu xiàn, wǒ zài měi gè guó jiā dāi de shí jiān dōu bú huì tàicháng, suī rán tíng liú búliǎo duō jiǔ, dàn wǒ měi tiān dōu hěn gāo xìng. o, duì le, wǒ hái méi yǒu jié hūn, yě méi yǒu háizi.

wǒ chū shēng yú yī jiǔ jiǔ èr nián sān yuè yī rì, jīn nián èr shí qī suì. wǒ méi yǒu xiōng dì jiě mèi, bà ba mā ma jiùzhǐyǒu wǒyígè hái zi, wǒ xiàn zài zì jǐ zhù zài běi jīng de gōng yù lǐ. wǒ de bà ba shìyìmíng yī shēng, mā ma shìyìmíng zhōng xué jiào shī, tā men zhù zài shàng hǎi. wǒ de fù mǔ yǎng le yìtiáo kě ài de xiǎo gǒu, míng zì jiào dòudou, měi cì huí jiā, wǎn shàng wǒ dōu huì dài tā qù gōng yuán sàn bù. shàng hǎi yǒu wǒ hěn duō xiǎo shí hòu de péng yǒu, tā men yǒu de yǐ jīng jié hūn shēng zǐ, yǒu de hái zài jì xù shàng xué. wǒ men yǒu shí huì yuē hǎo jiàn gè miàn, yìtóng tán tán xué xí, gōng zuò hé shēng huó zhōng de shì. zǒng zhī, wǒ duì xiàn zài hěn mǎn yì. xièxienǐ lái tīng wǒ de gù shì, zài jiàn.

Now, let's analyze this paragraph sentence by sentence.

大家早上好，我叫张阳，来自中国，很高兴认识大家。（dà jiā zǎo shàng hǎo, wǒ jiào zhāng yáng, lái zì zhōng guó, hěn gāo xìng rèn shí dà jiā）。

Good morning, everyone. My name is Zhang Yang. I'm from China; nice to meet you all.

In most places, you will get a warm and friendly response to your enthusiasm in speaking Chinese. A conversation can be struck and acquaintances made with just a few words.

The most often used greeting, appropriate for all occasions, is 你好（nǐ hǎo）. That said, when Chinese people meet, various amenities and civilities are exchanged. For instance:

你好! 好久不见，最近好吗（nǐ hǎo! hǎo jiǔ bú jiàn, zuì jìn hǎo ma）?

How are you? We haven't seen each other forsuch a long time.How are you lately?工作怎么样? 忙吗（gōng zuò zěn me yàng? máng ma）?

How's your work? Have you been busy?

身体好吗? 家里人都好吧（shēn tǐ hǎo ma? jiā lǐ rén dōu hǎo ba）?

Are you well? Is your family well?

你去哪儿（nǐ qù nǎ ér）?

Where are you going?

吃了吗（chī le ma）?

Have you eaten yet?

孩子学习怎么样（hái zixué xí zěn me yàng）?

How are the children doing in their studies?

听说你前些天去外地了，什么时候回来的（tīng shuō nǐ qián xiē tiān qù wài dì le, shén me shí hòu huí lái de）？

I heard that you went away a few days ago. When did you get back?

你好像瘦了（nǐ hǎo xiàng shòu le）？

You seem to be losing weight.

几天不见，你更漂亮了（jǐ tiān bú jiàn, nǐ gèng piàoliàng le）！

I haven't seen you for a few days; you've become prettier!

冷吗？**你穿的太少了**，**小心**别感冒（lěng ma？nǐ chuān de tài shǎo le, xiǎo xīn bié gǎn mào）！

Aren't you cold? You're wearing so little, be careful not to catch a cold!

这件衣服挺漂亮的，是新买的（zhè jiàn yī fú tǐng piàoliàng de, shì xīn mǎi de）？

This is a beautiful dress; did you just buy it?

The other party may give a truthful and factual answer or just a brief answer like 还可以（hái kě yǐ, passable）, **挺好的**（tǐng hǎo de, quite well）, **不太忙**（bú tài máng, not very busy）, **我出去了一趟**（wǒ chū qù le yítàng, I went away）, **吃了**（chī le, I had dinner）. Thesequestions indicate that the person asking them is concerned about you or interested in you. There's no reason to feel uncomfortable or upset since they're just amenities.

When coming across someone, the Chinese don't often say **你好**（nǐ hǎo, how are you）or **早上好**（zǎo shàng hǎo, good morning）. They are used to asking questions about what you are doing or what you're about to do in accordance with the time or situation. For instance: **上**课去呀（shàng kè qù ya, going to class?）? **出去呀**（chū qù ya, going out?）? **回来啦**（huí láila, you're back?）? **洗**

衣服呢（xǐ yī fú ne, doing laundry?）? 吃饭呢（chī fàn ne, eating?）?, Etc.

When parting from each other, some common civilities include but are limited to:

我还有点儿别的事，改天咱们好好儿聊聊（wǒ hái yǒu diǎn ér bié de shì, gǎi tiān zán men hǎo hǎo ér liáoliao）。

I have something else to attend to, so let's have a chat some other time.

有空儿来家里坐坐（yǒu kōng ér lái jiā lǐ zuòzuo）。

Come and visit us when you have time.

But this may just be polite convention, and may not necessarily be an invitation. Only when the date and time is given is it meant as an invitation.

"我叫（wǒ jiào）……" is the answer to "你叫什么名字（nǐ jiào shénme míngzi）?" ——What is your name?

你叫什么名字（nǐ jiào shénme míng zi）is used to ask someone for his or her full name. 您（nín） is a more polite form of 你（nǐ）. It is usually used for seniors or people of an older generation or a higher rank. It can also be used for people of the same age in order to sound more formal and polite. The answer can also be 我是（wǒ shì）…, usually giving both the surname and the first name.

We can use a respectful and polite way of asking for the surname of someone you have just met for the first time: 您贵姓（nín guì xìng）? This person would reply with "免贵姓（miǎn guì xìng）……"

A Chinese name starts with the family name and ends with the given name. There are over 5,000 Chinese family names, among which more than 200 are commonly seen. 张（zhāng）, 王（wáng）, 李（lǐ）, and 赵（zhào） are the most common ones. Such family names that have only one character are known as single-character surnames. Most Chinese people have a single-character surname. There are surnames with two or more characters also, which are called compound-character surnames, such as **欧阳** （ōu yáng）, **上官** （shàng guān）, and 诸葛（zhū gě）. Try to find your own Chinese name!

A person can be addressed with his/her family name followed by his/her job or profession. For instance, 张阳（zhāng yáng） is a teacher, so we can call her 张老师（zhāng lǎo shī）- literally, it means Teacher Zhang.

"**来自中国**（lái zì zhōng guó）" is the answer to "**你是哪国人**（nǐ shì nǎ guó rén）?" ——Where are you from?

It is used to inquire the nationality of someone having the same meaning with "**你从哪儿来**（nǐ cóng nǎ ér lái）?"

You can also reply by saying "**我是从……来的**（wǒ shì cóng ……lái de）" This structure is used to explain the place where you come from.

我很高兴认识你/**您**（wǒ hěn gāo xìng rèn shinǐ /nín）。

It's nice to meet you.

It is used when meeting someone for the first time. The answer is "**我也是**（wǒ yě shì）" which means "me, too". If it's not the first time, you need to say "**我很高**兴见到你/**您**（wǒ hěn gāo xìng jiàn dào nǐ /nín）" which means "it's good to see you". The answer can be the same.

五年前，我大学毕业并取得学士学位，我的专业是中国文学（wǔ nián qián, wǒ dà xué bì yè bìng qǔ dé xué shì xué wèi, wǒ de zhuān yè shì zhōng guó wén xué）。

Five years ago, I graduated from university with a bachelor's degree. My major was Chinese Literature.

With this sentence you can talk about your education, your major, and even your campus life. Questions you may hear Chinese people ask include:

你是大学生吗（nǐ shì dà xué shēng ma）？

Are you a university student?

大几了（dà jǐ le）？

What grade?

什么专业（shén me zhuān yè）？

What is your major?

我当时的梦想是成为一名记者，因此毕业后，我到处寻找工作，在不同的报社实习（wǒ dāng shí de mèng xiǎng shì chéng wéi yì míng jì zhě, yīn cǐ bì yè hòu, wǒ dào chù xún zhǎo gōng zuò, zài bú tóng de bào shè shí xí）。

My dream by then was to be a journalist. Therefore, after graduation, I looked for jobs everywhere, and did internship at many different newspaper offices.

This can be used to talk about your past experiences. Because verbs in Chinese do not need to change according to the tense, talking about the past, present, or future has no difference for the verbs. You need only add different adverbials of time.

现在我是一个网络小说作者，我很喜欢我现在的工作，因为我有时间可以到处旅行（xiàn zài wǒ shìyígè wǎng luò xiǎo shuō zuò zhě, wǒ hěn xǐ huān wǒ xiàn zài de gōng zuò, yīn wéi wǒ yǒu shí jiān kě yǐ dào chù lǚxíng）。

I'm now making a living by writing novelsonline. I love what I am doing right now because I have plenty of time to travel all over the world.

This can be used to introduce your current situation.

我去过很多国家，比如日本、韩国、美国和澳大利亚（wǒ qù guò hěn duō guó jiā, bǐ rú rì běn, hán guó, měi guó hé ào dà lì yà）。

I've been to many different countries, such as Japan, South Korea, America, and Australia.

Each country has their Chinese name, as well as major cities, famous places, beautiful sights, cuisine, celebrities, movies, etc. You have to remember these proper nouns every time you learn them. A sidenote--Hong Kong and Taiwan may use different versions of these proper nouns. Don't worry about it too much for now. Rome was not built in a day.

每个国家都有各自的特色，我特别喜欢美国的现代和繁华（měi gè guó jiā dōu yǒu gè zì de tè sè, wǒ tè bié xǐ huān měi guó de xiàn dài hé fán huá）。

Every country has its own characteristics. I especially like the prosperous and moderness of America.

"我喜欢（wǒ xǐ huān）……" is used to express someone's affirmation towards something, the negationis "我不喜欢（wǒ bù xǐ huān）……"

By changing the pronoun or adding the particle, we can form many different sentences, for example:

你喜欢美国的什么呢（nǐ xǐ huān měi guó de shénme ne）？

What do you like about America?

她应该喜欢唱歌吧（tā yīng gāi xǐ huān chàng gē ba）？

She likes to sing, doesn't she?

在独自旅行的时候，我结识了很多朋友（zài dú zì lǚxíngde shí hòu, wǒ jié shí le hěn duō péng yǒu）。

While travelling alone, I met and became friends with many different people.

Here, you can add your own travel stories to make your speech more interesting.

因为资金有限，我在每个国家呆的时间都不会太长，虽然停留不了多久，但我每天都很高兴（yīn wéi zī jīn yǒu xiàn, wǒ zài měi gè guó jiā dāi de shí jiān dōu bú huì tàicháng, suī rán tíng liú búliǎoduō jiǔ, dàn wǒ měi tiān dōu hěn gāo xìng）。

Because of my limited budget, I couldn't stay long in the countries I travelled to. Though I couldn't stay for a long time, I felt happy every day when I was there.

When someone asks you "how did you enjoy your trip?" you can also answer like so.

哦，对了，我还没有结婚，也没有孩子（ o, duì le, wǒ hái méi yǒu jié hūn, yě méi yǒu hái zi）。

Oh right, I still haven't got married, and I don't have anychild.

结婚（jié hūn）here, 结（jié）is a verb, **婚**（hūn） is marriage,combined together, 结婚（jié hūn）means to get married.. Similar, **离婚**（lí hūn），to get divorced；订婚（dìng hūn），to get engaged.

我出生于 1992 年 3 月 1 日，今年 27 岁 （wǒ chū shēng yú yī jiǔ jiǔ èr nián sān yuè yī rì, jīn nián èr shí qī suì）。I was born in Mar. 1, 1992. I'm 27 years old.

Compared with English, Chinese people use the time order of year-month-day-hour-minute-second. Try to get out of the standard English format when speaking Chinese.

As we mentioned earlier, in traditional Chinese culture, age is not considered private. It is a topic often brought up in social occasions, so don't feel uncomfortable when receiving questions asking about your age. In addition, when seniors meet you again after a long time, they may say "**你胖了**（nǐ pàng le）" which literally means "you've gotten fat", but actually they just mean "you've been well" or "you are in good health". No neeed to be offended.

我没有兄弟姐妹，爸爸妈妈就只有我一个孩子，我现在自己住在北京的公寓里（wǒ méi yǒu xiōng dì jiě mèi, bàbamābajiùzhǐyǒu wǒyígè hái zi, wǒ xiàn zài zì jǐ zhù zài běi jīng de gōng yù lǐ）。

I have no brothers or sisters. I'm my parents' only child. I live in an apartment in Beijing by myself.

In China, people often ask about their friends' parents or children during conversations to show respect and concern, and people asked are normally pleased about this. Therefore, talking about family is one of the most important aspects in a conversation. In Chinese, the pronouns 哥哥/弟弟/姐姐/妹妹（gē ge/ dì di/ jiě jie/ mèi mei） equate to older / younger brother and older / younger sister in English. No adjective is needed to modify the pronoun.

Because of the one-child policy, most Chinese families have been single-child households. Citizens that lived in the city were allowed to give birth to one child while citizens that lived in the countryside were allowed to give birth to a second only if the first was a girl. If people broke the rule, they had to pay for a huge penalty. Now, however, the Chinese government allows all the citizens to give birth to two children.

我的爸爸是一名医生，妈妈是一名中学教师，他们住在上海（wǒ de bàbashìyìmíng yī shēng, māmashìyìmíng zhōng xué jiào shī, tā men zhù zài shàng hǎi）。

My father is a doctor and my mother is a middle school teacher; they live in Shanghai now.

When talking about occupation, just remember the sentence structure: personal pronoun + 是（shì）+ 一位/一名（**yí** wèi/ yì míng）+ occupation. For the places the person is working: personal pronoun + work in + places/ companies. Sometimes, the latter can be used to answer the question of occupation. For example:

你爸爸做什么工作（nǐ bà bà zuòshén me gōng zuò）？——他是一名翻译（tā shìyì míng fān yì）。

What is your father's job? ——He's a translator.

她老公做什么工作（tā lǎo gōng zuòshén me gōng zuò）？——她老公在一家研究所工作（tā lǎo gōng zài yì jiā yán jiū suǒ gōng zuò）。

What is her husband's job? ——Her husband works in a research institute.

我的父母养了一条可爱的小狗，名字叫豆豆，每次回家，晚上我都会带它去公园散步（wǒ de fù mǔ yǎng le yì **tiáo kě ài de xiǎo gǒu, míng zì jiào dòudou, měi cì huí jiā, wǎn shàng wǒ dōu huì dài tā qù gōng yuán sàn bù）。**

My parents have a very lovely dog called Doudou; I walk it through the park every time I go home.

In China, cats and dogs are as popular as they are in many other countries. When naming pets, Chinese people often use some cute names like they use tochildren. Some common pet names are 贝贝（bèibei）, 豆豆（dòudou）, 欢欢（huānhuan）, 乐乐（lè le）, 小花（xiǎo huā）, 喵喵（miāomiao）, etc. So when you are trying to choose a Chinese name, please avoid these names. Just imagine Chinese people choosing their English name as Honey, Sweety, Hero, April, Precious...you can't helplaughing, right? So it's best to avoid these names.

上海有我很多小时候的朋友，他们有的已经结婚生子，有的还在继续上学（shàng hǎi yǒu wǒ hěn duō xiǎo shí hòu de péng yǒu, tā men yǒu de yǐ jīng jié hūn shēng zǐ, yǒu de hái zài jì xù shàng xué）。

I have many friends in Shanghai whom I've known since a young age. Some of them have already gotten married and even had kids; some of them are still students.

In Chinese, **有的**（yǒu de）……**有的**（yǒu de）……is a really common structure. This structure indicates a parallel relationship. We can use it in many other situations as well. For example:

他们有的人睡觉，有的人看书（tā men yǒu de rén shuì jiào， yǒu de rén kàn shū）。

Some of them are sleeping while some of them are reading a book.

公园里有的人散步，有的人跳舞（gōng yuán lǐ yǒu de rén sàn bù， yǒu de rén tiào wǔ）。

There are many people in the park; some of them are walking while some of them are dancing.

我们有时会约好见个面，一同谈谈学习、工作和生活中的事（wǒ men yǒu shí huì yuē hǎo jiàn gè miàn, yì **tóng tán tan xué xí, gōng zuò hé shēng huó zhōng de shì）。**

Sometimes, we'll pick a time and get together to talk about things thosehappened during studies, work, or daily life.

Sometimes among friends, especially among those who have the same aspirations and interests, a periodic talk is held and it's somewhat of an academic discussion. A periodic talk is usually prearranged and requires some preparations. People would talk about a certain aspect of work or study so as to exchange thoughts and share common ideas. So if you really want to start this part of the conversation, you need to learn a lot and of course, keep learning. We will provide more topics in our advanced books.

总之，我对现在很满意（zǒng zhī, wǒ duì xiàn zài hěn mǎn yì）。

All in all, I'm very satisfied with my current situation.

When someone asks you "are you happy?" or questions like this, you can then introduce your current situation and come up with your conclusion in the end by using this sentence. Some examples of positive situations are:

我现在很快乐（wǒ xiàn zài hěn kuài lè）。

I'm pretty happy now.

我很享受现在的生活（wǒ hěn xiǎng shòu xiàn zài de shēng huó）。

I'm enjoying my life right now.

For negative conclusions, expect putting 不（bù）to the proper positions of the sentences, you can use the word like 难过/失落/寂寞（nán guò / shī luò / jì mò ）instead of 满意/快乐/享受（mǎn yì/ kuài lè/ xiǎng shòu）。For example:

我现在很寂寞（wǒ xiàn zài hěn jì mò）。

I'm really lonely right now.

现在的生活让我很失落（xiàn zài de shēng huó ràng wǒ hěn shī luò）。

I feel very sorry for myself.

谢谢你来听我的故事，再见（xièxienǐ lái tīng wǒ de gù shì, zài jiàn）。

Thank you for listening to my story. Goodbye.

The respond to 谢谢（xièxie） is 不谢/不用谢/不客气（bú xiè/ bú yòng xiè/ bú kè qì） which means "you're welcome", or "my pleasure".

As in English, there are many ways in Chinese to express "goodbye" or "see you later". When parting with someone, you may also include the time or location at which you will again see the other party, for example:

明天见（míng tiān jiàn）。

See you tomorrow.

一会儿见（yí huì ér jiàn）。

See you soon.

下周见（xià zhōu jiàn）。

See you next week.

门口见（mén kǒu jiàn）。

See you at the gate.

You can also use 一路平安/一路顺风（yí lù píng ān /yí lù shùn fēng） to say goodbye or to wish someone a safe journey.

Last but not least, asking about other people's stories is as interesting as telling them your own stories. In order to start and continue an exchange of stories, get to learn the questions listed. We're expected to come up with questions as well as giving responses.

Chapter 6: Daily Life and Social Activity

After learning some things related to grammar, we can finally go back to the practicing. Because this book is limited in length, we will only focus on different sentences in this chapter. For more explanations and language points, please refer to our advanced books.

In a Restaurant

你想吃什么（nǐ xiǎng chī shén me）？

What do you want to eat?

有沙拉吗（yǒu shā lā ma）？

Is there any salad?

这里面是什么（zhè lǐ miàn shì shén me）？

What's in this dish?

我要这个（wǒ yào zhè gè）。

I want this.

给我两碗米饭（gěi wǒ liǎng wǎn mǐ fàn）。

Two bowls of rice, please.

米饭和菜一起上（mǐ fàn hé cài yì qǐ shàng）。

Please bring the rice and dish together.

还要些什么（hái yào xiē shén me）？

What else do you want?

就要这些（jiù yào zhè xiē）。

These will be enough.

不要了（bú yào le）。

Nothing else.

我们不吃螃蟹（wǒ men bù chī páng xiè）。

We don't like to eat crab.

再来一瓶果汁（zài lái yì píng guǒ zhī）。

A cup of juice, please.

我要买单（wǒ yào mǎi dān）。

I'll pay the bill.

我们要发票和收据（wǒ men yào fā piào hé shōu jù）。

Wewant the receipt and invoice.

可以打包吗（kě yǐ dǎ bāo ma）？

Can I pack the remaining food?

In a Shop

您要买什么（nín yào mǎi shén me）？

What do you want to buy?

我看看（wǒ kànkan）。

Let me see.

这个多少钱（zhè gè duō shǎo qián）？

How much is this?

打折吗（dǎ zhé ma）？

Can I get a discount?

太贵了（tài guì le）。

(That's) too expensive.

能便宜一点吗（néng pián yiyìdiǎn ma）？

Can you make it a little cheaper?

还有别的颜色吗（hái yǒu bié de yán sè ma）？

Do you have another color?

有没有更好的（yǒu méi yǒu gèng hǎo de）？

Do you havea better one?

能换一个吗（néng huàn yí gè ma）？

Can you show me another one?

我喜欢这条裤子（wǒ xǐ huān zhè tiáo kùzi）。

I like these pants.

能试一试吗（néng shìyí shì ma）？

Can I try them on?

In a Taxi

你要去哪里（nǐ yào qù nǎ lǐ）？

Where are you going?

去超市（qù chāo shì）。

I'm going to the supermarket.

请开一下后备箱（qǐng kāi yí xià hòu bèi xiāng）。

Please open the trunk.

你知道怎么去超市吗（nǐ zhī dào zěn me qù chāo shì ma）？

Do you know how to get to the supermarket?

请快一点（qǐng kuài yì diǎn）。

Please hurry up.

请不要开太快（qǐng bú yào kāi tài kuài）。

Please don't drive too fast.

大概要多少时间（dà gài yào duō shǎo shí jiān）？

How long do you need to go there?

你能停一下吗（nǐ néng tíng yíxià ma）？

Can you stop for a minute?

你能等我十分钟吗（nǐ néng děng wǒ shí fèn zhōng ma）？

Can you wait for me for like ten minutes?

你有零钱吗（nǐ yǒu líng qián ma）？

Do you have change?

去机场多少钱（qù jī chǎng duō shǎo qián）？

How much from here to the airport?

On the Road

请问公园怎么走（qǐng wèn gōng yuán zěn me zǒu）？

Could you please tell me how to get to the park?

洗手间在什么地方（xǐ shǒu jiān zài shén me dì fāng）？

Can you show me the way to the toilet?

附近有饭店吗（fù jìn yǒu fàn diàn ma）？

Are there any restaurants nearby?

这趟车去不去机场（zhè tàng chē qù bú qù jī chǎng）？

Is this vehicle heading to the airport?

向前直走（xiàng qián zhí zǒu）。

Go straight.

向左拐（xiàng zuǒ guǎi）。

Turn left.

你得去马路对面坐车（nǐděiqù mǎ lù duì miàn zuò chē）。

You have to get a taxi across the street.

这是什么地方（zhè shì shén me dì fāng）？

What is this place?

我们现在在哪里（wǒ men xiàn zài zài nǎ lǐ）？

Where are we?

走这边还是那边（zǒu zhè biān hái shì nà biān）？

Shall we go this way or that way?

去火车站到哪下（qù huǒ chē zhàn dào nǎ xià）？

Where should I get off the bus if I need to go to the train station?

Things Related to Time

现在几点了（xiàn zài jǐ diǎn le）？

What time is it now?

今天几号（jīn tiān jǐ hào）？

What day is today?

明天星期几（míng tiān xīng qī jǐ）？

What day is tomorrow?

你什么时候有空（nǐ shén me shí hòu yǒu kòng）？

When will you be free?

周末我没时间（zhōu mò wǒ méi shí jiān）。

I'm busy on the weekend.

你几点到几点上班（nǐ jǐ diǎn dào jǐ diǎn shàng bān）。

What time do you work?

我明天九点来找你（wǒ míng tiān jiǔ diǎn lái zhǎo nǐ）。

I'll come to get you tomorrow at 9 o'clock.

请晚上八点后打电话（qǐng wǎn shàng bā diǎn hòu dǎ diàn huà）。

Please call me after 8pm.

你等多久了（nǐ děng duō jiǔ le）？

How long you have been waiting?

我们在这学习一个月（wǒ men zài zhè xué xíyígè yuè）。

We will study here for a month.

火车几点开（huǒ chē jǐ diǎn kāi）？

When will the train leave?

飞机什么时候起飞（fēi jīshénme shí hòu qǐ fēi）？

When will the plane depart?

明天几点到北京（míng tiān jǐ diǎn dào běi jīng）？

When will you arrive in Beijing tomorrow?

你们哪天回家（nǐ men nǎ tiān huí jiā）？

What day are you going back home?

你打算什么时候再来（nǐ dǎ suàn shén me shí hòu zài lái）？

When are you planning to come back?

Business Negotiation

鉴于这几年的良好合作关系，我们准备接受你方的价格（jiàn yú zhè jǐ nián de liáng hǎo hé zuò guān xì, wǒ men zhǔn bèi jiē shòu nǐ fāng de jià gé）。

In view of our good cooperation over the past few years, we are prepared to accept your offer.

我认为我们应该各自折中一下以便业务成交（wǒ rèn wéi wǒ men yīng gāi gè zìzhézhōng yíxià yǐ biàn yè wù chéng jiāo）。

I think we should come to a compromise with each other so as to close the deal.

若双方各自做些让步，生意是很容易达成的（ruò shuāng fāng gè zì zuò xiē ràng bù, shēng yì shì hěn róng yì dá chéng de）。

Business is quite possible if both sides make some concessions.

我们准备降低价格（wǒ men zhǔn bèi jiàng dī jià gé）。

We're ready to decrease the price.

百分之十的折扣太离谱了，我们准备给你百分之四（bǎi fèn zhī shí de zhékòu tài lí pǔ le, wǒ men zhǔn bèi gěi nǐ bǎi fèn zhī sì）。

A 10% discount is off the table, but we're willing to offer you 6%

Asking for Help

对不起，我要下车（duì bú qǐ， wǒ yào xià chē）。

Sorry, I need to get off (the vehicle).

你能帮我一个忙吗（nǐ néng bāng wǒyí gè máng ma）？

Can you do me a favor?

麻烦你帮帮我吧（má fán nǐ bāng bang wǒ ba）。

Please help me.

你有什么事（nǐ yǒu shén me shì）？

What's up?

你怎么了（nǐ zěn me le）？

What happened?

请送我去医院（qǐng sòng wǒ qù yī yuàn）。

Please take me to the hospital.

快叫警察（kuài jiào jǐng chá）！

Call the police!

救命（jiù mìng）！

Help!

怎么办（zěn me bàn）？

What should I do?

我迷路了（wǒ mí lù le）。

I'm lost.

我的机票丢了（wǒ de jī piào diū le）。

I lost my plane ticket.

可以用一下你的手机吗（kě yǐ yòng yíxià nǐ de shǒu jī ma）？

Can I borrow your cellphone?

你真是太好了（nǐ zhēn shì tài hǎo le）！

That's so nice of you.

非常感谢（fēi cháng gǎn xiè）！

Thank you so much.

Saying Goodbye

时间过得真快（shí jiān guò dé zhēn kuài）。

Time flies.

我们来跟您告别（wǒ men lái gēn nín gào bié）。

We've come to say goodbye to you.

请收下这个小礼物（qǐng shōu xià zhè gè xiǎo lǐ wù）。

Please accept this small gift.

希望你喜欢（xī wàng nǐ xǐ huān）。

I hope you like it.

你给了我很多帮助（nǐ gěi le wǒ hěn duō bāng zhù）。

You've helped me a lot.

感谢你为我们做的一切（gǎn xiè nǐwèi wǒ men zuò de yíqiē）。

Thank you for everything you've done for us.

希望以后还能再见面（xī wàng yǐ hòu hái néng zài jiàn miàn）。

I hope we can see each other again in the future.

能给我您的联系地址吗（néng gěi wǒ nín de lián xì dì zhǐ ma）？

Can you give me your contact address?

你有电子邮箱地址吗（nǐ yǒu diàn zǐ yóu xiāng dì zhǐ ma）？

Do you have an email address?

请一定要联系我（qǐng yídìng yào lián xì wǒ）。

Please contact me sometime.

我会想你的（wǒ huì xiǎng nǐ de）。

I'll miss you.

祝友谊地久天长（zhù yǒu yì dì jiǔ tiān zhǎng）。

Friendship lasts forever.

Conclusion

The above are some directions and suggestions about learning Chinese. You may use the book flexibly according to the actual situations. For total beginners, this is your entry-level Chinese learning material. We strive to make Chinese easier to learn so that our readers can study the language happily, effortlessly, and efficiently.

When laying stress on function, as well as listening and speaking drills, we have made every effort to observe the rules of language teaching by proceeding from the simple to the more complex and advancing in ordered steps. The examples are simple, practical, easy to lean and remember, and are representative of natural speech.

Here are some tips for you when you start or continue to learn to speak Chinese.

1. After you are familiar with the examples above, read them loudly and clearly. This is to use your listening ability to potentially strengthen your memory, and correct the pronunciation – you will find it much better than reading silently. That said, do make sure that you pronounce the sentences correctly.

2. Study frequently and form a habit. Spending a little time each day learning Chinese is better than learning it for quite a long time once a week. Always slice the study time into several short periods rather than in a continued long term. For example, you can use the time

when taking the bus, having a meal, queuing in the line, or in the bath to learn new knowledge and continuously review.

3. Make vocabulary cards. Handmade vocabulary cards can help you improve the character recognition capabilities. In accordance with part of speech (verbs, nouns, etc.) to itemize them, carry around, and have them available to reference at any time.

4. Bedtime review. Some people found that a quick five-minute review before going to sleep can enhance memory. This review should not be time-consuming and not suitable at midnight, because while your body is still awake, your brain is already trying to sleep.

5. Find yourself a practice partner. Find a Chinese pal and talk with him/her; you will not only learn how to speak Chinese correctly but also acquire a lot more knowledge about Chinese **culture** and life experience. They can strengthen their English in the meantime--two birds killed with one stone.

6. Once you are familiar with Chinese characters, you can block the Pinyin part – what you're doing is trying to understand the meaning of the sentences, not the pronunciation. Developing this habit will make your future learning easier.

7. Enroll in some language course so you can learn Chinese with experienced teachers who can help you precisely locate your current Chinese level and rapidly improve it via professional techniques.

Finally, just remember; don't be too harsh on yourself! Learning a language is a gradual process--you have to keep at it. To be honest, Chinese is one of the hardest languages to learn, so take your time. Once you feel comfortable with the basics of Chinese speech, consider taking a trip to China. Nothing can be better for learning the language than a journey to its native land!

Part 2: Chinese Short Stories

11 Simple Stories for Beginners Who Want to Learn Mandarin Chinese in Less Time While Also Having Fun

Introduction

In countries all over the world, many people are learning foreign languages. Everybody knows their native language but knowing another one is also very useful.

There are about 1,500 languages, and of course, Chinese is one of them. It is used not only in China but in many parts of the world. Today, the importance of being able to read Chinese is self-evident.

But what is the best way to learn Chinese? We should remember how we learned our own language when we were children. If we could learn a second language in the same way, it would not seem so difficult. Think of what a child does; he or she listens to what people say and tries to copy the words. When he or she wants something, they have to ask for it. They are using the language, speaking it, and thinking in it all the time. Thus, if a second language is also used as frequently, it will be learned very quickly.

The main purpose of this book is to provide you with a platform to improve your reading skills and your ability to use Chinese comprehensively so that you can easily read and learn.

Many learners are determined to improve their reading skills, so they try to expand their reading, but often feel confused because:

1. Chinese websites have a large number of words. They are hard to read, and they have no test questions.
2. Most of the reading materials on the market are old and difficult. Many of these materials are not properly written, the

language is not lively or authentic, and the test points are not accurate. Most importantly, they are boring and not attractive.

3. Most of the original Chinese reading stories and novels on the Internet are too long. Many learners do not have the time nor the energy to keep reading.

In response to this confusion, this book delivers a shortcut to improving your reading ability while retaining your interest. This guide has the following characteristics:

Unique material selection

This is an authentic book that covers a wide range of topics, including humorous stories, campus life, hobbies, social life, etc. The content of the stories is interesting, and the sentence construction lively.

Diverse questions

The question structure is not limited to multiple choice. Each story has a variety of questions to test your reading comprehension from multiple perspectives.

Self-supporting reading

To help you fully understand the reading material and correctly pronounce the language, an English translation and Chinese Pinyin have been added. Because grammar between Chinese and English is different, the content is not translated sentence by sentence. Instead, the intent is to strive to translate the language to fully comply with English habits, guaranteeing ease in your reading.

Open this book and immerse yourself. What are you waiting for? Come on!

Chapter 1: 老鼠开会 (lǎo shǔ kāi huì) – The Mice's Meeting

在一座房子里，住着很多老鼠. 他们每天都非常**快乐**.有一天，房屋的主人带回家一只猫，这只猫杀死了很多老鼠. 这让老鼠们感到非常悲伤，但它们对此也**毫无办法**. 于是，它们就向别的动物**求助**，但没有谁愿意帮助它们.

zài yí zuò fáng zǐ lǐ, zhù zhe hěn duō lǎo shǔ. tā men měi tiān dōu fēi cháng kuài lè. yǒu yì tiān, fáng wū de zhǔ rén dài huí jiā yì zhī māo, zhè zhī māo shā sǐ le hěn duō lǎo shǔ. zhè ràng lǎo shǔ men gǎn dào fēi cháng bēi shāng, dàn tā men duì cǐ yě háo wú bàn fǎ. yú shì, tā men jiù xiàng bié de dòng wù qiú zhù, dàn méi yǒu shuí yuàn yì bāng zhù tā men.

There were many mice in the house; every day was full of happiness. Then the owner of the house got a cat. The cat killed many of the mice. The mice became very sad, but they could do nothing about it. They asked for help from other animals, but no one would help them.

一只年纪最大的老鼠非常英明. 一天它对其他老鼠说,"所有的老鼠今天晚上都必须到我的洞里来，我们要**召开一个会议**，想一想怎么来对付那只猫."

yì zhī nián jì zuì dà de lǎo shǔ fēi cháng yīng míng. yì tiān tā duì qí tā lǎo shǔ shuō: "suǒ yǒu de lǎo shǔ jīn tiān wǎn shàng dōu bì xū dào wǒ de dòng lǐ lái, wǒ men yào zhào kāi yí gè huì yì, xiǎng yì xiǎng zěn me lái duì fù nà zhī māo."
The oldest mouse was very wise. He said to the mice one day, "All the mice must come to my hole tonight. We are going to have a meeting and think what we can do about this cat."
晚饭之后，所有的老鼠都来了. 众老鼠议论纷纷，但没有一个知道该怎么办. 最后，一只**聪明**的年轻老鼠站起来说："我们必须给猫系上一个**铃铛**，以后当猫来到附近时，我们听到铃铛响就赶快跑，然后把自己藏起来.这样，那只猫再也抓不到任何弟兄了."
wǎn fàn zhī hòu, suǒ yǒu de lǎo shǔ dōu lái le. zhòng lǎo shǔ yì lùn fēn fēn, dàn méi yǒu yí gè zhī dào gāi zěn me bàn. zuì hòu, yì zhī cōng míng de nián qīng lǎo shǔ zhàn qǐ lái shuō: "wǒ men bì xū gěi māo jì shàng yí gè líng dāng, yǐ hòu dāng māo lái dào fù jìn shí, wǒ men tīng dào líng dāng xiǎng jiù gǎn kuài pǎo, rán hòu bǎ zì jǐ cáng qǐ lái. zhè yàng, nà zhī māo zài yě zhuā bú dào rèn hé dì xiōng le."
After dinner, all the mice came. Many mice spoke, but none knew what to do. At last, a clever young mouse stood up and said, "We must tie a bell to the cat. Then, when the cat comes near, we will hear the bell and run away and hide. This way, the cat will not catch any more mice."
这位年长的老鼠听到这里高兴地说道,"这是一个很好的想法！如果哪位老鼠认为这是个不错的点子，请举起**爪子!**"
zhè wèi nián zhǎng de lǎo shǔ tīng dào zhè lǐ gāo xìng de shuō dào: "zhè shì yí gè hěn hǎo de xiǎng fǎ! rú guǒ nǎ wèi lǎo shǔ rèn wéi zhè shì gè bú cuò de diǎn zi, qǐng jǔ qǐ zhǎo zi!"
The oldest mouse was pleased and said, "A good idea! If any other mice think this is a good idea, please raise your paw!"
所有的老鼠都举起了它们的爪子.
suǒ yǒu de lǎo shǔ dōu jǔ qǐ le tā men de zhǎo zi.
All the mice raised their paws.

接下来，这只年纪最大的老鼠问,“谁愿意把这个铃铛系到猫的身上去?”
jiē xià lái, zhè zhī nián jì zuì dà de lǎo shǔ wèn: “shuí yuàn yì bǎ zhè gè líng dāng jì dào māo de shēn shàng qù?”
Then the oldest mouse said, “Who will tie the bell to the cat?”
它**四处看了看**，并没有任何老鼠回应.
tā sì chù kàn le kàn, bìng méi yǒu rèn hé lǎo shǔ huí yīng.
He looked around, but no mouse answered.
它又等了几分钟，但仍然没有任何声音.
tā yòu děng le jǐ fēn zhōng, dàn réng rán méi yǒu rèn hé shēng yīn.
He waited a few minutes, but still, no one answered.
最后它说道,“说一些事情并不**困难**，但困难的是去做这些事情.”
zuì hòu tā shuō dào, “shuō yì xiē shì qíng bìng bù kùn nán, dàn kùn nán de shì qù zuò zhè xiē shì qíng.”
At last, he said, “It’s easy to say things, but it’s difficult to do them.”

总结（zǒng jié）— Summary

自从猫来了以后，这伙老鼠的快乐日子就一去不复返了. 它们整日里闷闷不乐、寝食难安，遇到同伴被吃掉的日子，它们更是吓得魂飞魄散. 这天，老谋深算的老鼠爷决定召开一次秘密会议，来研究一下和猫打游击的战术问题，可是会议的结果却并不那么理想呢.
zì cóng māo lái le yǐ hòu, zhè huǒ lǎo shǔ de kuài lè rì zi jiù yí qù bú fù fǎn le. tā men zhěng rì lǐ mèn mèn bú lè、qǐn shí nán ān, yù dào tóng bàn bèi chī diào de rì zi, tā men gèng shì xià dé hún fēi pò sàn. zhè tiān, lǎo móu shēn suàn de lǎo shǔ yé jué dìng zhào kāi yí cì mì mì huì yì, lái yán jiū yí xià hé māo dǎ yóu jī de zhàn shù wèn tí, kě shì huì yì de jié guǒ què bìng bú nà me lǐ xiǎng ne.

Ever since the owner of the house got a cat, the happy days of this group of mice were gone forever. The mice were unhappy and nervous all day long. One day, the oldest wise mouse decided to hold a secret meeting to see what could be done about the cat. However, the results of the meeting were not so ideal.

词汇（cí huì）— Vocabulary

快乐（kuài lè）happy

毫无办法（háo wú bàn fǎ）nothing can be done

求助（qiú zhù）to ask for help

召开会议（zhào kāi huì yì）to have a meeting

聪明（cōng míng）clever

铃铛（líng dāng）bell

爪子（zhǎo zi）paw

四处看看（sì chù kàn kàn）to look around

最后（zuì hòu）at last

困难（kùn nán）difficult

练习与答案（liàn xí yǔ dá àn）— Questions and Answers

1. 老鼠们在哪里开会？

lǎo shǔ men zài nǎ lǐ kāi huì?

The mice had a meeting _______.

A. 在最年长老鼠的洞里.

zài zuì nián zhǎng lǎo shǔ de dòng lǐ.

in the oldest mouse's hole.

B. 在最大的洞里.

zài zuì dà de dòng lǐ.

in the biggest hole.

C. 在猫的房间.

zài māo de fáng jiān.

in the cat's room.

2. 老鼠们什么时候开会？

lǎo shǔ men shén me shí hòu kāi huì?

When did the mice have the meeting?

A. 在早上.

zài zǎo shàng.

in the morning.

B. 在晚饭前.

zài wǎn fàn qián.
before dinner.
C. 在晚上.
zài wǎn shàng.
at night.

3. 谁将去给猫系铃铛?
shuí jiāng qù gěi māo jì líng chēng?
Who would tie the bell to the cat?
A. 提出这个点子的年轻老鼠.
tí chū zhè gè diǎn zi de nián qīng lǎo shǔ.
The young mouse who had the idea.
B. 那只年纪最大的聪明老鼠.
nà zhī nián jì zuì dà de cōng míng lǎo shǔ.
The oldest, wise mouse.
C. 没有老鼠要去这么做.
méi yǒu lǎo shǔ yào qù zhè me zuò.
No mouse would do that.

4. 年轻老鼠认为给猫系上铃铛后有什么好处?
nián qīng lǎo shǔ rèn wéi gěi māo jì shàng líng dāng hòu yǒu shén me hǎo chù
What benefits did the young mice think tying a bell to the cat had?

5. 那只年长老鼠最后对会议的总结是什么?
nà zhī nián zhǎng lǎo shǔ zuì hòu duì huì yì de zǒng jié shì shén me?
What was the oldest mouse's summary of the meeting?

1. A
2. C
3. C
4. 老鼠们可以听到铃铛响后逃跑，然后把自己藏起来.
lǎo shǔ men kě yǐ tīng dào líng dāng xiǎng hòu táo pǎo, rán hòu bǎ zì jǐ cáng qǐ lái.
The mice could hear the bell and run and hide.

5. 说一些事情并不困难，但困难的是去做这些事情.

shuō yì xiē shì qíng bìng bù kùn nán, dàn kùn nán de shì qù zuò zhè xiē shì qíng.

It’s easy to say things, but difficult to do them.

Chapter 2: 两瓶墨水 (liǎng píng mò shuǐ) – Two Bottles of Ink

一位**药剂师**醒来看了一下表：三点四十五. 楼下商店的敲门声不断地传来，他下了床，穿上衣服和**拖鞋**，然后步子沉重地下楼打开了门.

yí wèi yào jì shī xǐng lái kàn le yí xià biǎo: sān diǎn sì shí wǔ. lóu xià shāng diàn de qiāo mén shēng bú duàn de chuán lái, tā xià le chuáng, chuān shàng yī fú hé tuō xié, rán hòu bù zi chén zhòng de xià lóu dǎ kāi le mén.

The chemist woke up and looked at the clock. A quarter to four. The knocking on the shop door downstairs was incessant. He got out of bed, put on his clothes and slippers, and groggily headed down to the shop, opening the door.

街上站着一个年轻人，他戴着厚厚的**眼镜**."你想买点什么?"药剂师问，"现在已经是深夜了."

jiē shàng zhàn zhe yí gè nián qīng rén, tā dài zhe hòu hòu de yǎn jìng. " nǐ xiǎng mǎi diǎn shén me? " yào jì shī wèn, " xiàn zài yǐ jīng shì shēn yè le. "

In the street stood a young man, wearing thick glasses. "What do you want?" said the chemist. "It's the middle of the night."

"是的，我感到很抱歉."这个男的说，"我非常需要一瓶墨水，我现在正写一首诗."

"shì de, wǒ gǎn dào hěn bào qiàn," zhè gè nán de shuō. " wǒ fēi cháng xū yào yì píng mò shuǐ, wǒ xiàn zài zhèng xiě yì shǒu shī. "

"Yes, it is, and I'm very sorry," said the man. "I'm in urgent need for a bottle of ink; I'm writing a poem."

店主很生气地答道,"这是一个药剂店."

"diàn," zhǔ hěn shēng qì de dá dào, "zhè shì yí gè yào jì diàn."

"This," the chemist said in an angry voice, "is a chemist shop."

"药剂店?"

"yào jì diàn?"

"A chemist shop?"

"是的，一个药剂店. 并且是一个不卖墨水的药剂店!"药剂师大声说.

"shì de, yí gè yào jì diàn. bìng qiě shì yí gè bú mài mò shuǐ de yào jì diàn!" yào jì shī dà shēng shuō.

"Yes, a chemist shop. And a chemist shop doesn't sell ink!" shouted the chemist.

"药剂店不卖墨水?"男子站在路上**重复**了一遍，"从没卖过?"

"yào jì diàn bú mài mò shuǐ?" nán zǐ zhàn zài lù shàng chóng fù le yí biàn, "cóng méi mài guò?"

"A chemist shop does not sell ink?" repeated the man in the street. "You've never sold ink?"

"从来没有!"药剂师说，"在我开这个店的 25 年里我从来没有卖过墨水."药剂师大声喊："走吧！我一生中从来没有听过这样的事，半夜三更地弄醒药剂师买墨水!"他愤怒地用力关上门，然后就上楼回他的卧室了. 半小时以后，他的妻子摇醒了他："亲爱的，醒一醒！楼下有人在敲门."

"cóng lái méi yǒu! " yào jì shī shuō. "zài wǒ kāi zhè gè diàn de èr shí wǔ nián lǐ wǒ cóng lái méi yǒu mài guò mò shuǐ." yào jì shī dà shēng hǎn, "zǒu ba! wǒ yì shēng zhōng cóng lái méi yǒu tīng guò zhè yàng de shì, bàn yè sān gēng de nòng xǐng yào jì shī mǎi mò shu!" tā fèn nù de yòng lì guān shàng mén, rán hòu jiù shàng lóu huí tā de wò shì le. bàn xiǎo shí yǐ hòu, tā de qī zǐ yáo xǐng le tā. "qīn ài de, xǐng yì xǐng! lóu xià yǒu rén zài qiāo mén."

"Never!" said the chemist. "In twenty-five years of running this shop, I have never had any ink." The chemist then shouted, "Go away! I have never heard anything like it in all my life, waking a chemist at this time of night to ask for ink!" He shut the door angrily and went up to his bedroom. Half an hour later, his wife shook him. "Dear, wake up! There is someone knocking downstairs."

药剂师从**枕头**上抬起头："这能是谁呢?"

yào jì shī cóng zhěn tóu shàng tái qǐ tóu. "zhè néng shì shuí ne?"

The chemist raised his head from his pillow. "Who could it be now?"

"四点半！好吧，我不再下楼了. 无论是谁，让他敲去吧. 他为什么不去找个日夜都营业的药剂店呢?"

"sì diǎn bàn! hǎo ba, wǒ bú zài xià lóu le. wú lùn shì shuí, ràng tā qiāo qù ba. tā wéi shén me bú qù zhǎo gè rì yè dōu yíng yè de yào jì diàn ne?"

"Half past four! Well, I'm not going down again. Let him knock, whoever he is. Why doesn't he go and find an all-night chemist's?"

"亲爱的,"他的妻子说，"也许是有非常**严重**的事情呢，可能是有人病得非常严重啊."

"qīn ài de," tā de qī zǐ shuō, "yě xǔ shì yǒu fēi cháng yán zhòng de shì qíng ne, kě néng shì yǒu rén bìng dé fēi cháng yán zhòng a."

"Dear," said his wife, "it might be something terribly serious. Someone may be very ill."

药剂师又一次起床，一路直奔楼下的商店. 外面的大路上站着刚来过的那个人."你好啊!"他问道，而且笑得很灿烂，"我希望我没有把你弄醒. 我已经设法找到墨水了，并且我记得你对我说过，你这 25 年来从来都没有墨水，所以我也给你买了一瓶."

yào jì shī yòu yí cì qǐ chuáng, yí lù zhí bèn lóu xià de shāng diàn. wài miàn de dà lù shàng zhàn zhe gāng lái guò de nà gè rén. "nǐ hǎo a!" tā wèn dào, ér qiě xiào dé hěn càn làn, "wǒ xī wàng wǒ méi yǒu bǎ nǐ nòng xǐng. wǒ yǐ jīng shè fǎ zhǎo dào mò shuǐ le, bìng qiě wǒ jì

dé nǐ duì wǒ shuō guò, nǐ zhè èr shí wǔ nián lái cóng lái dōu méi yǒu mò shuǐ, suǒ yǐ wǒ yě gěi nǐ mǎi le yì píng."
The chemist got out of bed again and made his way down to the shop. Outside in the street stood the same man who had come before. "Hello again!" he said, smiling brightly, "I hope I didn't wake you up. I managed to find the ink. And I remembered what you said. You have not had any ink for twenty-five years, so I brought a bottle for you too."

总结（zǒng jié）— Summary

中国人常说"礼多人不怪"，但是如果过于迂腐，就会做出费力不讨好的事情来. 本文中的这位年轻人酷爱吟诗赋词，这天半夜里突然来了灵感，正当他准备挥毫泼墨之际，却发现没有墨水了，于是他急忙就近敲开了一家药剂店的门，给药剂师带去了极大的困扰.
zhōng guó rén cháng shuō "lǐ duō rén bú guài." dàn shì rú guǒ guò yú yū fǔ, jiù huì zuò chū fèi lì bù tǎo hǎo de shì qíng lái. běn wén zhōng de zhè wèi nián qīng rén kù ài yín shī fù cí, zhè tiān bàn yè lǐ tū rán lái le líng gǎn, zhèng dāng tā zhǔn bèi huī háo pō mò zhī jì, què fā xiàn méi yǒu mò shuǐ le, yú shì tā jí máng jiù jìn qiāo kāi le yì jiā yào jì diàn de mén, gěi yào jì shī dài qù le jí dà de kùn rǎo.

There is a saying in China that goes, "One with too much etiquette will never be blamed." But if you are too pedantic, you will not be thanked for doing good things. The young man in this story is passionate about writing poetry. In the middle of the night, he suddenly came to inspiration. Just as he was preparing to write down his work, he found he had no ink. So, he hurriedly knocked on the door of a nearby chemist, causing a lot of trouble for the chemist.

词汇（cí huì）— Vocabulary

药剂师（yào jì shī）chemist
拖鞋（tuō xié）slipper
眼镜（yǎn jìng）glasses
重复（chóng fù）to repeat

枕头（zhěn tóu）pillow

严重（yán zhòng）serious

练习与答案（liàn xí yǔ dá àn）— Questions and Answers

1. 这人半夜叫醒药剂师是因为什么？

zhè rén bàn yè jiào xǐng yào jì shī shì yīn wéi shén me?

The man woke the chemist at midnight _______.

A. 因为他疯了.

yīn wéi tā fēng le.

because he was crazy.

B. 因为他那时特别需要墨水.

yīn wéi tā nà shí tè bié xū yào mò shuǐ.

because he desperately needed ink.

C. 因为他喝多了.

yīn wéi tā hē duō le.

because he was drunk.

2. 为什么妻子第二次叫醒了药剂师？

wèi shén me qī zǐ dì èr cì jiào xǐng le yào jì shī?

Why did the chemist's wife wake him up for the second time?

A. 因为她知道有人来送墨水.

yīn wèi tā zhī dào yǒu rén lái sòng mò shuǐ.

Because she knew that someone was coming to give them some ink.

B. 因为她听到有人敲门.

yīn wèi tā tīng dào yǒu rén qiāo mén.

Because she heard someone knocking at the door.

C. 因为她害怕下楼.

yīn wèi tā hài pà xià lóu.

Because she was afraid to go downstairs.

3. 以下哪一项不是真的？

yǐ xià nǎ yí xiàng bú shì zhēn de?

Which of the following is NOT true?

A. 三点四十五的时候，药剂师第一次醒来.

sān diǎn sì shí wǔ de shí hòu, yào jì shī dì yī cì xǐng lái.
At a quarter to four, the chemist was woken up for the first time.

B. 药剂店里二十年从未有过墨水.
yào jì diàn lǐ èr shí nián cóng wèi yǒu guò mò shuǐ.
In twenty years, the shop had never had any ink.

C. 年轻人第二次来的时候四点半.
nián qīng rén dì èr cì lái de shí hòu sì diǎn bàn.
The man came for the second time at half-past four.

4. 药剂师第一次下楼跟年轻人对话的反应是什么?
yào jì shī dì yī cì xià lóu gēn nián qīng rén duì huà de fǎn yìng shì shén me?
What was the chemist's reaction the first time he talked to the young man?

5. 药剂师第二次见到年轻人会是什么反应?
yào jì shī dì èr cì jiàn dào nián qīng rén huì shì shén me fǎn yìng?
How would the chemist react if he saw the young man for the second time?

1. B
2. B
3. B
4. 他很生气并且大声讲话.
tā hěn shēng qì bìng qiě dà shēng jiǎng huà.
He was angry and spoke loudly.
5. 他会比之前更生气.
tā huì bǐ zhī qián gèng shēng qì.
He would be even angrier than the first time.

Chapter 3: 你收藏钱币吗 (nǐ shōu cáng qián bì ma) – Do You Collect Coins?

许多人想买古老的钱币，但是在你**付款**之前要**小心**，你可能会买到一枚十足的**假币**.
xǔ duō rén xiǎng mǎi gǔ lǎo de qián bì, dàn shì zài nǐ fù kuǎn zhī qián yào xiǎo xīn, nǐ kě néng huì mǎi dào yì méi shí zú de jiǎ bì.
Many people want to buy old and ancient coins. But before you part with your hard-earned money, watch out! You may be buying a coin that's fake.
专家告诉我们，制造假币的历史可以**回溯**到两千年前. 在古代，制造假币的人会被**处以死刑**，但现在制造和销售假币却成为一种常见的**商业活动**.
zhuān jiā gào sù wǒ men, zhì zào jiǎ bì de lì shǐ kě yǐ huí sù dào liǎng qiān nián qián. zài gǔ dài, zhì zào jiǎ bì de rén huì bèi chù yǐ sǐ xíng. dàn xiàn zài zhì zào hé xiāo shòu jiǎ bì què chéng wéi yì zhǒng cháng jiàn de shāng yè huó dòng.

Experts tell us that the creation of fake coinage goes back 2,000 years. In the old days, those who faked coins would be put to death. But now, creating and selling fake coins is a regular business activity.
一些假币造的很完美，以至于它们被载入钱币书中，**收藏家愿意**为这些钱币出高价，他们常设法得到它们. 一枚假币被当作假币出售是一回事，但是当它被当作真品出售时，那就完全是另外一种情况了. 最好的**建议**是，你要从**名声好**的商家那里买钱币.
yì xiē jiǎ bì zào de hěn wán měi, yǐ zhì yú tā men bèi zǎi rù qián bì shū zhōng, shōu cáng jiā yuàn yì wéi zhè xiē qián bì chū gāo jià, tā men cháng shè fǎ dé dào tā men. yì méi jiǎ bì bèi dāng zuò jiǎ bì chū shòu shì yì huí shì, dàn shì dāng tā bèi dāng zuò zhēn pǐn chū shòu shí, nà jiù wán quán shì lìng wài yì zhǒng qíng kuàng le. zuì hǎo de jiàn yì shì, nǐ yào cóng míng shēng hǎo de shāng jiā nà lǐ mǎi qián bì.
Some fake coins are made so well that they are written in coin collector books, and collectors are willing to pay a lot more money for these coins. They are always trying to get them. It is one thing to buy a fake coin when it's sold as a fake, but it's another thing to buy a fake coin when it's sold as the real thing. The best advice is always to buy from a reputable dealer.
如果能证明是假币的话，商家应该让你退货. 但如果你自己单独出行其他国家，这条建议就很难**遵从**了.
rú guǒ néng zhèng míng shì jiǎ bì de huà, shāng jiā yīng gāi ràng nǐ tuì huò. dàn rú guǒ nǐ zì jǐ dān dú chū xíng qí tā guó jiā, zhè tiáo jiàn yì jiù hěn nán zūn cóng le.
The dealer will take back a coin if it should prove to be fake, but advice is hard to follow if you visit other countries by yourself.
你有可能买泥土中刚挖出来的钱币，而不是从钱币卖家那里买货. 但许多假币确实也是刚挖出来的. 假币被偷偷埋起来，然后当着你的面又挖出来，就连钱币卖家自己也可能**上当**.
nǐ yǒu kě néng mǎi ní tǔ zhōng gāng wā chū lái de qián bì, ér bú shì cóng qián bì mài jiā nà lǐ mǎi huò. dàn xǔ duō jiǎ bì què shí yě shì gāng wā chū lái de. jiǎ bì bèi tōu tōu mái qǐ lái, rán hòu dāng zhe nǐ

de miàn yòu wā chū lái, jiù lián qián bì mài jiā zì jǐ yě kě néng shàng dāng.
You might buy coins "from the soil" rather than from a dealer, and many of these fake coins do come right from the soil. These fake coins are buried in secret and are then dug up in front of you. The dealers themselves can be fooled by this.
还有另外一条诡计：商家把一枚**罕见**的钱币放在一些常见的真币中. 买家看见这一大堆都是真币，就会认为那枚稀少的钱币也是真货. 当出现这样的情况时，买家就难免要**上钩**. 所以当你决定买钱币时，一定要当心！
hái yǒu lìng wài yì tiáo guǐ jì: shāng jiā bǎ yì méi hǎn jiàn de qián bì fàng zài yì xiē cháng jiàn de zhēn bì zhōng. mǎi jiā kàn jiàn zhè yí dà duī dōu shì zhēn bì, jiù huì rèn wéi nà méi xī shǎo de qián bì yě shì zhēn huò. dāng chū xiàn zhè yàng de qíng kuàng shí, mǎi jiā jiù nán miǎn yào shàng gōu. suǒ yǐ dāng nǐ jué dìng mǎi qián bì shí, yí dìng yào dāng xīn!
There is another trick. The dealer places a copy of a rare coin among some real but common coins. When the buyer sees the real coins, the buyer then thinks that the rare coin is real too. When this happens, the buyer has been tricked. So if you decide to buy old coins, be careful!

总结（zǒng jié）— Summary

有人爱集，有人爱收藏，而古钱币更是收藏家们热衷的收集对象. 但是收集钱币也很容易上当受骗，因为现代人的伪造技术极为高超，完全可以以假乱真. 在一大堆锈迹斑斑的古钱币中也许就只有那么一两枚是真货，而其余的全是鱼目混珠的赝品！你需要一双慧眼！记住我们教你的这几招！
yǒu rén ài jí yóu, yǒu rén ài shōu cáng. ér gǔ qián bì gèng shì shōu cáng jiā men rè zhōng de shōu jí duì xiàng. dàn shì shōu jí qián bì yě hěn róng yì shàng dàng shòu piàn, yīn wèi xiàn dài rén de wěi zào jì shù jí wéi gāo chāo, wán quán kě yǐ yǐ jiǎ luàn zhēn. zài yí dà duī xiù jì bān bān de gǔ qián bì zhōng yě xǔ jiù zhǐ yǒu nà me yì liǎng méi

shì zhēn huò, ér qí yú de quán shì yú mù hùn zhū de yàn pǐn! nǐ xū yào yì shuāng huì yǎn! jì zhù wǒ men jiāo nǐ de zhè jǐ zhāo!

Some people love to collect stamps; some people love to collect different things. Many collectors like to collect ancient coins. Collecting coins can be very risky because modern forgery techniques are extremely good, making it hard to distinguish imitation and authentic coins. Among a lot of rusty "ancient" coins, perhaps only one or two would be real, while the rest are just fake! You need to look carefully and remember what we have taught you here!

词汇（cí huì）— Vocabulary

付款（fù kuǎn）to pay

小心（xiǎo xīn）be careful

假币（jiǎ bì）fake coin

回溯（huí sù）to go back

处以死刑（chù yǐ sǐ xíng）put to death

商业活动（shāng yè huó dòng）business activity

收藏家（shōu cáng jiā）collector

愿意（yuàn yì）be willing to

建议（jiàn yì）advice

名声好（míng shēng hǎo）reputable

遵从（zūn cóng）to follow

上当（shàng dāng）to be fooled

罕见（hǎn jiàn）rare

上钩（shàng gōu）to be tricked

练习与答案（liàn xí yǔ dá àn）— Questions and Answers

1. 本文主要讲什么？

běn wén zhǔ yào jiǎng shén me?

This article is mainly about _______.

A. 讲现今的钱币.

jiǎng xiàn jīn de qián bì.
today's coins.

B. 讲钱币的制作历史.
jiǎng qián bì de zhì zuò lì shǐ.
how old coins were made.

C. 讲假币.
jiǎng jiǎ bì.
fake coins.

2. 上钩买假币的人大多数通常是哪种人?
shàng gōu mǎi jiǎ bì de rén dà duō shù tōng cháng shì nǎ zhǒng rén?
People who are tricked into buying fake coins are most often ________.

A. 钱币收藏家.
qián bì shōu cáng jiā.
coin collectors.

B. 呆在家里的人.
dāi zài jiā lǐ de rén.
people who stay at home.

C. 去另一个国家的游客.
qù lìng yí gè guó jiā de yóu kè.
visitors to another country.

3. 当你买钱币时，应该记住的最重要的一点是什么?
dāng nǐ mǎi qián bì shí, yīng gāi jì zhù de zuì zhòng yào de yì diǎn shì shén me?
When you buy a coin, the most important thing to remember is ________.

A. 从名声好的商家那里购买钱币.
cóng míng shēng hǎo de shāng jiā nà lǐ gòu mǎi qián bì.
to buy coins from reputable dealers.

B. 尽可能少付钱.
jìn kě néng shǎo fù qián.
to pay as little money as possible.

C. 不要在外国购买钱币.

bú yào zài wài guó gòu mǎi qián bì.

not to buy them in a foreign country.

4. 为什么有商家会将一枚罕见的假币放在一堆常见的真币里？

wéi shén me yǒu shāng jiā huì jiāng yì méi hǎn jiàn de jiǎ bì fàng zài yì duī cháng jiàn de zhēn bì lǐ?

Why does the dealer place a copy of a rare coin among some real but common coins?

5. 在古代制造假币会怎么样？

zài gǔ dài zhì zào jiǎ bì huì zěn me yàng?

What would happen if you faked coins in ancient times?

1. C
2. C
3. A
4. 因为买家看见这一大堆都是真币，就会认为那枚稀少的假币也是真货.

yīn wèi mǎi jiā kàn jiàn zhè yí dà duī dōu shì zhēn bì, jiù huì rèn wéi nà méi xī shǎo de jiǎ bì yě shì zhēn huò.

Because the buyer sees the real coins and then thinks that the rare fake coin is real too.

5. 你会被判死刑.

nǐ huì bèi pàn sǐ xíng.

You would be put to death.

Chapter 4: 我的第一次约会 (wǒ de dì yī cì yuē huì) – My First Date

我对凯伦钟情已久了. 一天，我**鼓起勇气**邀请她和我一起去一家**露天汽车影院**看电影. 她欣然接受了.
wǒ duì kǎi lún zhōng qíng yǐ jiǔ le. yì tiān, wǒ gǔ qǐ yǒng qì yāo qǐng tā hé wǒ yì qǐ qù yì jiā lù tiān qì chē yǐng yuàn kàn diàn yǐng. tā xīn rán jiē shòu le.
I've had a crush on Karen for a long time. One day, I plucked up my courage to ask her to the drive-in to see a film with me. She said yes!
晚上，我穿上最得体的衣服，带上足够的钱之后，把她接上我的车并驶向那家影院. 凯伦当时穿了一件蓝色的裙子，她的秀发在风中飘舞，我感觉棒极了！我对自己说，这次**约会**没什么需要紧张的.
wǎn shàng, wǒ chuān shàng zuì dé tǐ de yī fu, dài shàng zú gòu de qián zhī hòu, bǎ tā jiē shàng wǒ de chē bìng shǐ xiàng nà jiā yǐng yuàn. kǎi lún dāng shí chuān le yí jiàn lán sè de qún zǐ, tā de xiù fà zài fēng zhōng piāo wǔ, wǒ gǎn jué bàng jí le! wǒ duì zì jǐ shuō, zhè cì yuē huì méi shén me xū yào jǐn zhāng de.

In the evening, I put my best clothes on carefully and made sure I had enough money. I picked up her up, and we headed for the drive-in. Karen wore a blue dress; her beautiful hair flew in the wind. I felt wonderful. Dating is a piece of cake, I thought.
不一会儿，天黑了，电影开始了. 凯伦坐在后座上看. 我开始揣测我要不要我**握住她的手**. 可直至电影演到一半了，我还在犹豫，不知道该如何去做.
bù yí huì ér, tiān hēi le, diàn yǐng kāi shǐ le. kǎi lún zuò zài hòu zuò shàng kàn. wǒ kāi shǐ chuāi cè wǒ yào bú yào wò zhù tā de shǒu. kě zhí zhì diàn yǐng yǎn dào yí bàn le, wǒ hái zài yóu yù, bù zhī dào gāi rú hé qù zuò.
Soon it was dark, and the film began. Karen sat in the back seat. I thought that maybe I could hold her hand. By the middle of the film, I was still thinking about how to go about it.
"我有点**渴**了,"凯伦忽然说. 我说,"我去买些饮料!"我当时几乎是从车上跳出去的. 我冲过黑暗的街道，在附近的一家商店里买了**可乐**、**爆米花**和 M&M 豆. 之后，我转身跑回我停车的方向.
"wǒ yǒu diǎn kě le," kǎi lún hū rán shuō. wǒ shuō, "wǒ qù mǎi xiē yǐn liào!" wǒ dāng shí jī hū shì cóng chē shàng tiào chū qù de. wǒ chōng guò hēi àn de jiē dào, zài fù jìn de yì jiā shāng diàn lǐ mǎi le kě lè、bào mǐ huā hé M&M dòu. zhī hòu, wǒ zhuǎn shēn pǎo huí wǒ tíng chē de fāng xiàng.
"I'm thirsty," Karen said suddenly. "I'll buy something!" I said, almost jumping out of the car. I ran through the dark rows to a nearby shop and bought some coke, popcorn, and M&Ms. I turned and went back to my car.
我的车在哪里？在黑暗中，所有的车看起来都一样. 我分不清哪一部车是我的. 在黑暗之中四处搜寻了好久，我有些**饿**了. 所以，我一个人吃了很多爆米花，还喝光了两瓶可乐.
wǒ de chē zài nǎ lǐ? zài hēi àn zhōng, suǒ yǒu de chē kàn qǐ lái dōu yí yàng. wǒ fēn bù qīng nǎ yí bù chē shì wǒ de. zài hēi àn zhī zhōng sì chù sōu xún le hǎo jiǔ, wǒ yǒu xiē è le. suǒ yǐ, wǒ yí gè rén chī le hěn duō bào mǐ huā, hái hē guāng le liǎng píng kě lè.

Where's my car? In the dark, all the cars look the same. I couldn't find which one was mine. After running around in the dark for a long time, I was hungry. I ended up eating a lot of popcorn and drank both cans of coke by myself.

终于，我找到了我的车. 凯伦看着我，双眼含泪，问："我的**饮料**呢？"我把 M&M 豆给了她——那是我当时手中仅有的东西.

zhōng yú, wǒ zhǎo dào le wǒ de chē. kǎi lún kàn zhe wǒ, shuāng yǎn hán lèi, wèn: "wǒ de yǐn liào ne?" wǒ bǎ M&M dòu gěi le tā—nà shì wǒ dāng shí shǒu zhōng jǐn yǒu de dōng xi.

Finally, I found the car. Karen was looking at me, her eyes full of tears. "Where's my drink?" she asked. I gave her the M&Ms—it was all I had left.

我们默默无语地看完了**剩下**的电影. 从此之后，凯伦再也不跟我一起出来了.

wǒ men mò mò wú yǔ de kàn wán le shèng xià de diàn yǐng. cóng cǐ zhī hòu, kǎi lún zài yě bù gēn wǒ yì qǐ chū lái le.

We watched the rest of the film and said nothing. After that, Karen never went out with me again.

总结（zǒng jié）— Summary

这位男生那时真是春风得意因为他钟情已久的漂亮女生欣然接受了他的邀请，要和他一起去看电影，兴奋万分的他驾车带着女孩去了一家露天汽车影院. 但是，他的表现却没能打动女孩的心扉，他所期待的激动人心的时刻最后也没有出现. 反而是女孩再也不跟他一起出来了.

zhè wèi nán shēng nà shí zhēn shì chūn fēng dé yì, yīn wéi tā zhōng qíng yǐ jiǔ de piào liàng nǚ shēng xīn rán jiē shòu le tā de yāo qǐng yào hé tā yì qǐ qù kàn diàn yǐng, xīng fèn wàn fēn de tā jià chē dài zhe nǚ hái qù le yì jiā lù tiān qì chē yǐng yuàn. dàn shì, tā de biǎo xiàn què méi néng dǎ dòng nǚ hái de xīn fēi. tā suǒ qī dài de jī dòng rén xīn de shí kè zuì hòu yě méi yǒu chū xiàn. fǎn ér shì nǚ hái zài yě bù gēn tā yì qǐ chū lái le.

The boy was really happy at the time because his crush finally accepted his invitation to go to a movie with him. He was very excited and drove the girl to a drive-in. However, his performance did not move the girl's heart. The exciting moment he was looking forward to didn't appear at the end. Instead, the girl never went out with him again.

词汇（cí huì）— Vocabulary

鼓起勇气（gǔ qǐ yǒng qì）pluck up one's courage

露天汽车影院（lù tiān qì chē yǐng yuàn）drive-in

约会（yuē huì）to date

握住手（wò zhù shǒu）take one's hand

渴（kě）thirsty

可乐（kě lè）Coke

爆米花（bào mǐ huā）popcorn

饿（è）hungry

饮料（yǐn liào）drink

剩下（shèng xià）the rest of

练习与答案（liàn xí yǔ dá àn）— Questions and Answers

1. 男孩要求凯伦去露天汽车影院做什么？

nán hái yào qiú kǎi lún qù lù tiān qì chē yǐng yuàn zuò shén me?

The boy invited Karen to the drive-in _______.

A. 喝咖啡.

hē kā fēi.

to drink coffee.

B. 吃晚餐.

chī wǎn cān.

to have dinner.

C. 看电影.

kàn diàn yǐng.

to see a film.

2. 在去露天汽车影院的路上，男孩为什么感觉棒极了？

zài qù lù tiān qì chē yǐng yuàn de lù shàng, nán hái wéi shén me gǎn jué bàng jí le?
On the way to the drive-in, the boy felt wonderful because ________.

A. 因为女孩亲了他.
yīn wèi nǚ hái qīn le tā.
the girl kissed him.

B. 因为他身边的女孩很可爱.
yīn wèi tā shēn biān de nǚ hái hěn kě ài.
the girl beside him was lovely.

C. 因为女孩牵着他的手.
yīn wèi nǚ hái qiān zhe tā de shǒu.
the girl was holding his hand.

3. 为什么男孩花了好长时间才找到自己的车？
wéi shén me nán hái huā le hǎo cháng shí jiān cái zhǎo dào zì jǐ de chē?
It took the boy a long time to find his car because ________.

A. 因为那里有太多车而且看起来很像.
yīn wèi nà lǐ yǒu tài duō chē ér qiě kàn qǐ lái hěn xiàng.
there were too many cars there, and they looked the same.

B. 因为女孩不在车里.
yīn wèi nǚ hái bú zài chē lǐ.
the girl was not in the car.

C. 因为女孩出去买爆米花了.
yīn wèi nǚ hái chū qù mǎi bào mǐ huā le.
the girl went out to buy popcorn.

4. 男孩去商店都买了些什么？
nán hái qù shāng diàn dōu mǎi le xiē shén me?
What did the boy buy from the shop?

A. 可乐、爆米花和 M&M 豆.
kě lè、bào mǐ huā hé M&M dòu
coke, popcorn and M&Ms.

B. 可乐、热狗和爆米花.

kě lè、rè gǒu hé bào mǐ huā.

coke, a hotdog, and popcorn.

C. 可乐、面包和 M&M 豆.

kě lè、miàn bāo hé M&M dòu.

Coke, bread and M&Ms.

5. 男孩在接凯伦去露天汽车影院看电影前做了什么准备？

nán hái zài jiē kǎi lún qù lù tiān qì chē yǐng yuàn kàn diàn yǐng qián zuò le shén me zhǔn bèi?

What did the boy do to prepare for his date with Karen?

6. 男孩在商店买完东西后做了什么？

nán hái zài shāng diàn mǎi wán dōng xī hòu zuò le shén me?

What did the boy do after buying things from the shop?

7. 当男孩最终找到自己的车的时候，凯伦为什么双眼含泪？

dāng nán hái zuì zhōng zhǎo dào zì jǐ de chē de shí hòu, kǎi lún wèi shén me shuāng yǎn hán lèi?

Why were Karen's eyes full of tears when the boy finally found his car?

1. C
2. B
3. A
4. A
5. 他穿上了他最得体的衣服并带上了足够的钱.

tā chuān shàng le tā zuì dé tǐ de yī fú bìng dài shàng le zú gòu de qián.

He put on his best clothes and made sure he had enough money.

6. 他找不到自己的车，他吃了爆米花并喝光了两瓶可乐.

tā zhǎo bú dào zì jǐ de chē, tā chī le bào mǐ huā bìng hē guāng le liǎng píng kě lè.

He couldn't find his car, so he ate the popcorn and drank both cans of coke.

7. 因为她渴了并且已经等了很久.

yīn wèi tā kě le bìng qiě yǐ jīng děng le hěn jiǔ.

Because she was thirsty and waited for quite a long time.

Chapter 5: 会说话的猫 (huì shuō huà de māo) – The Talking Cat

艾琪有一只名叫**冥王星**的黑猫. 艾琪很喜欢它. 她觉得冥王星很通人性. 当艾琪洗刷的时候, 冥王星也洗刷. 当艾琪照**镜子**的时候, 冥王星也照镜子. 如果艾琪**自言自语**, 冥王星也张开自己的嘴好像也在自言自语.

ài qí yǒu yì zhī míng jiào míng wáng xīng de hēi māo. ài qí hěn xǐ huān tā. tā jué dé míng wáng xīng hěn tōng rén xìng. dāng ài qí xǐ shuā de shí hòu, míng wáng xīng yě xǐ shuā. dāng ài qí zhào jìng zi de shí hòu, míng wáng xīng yě zhào jìng zi. rú guǒ ài qí zì yán zì yǔ, míng wáng xīng yě zhāng kāi zì jǐ de zuǐ hǎo xiàng yě zài zì yán zì yǔ.

Aggie had a black cat named Pluto. Aggie liked it very much. She thought Pluto was wonderful. When Aggie washed herself, Pluto washed itself. When Aggie looked at herself in the mirror, it looked at itself in the same mirror. If Aggie talked to herself, Pluto opened its mouth just as if it was talking to itself.

这使艾琪产生了一个有趣的想法. 她决定教冥王星说话. 她想, "我会让冥王星吃和我一样的食物. 这样说不定能帮它开口说话."

zhè shǐ ài qí chǎn shēng le yí gè yǒu qù de xiǎng fǎ. tā jué dìng jiāo míng wáng xīng shuō huà. tā xiǎng, "wǒ huì ràng míng wáng xīng chī hé wǒ yí yàng de shí wù. zhè yàng shuō bú dìng néng bāng tā kāi kǒu shuō huà."

This gave Aggie a funny idea. She decided to try to teach Pluto to talk. Aggie thought, "I'll give the cat the same food as I eat. I'm sure that will help him learn how to speak."

接着，艾琪让冥王星坐在桌前的**椅子**上开始教它说话.

jiē zhe, ài qí ràng míng wáng xīng zuò zài zhuō qián de yǐ zǐ shàng kāi shǐ jiāo tā shuō huà.

Aggie then let Pluto sit in a chair by the table and began to teach him.

当艾琪吃奶油面包的时候，冥王星也吃. 当艾琪喝**咖啡**的时候，冥王星也喝. 一天，当艾琪和冥王星边喝咖啡边**抽烟**的时候，艾琪又有想法了：她有一只好讲话的老**鹦鹉**. 它跟自己讲话，也和艾琪及冥王星讲话.

dāng ài qí chī nǎi yóu miàn bāo de shí hòu, míng wáng xīng yě chī. dāng ài qí hē kā fēi de shí hòu, míng wáng xīng yě hē. yì tiān, dāng ài qí hé míng wáng xīng biān hē kā fēi biān chōu yān de shí hòu, ài qí yòu yǒu xiǎng fǎ le: tā yǒu yì zhī hào jiǎng huà de lǎo yīng wǔ. tā gēn zì jǐ jiǎng huà, yě hé ài qí jí míng wáng xīng jiǎng huà.

When Aggie ate bread and butter, Pluto did the same. When Aggie drank coffee, Pluto drank too. One day when Aggie and Pluto were drinking coffee and smoking cigarettes, Aggie had another idea: she had an old parrot that was always talking. It talked to itself, it talked to Aggie, and to Pluto.

艾琪很讨厌鹦鹉跟她讲话. 她自言自语到，"如果冥王星吃了这只鹦鹉的话，它肯定能讲话了."

ài qí hěn tǎo yàn yīng wǔ gēn tā jiǎng huà. tā zì yán zì yǔ dào, " rú guǒ míng wáng xīng chī le zhè zhī yīng wǔ de huà, tā kěn dìng néng jiǎng huà le. "

Aggie hated the parrot, so she said to herself, "If Pluto eats the parrot, I'm sure he'll definitely start talking."

于是，她就把这只鹦鹉杀了，油炸后喂给了冥王星.

yú shì, tā jiù bǎ zhè zhī yīng wǔ shā le, yóu zhà hòu wèi gěi le míng wáng xīng.

She killed the parrot and cooked it in butter, then gave it to Pluto.

冥王星在桌上享受这顿美食. 它用**刀、叉**吃着，像个**绅士**. 当它吃完后，突然冲着艾琪喊到，“小心!”艾琪盯着它. 她很吃惊因为她竟然听到冥王星讲话了. 同时，一大块**天花板**落下来砸到了她的头上.
míng wáng xīng zài zhuō shàng xiǎng shòu zhè dùn měi shí. tā yòng dāo、chā chī zhe ， xiàng gè shēn shì. dāng tā chī wán hòu, tū rán chōng zhe ài qí hǎn dào, “xiǎo xīn!” ài qí dīng zhe tā. tā hěn chī jīng yīn wéi tā jìng rán tīng dào míng wáng xīng jiǎng huà le. tóng shí, yí dà kuài tiān huā bǎn luò xià lái zá dào le tā de tóu shàng.
Pluto sat at the table and helped himself to the food. Pluto ate very politely with a knife and fork like a gentleman. When Pluto finished every bit of the parrot, suddenly he turned to Aggie and shouted, “Look out!” Aggie was so astonished looking at him that she hardly heard what Pluto said, and a massive piece of the ceiling fell on her head.
冥王星说,“艾琪用五年的时间教我说话，当我能讲话的时候，她却不听.”
míng wáng xīng shuō: “ ài qí yòng wǔ nián de shí jiān jiāo wǒ shuō huà, dāng wǒ néng jiǎng huà de shí hòu, tā què bù tīng.”
Pluto said, “Aggie spent five years trying to get me to talk, and when I finally speak, she doesn’t listen.”

总结（zǒng jié）— Summary

你能教会猫说人话吗？艾琪就做到了，并且这只猫说出的是流利的中文！她用了什么高科技的手段呢？一般人能掌握吗？不要担心，只要熟读本文，保证你也一学就会，但灵验不灵验，只有艾琪知道; 我们可不敢打保票.
nǐ néng jiāo huì māo shuō rén huà ma? ài qí jiù zuò dào le, bìng qiě zhè zhī māo shuō chū de shì liú lì de zhōng wéntā yòng le shén me gāo kē jì de shǒu duàn ne? yì bān rén néng zhǎng wò ma? bú yào dān xīn, zhǐ yào shú dú běn wén, bǎo zhèng nǐ yě yì xué jiù huì, dàn líng yàn bù líng yàn, zhī yǒu ài qí zhī dào, wǒ men kě bù gǎn dǎ bǎo piào.

Can you teach a cat to speak like a person? Aggie did. She taught a cat to speak fluent Chinese. What kind of high-tech means did she use? Can ordinary people master it? Don't worry, just read this story and make sure you understand it well; then you can try to teach a cat to speak. As for the result, only Aggie knows; we can't guarantee anything.

词汇（cí huì）— Vocabulary

冥王星（míng wáng xīng）Pluto

镜子（jìng zi）mirror

自言自语（zì yán zì yǔ）talk to oneself

椅子（yǐ zi）chair

咖啡（kā fēi）coffee

抽烟（chōu yān）to smoke

鹦鹉（yīng wǔ）parrot

刀（dāo）knife

叉（chā）fork

绅士（shēn shì）gentleman

天花板（tiān huā bǎn）ceiling

练习与答案（liàn xí yǔ dá àn）— Questions and Answers

1. 艾琪有个什么有趣的想法？

ài qí yǒu gè shén me yǒu qù de xiǎng fǎ?

Aggie's fun idea was _______.

A. 教冥王星饮酒.

jiāo míng wáng xīng yǐn jiǔ.

to teach Pluto how to drink.

B. 教冥王星坐在桌子上.

jiāo míng wáng xīng zuò zài zhuō zi shàng.

to teach Pluto how to sit by the table.

C. 教冥王星讲话.

jiāo míng wáng xīng jiǎng huà.

to teach Pluto how to talk.

2. 冥王星是什么？

míng wáng xīng shì shén me?

Pluto was _______.

A．一条很大的狗.

yì tiáo hěn dà de gǒu.

a very big dog.

B．一只聪明的猫.

yì zhī cōng míng de māo.

a clever cat.

C．一头愚蠢的驴.

yì tóu yú chǔn de lǘ.

a stupid donkey.

3. 下列哪一项是正确的？

xià liè nǎ yí xiàng shì zhèng què de?

Which of the following is true?

A．艾琪杀死了鹦鹉.

ài qí shā sǐ le yīng wǔ.

Aggie killed the parrot.

B．艾琪用了六年教猫说话.

ài qí yòng le liù nián jiāo māo shuō huà.

Aggie spent six years teaching the cat to talk.

C．天花板落在了冥王星的头上.

tiān huā bǎn luò zài le míng wáng xīng de tóu shàng.

The ceiling fell on Pluto's head.

4. 艾琪为了让冥王星开口说话都做了什么？

ài qí wèi le ràng míng wáng xīng kāi kǒu shuō huà dōu zuò le shén me?

What did Aggie do in order to help Pluto to speak?

A．她给冥王星吃和自己吃的一样的食物.

tā gěi míng wáng xīng chī hé zì jǐ chī de yí yàng de shí wù

She gave Pluto the same food she ate.

B．她让冥王星看电视.

tā ràng míng wáng xīng kàn diàn shì.

She let Pluto watch TV.

C. 她给冥王星读故事书.

tā gěi míng wáng xīng dú gù shì shū.

She read Pluto storybooks.

5. 艾琪为什么要杀掉鹦鹉？

ài qí wèi shén me yào shā diào yīng wǔ?

Why did Aggie kill the parrot?

6. 冥王星第一次开口说话的目的是什么？

míng wáng xīng dì yī cì kāi kǒu shuō huà de mù de shì shén me?

What was the purpose of Pluto's first words?

7. 为什么艾琪没有听冥王星的话？

wèi shén me ài qí méi yǒu tīng míng wáng xīng de huà?

Why didn't Aggie listen to Pluto?

1. C
2. B
3. A
4. A
5. 因为她很讨厌鹦鹉跟她讲话，而且认为吃掉鹦鹉后，冥王星就能讲话了.

yīn wèi tā hěn tǎo yàn yīng wǔ gēn tā jiǎng huà, ér qiě rèn wéi chī diào yīng wǔ hòu, míng wáng xīng jiù néng jiǎng huà le.

Because she hated the parrot, and she thought after eating the parrot, Pluto would start to speak.

6. 警告艾琪天花板掉下来了.

jǐng gào ài qí tiān huā bǎn diào xià lái le.

To warn Aggie about the falling ceiling.

7. 因为她对终于听到冥王星说话感到吃惊.

yīn wèi tā duì zhōng yú tīng dào míng wáng xīng shuō huà gǎn dào chī jīng.

Because she was so astonished that she hardly heard what Pluto said.

Chapter 6: 打赌(dǎ dǔ) – A Bet

贝克先生在一个大工厂里工作，他一直很忙，几乎没有时间休息. 有一年**夏天**，他决定去海边**度假**. 一个**酷热**的下午，贝克先生走进一个**餐馆**，坐在桌前想喝点东西.

bèi kè xiān shēng zài yí gè dà gōng chǎng lǐ gōng zuò, tā yì zhí hěn máng, jī hū méi yǒu shí jiān xiū xi. yǒu yì nián xià tiān, tā jué dìng qù hǎi biān dù jià. yí gè kù rè de xià wǔ, bèi kè xiān shēng zǒu jìn yì gè cān guǎn, zuò zài zhuō qián xiǎng hē diǎn dōng xi.

Mr. Baker worked in a big factory. He was busy all the time and had little time to rest. One summer, he decided to spend his holiday by the sea. One afternoon it was very hot. Mr. Baker came into a restaurant, sat at a table, and wanted to drink.

就在这时一个老人走向他说，“很高兴见到你，年轻人.”贝克先生说：“你好，老大爷.”他让老人挨着他坐下.“你能和我一起喝点吗?”

jiù zài zhè shí yí gè lǎo rén zǒu xiàng tā shuō, “hěn gāo xìng jiàn dào nǐ, nián qīng rén.” bèi kè xiān shēng shuō, “nǐ hǎo, lǎo dà ye,” tā ràng lǎo rén āi zhe tā zuò xià. “nǐ néng hé wǒ yì qǐ hē diǎn ma?”

Just then, an old man came up to him and said, "Nice to meet you, son." "Nice to meet you too, paps," Mr. Baker replied and invited the old man to sit next to him. "Would you mind joining me?"
老人说,"谢谢你，年轻人. 你以前来过这儿吗?"
lǎo rén shuō, "xiè xie nǐ, nián qīng rén. nǐ yǐ qián lái guò zhè ér ma?"
"Thank you, young man," said the old man. "Have you been here before?"
"没有，我从来没来过,"年轻的贝克先生说.
"méi yǒu, wǒ cóng lái méi lái guò," nián qīng de bèi kè xiān shēng shuō.
"No, I haven't," said the young Mr. Baker.
"你看起来很孤独，不是吗?"这个老人说."让我们打个赌，好吗?"
"nǐ kàn qǐ lái hěn gū dú, bú shì ma?" zhè gè lǎo rén shuō. "ràng wǒ men dǎ gè dǔ, hǎo ma?"
"You look lonely, don't you?" said the old man. "Let's have a bet, shall we?"
贝克先生非常感兴趣."噢，我很**乐意**."他说."但是我们赌什么呢?"
bèi kè xiān shēng fēi cháng gǎn xìng qù. "o, wǒ hěn lè yì." tā shuō. "dàn shì wǒ men dǔ shí me ne?"
Mr. Baker was intrigued. "Oh, I'm glad to," he said. "But what shall we bet on?"
"我能咬住我的左**眼球**,"这个老人说."我跟你赌五美元."
"wǒ néng yǎo zhù wǒ de zuǒ yǎn qiú," zhè gè lǎo rén shuō. "wǒ gēn nǐ dǔ wǔ měi yuán."
"I can bite my left eyeball," said the old man. "I'll bet you five dollars."
"这不可能,"贝克暗自想，然后他在桌子上放了五美元. 这个老人扣下他的**玻璃**眼睛，把它放到嘴里轻轻地咬了咬. 贝克非常吃惊，但他不得不把钱给了这位老人.
"zhè bù kě néng," bèi kè àn zì xiǎng, rán hòu tā zài zhuō zi shàng fàng le wǔ měi yuán. zhè gè lǎo rén kòu xià tā de bō lí yǎn jīng, bǎ tā

fàng dào zuǐ lǐ qīng qīng de yǎo le yǎo. bèi kè fēi cháng chī jīng, dàn tā bù dé bù bǎ qián gěi le zhè wèi lǎo rén.
“That’s impossible,” Mr. Baker said to himself and put five dollars on the table. The old man took out his glass eyeball, put it into his mouth, and gently bit it. Mr. Baker was surprised and had to give the money to him.
“没关系，年轻人,”老人笑着说.“我会给你一次机会并且你可以把钱赢回去. 我能咬住我的右眼. 我跟你赌十美元.”
“méi guān xì, nián qīng rén, ” lǎo rén xiào zhe shuō. “ wǒ huì gěi nǐ yí cì jī huì bìng qiě nǐ kě yǐ bǎ qián yíng huí qù. wǒ néng yǎo zhù wǒ de yòu yǎn. wǒ gēn nǐ dǔ shí měi yuán.”
“It doesn’t matter, young man,” the old man said with a smile. “I’ll give you a chance, and you can win the money back. I can also bite my right eye. I’ll bet you ten dollars.”
“我确信他能够看到东西，我一定会赢他的钱,”贝克想，所以他拿出十美元放在桌子上.
“wǒ què xìn tā néng gòu kàn dào dōng xi, wǒ yí dìng huì yíng tā de qián, ” bèi kè xiǎng, suǒ yǐ tā ná chū shí měi yuán fàng zài zhuō zi shàng.
“I’m sure he’s able to see, and I have to win back my money,” Mr. Baker thought. So, he brought out ten dollars and put it on the table.
但是当这个老人摘下他的**假牙**开始咬他的右眼时，贝克更加吃惊了. 随后，老人把钱放进**口袋**里扬长而去.
dàn shì dāng zhè gè lǎo rén zhāi xià tā de jiǎ yá kāi shǐ yǎo tā de yòu yǎn shí, bèi kè gèng jiā chī jīng le. suí hòu, lǎo rén bǎ qián fàng jìn kǒu dài lǐ yáng cháng ér qù.
But he was even more surprised, as the old man took out his false teeth and began to bite his right eye. Then, the old man put the money into his pocket and went away.

总结（zǒng jié）— Summary

人们往往会犯经验主义的错误，以为从常识中得来的判断定然没错. 而有些人正是巧妙地利用了人们的这种思维定式来产生出其不意的效果，让人在惊讶中犯下意外的错误. 这个故事就是讲述一位老人如何利用人们的习惯思维来让年轻的贝克先生进入圈套中的.

rén men wǎng wǎng huì fàn jīng yàn zhǔ yì de cuò wù, yǐ wéi cóng cháng shí zhōng dé lái de pàn duàn dìng rán méi cuò. ér yǒu xiē rén zhèng shì qiǎo miào de lì yòng le rén men de zhè zhǒng sī wéi dìng shì lái chǎn shēng chū qí bú yì de xiào guǒ, ràng rén zài jīng yà zhōng fàn xià yì wài de cuò wù. zhè gè gù shì jiù shì jiǎng shù yí wèi lǎo rén rú hé lì yòng rén men de xí guàn sī wéi lái ràng nián qīng de bèi kè xiān shēng jìn rù quān tào zhōng de.

People often make empirical mistakes: they believe that judging from common sense is certainly correct. However, some people cleverly take advantage of people's mindsets to produce unexpected results, leading people to make unexpected mistakes in surprise. This story is about how an old man uses people's mindsets to lure young Mr. Baker into the trap.

词汇（cí huì）— Vocabulary

工厂（gōng chǎng）factory

夏天（xià tiān）summer

度假（dù jiǎ）to spend the holiday

酷热（kù rè）hot

餐馆（cān guǎn）restaurant

乐意（lè yì）be glad to

眼球（yǎn qiú）eyeball

玻璃（bō lí）glass

假牙（jiǎ yá）false teeth

口袋（kǒu dài）pocket

练习与答案（liàn xí yǔ dá àn）— Questions and Answers

1. 贝克先生去海边做什么？

bèi kè xiān shēng qù hǎi biān zuò shén me?

Mr. Baker went to the seaside ________.

A. 游泳.

yóu yǒng.
to swim.

B. 打赌.
dǎ dǔ.
to bet.

C. 度假.
dù jiǎ.
to have a holiday.

2. 老人为什么来跟贝克先生打招呼？
lǎo rén wèi shén me lái gēn bèi kè xiān shēng dǎ zhāo hū?
The old man said hello to Mr. Baker because _______.

A. 因为他们是好朋友.
yīn wèi tā men shì hǎo péng yǒu.
they were good friends.

B. 因为他想和贝克先生喝一杯.
yīn wèi tā xiǎng hé bèi kè xiān shēng hē yì bēi.
he wanted to drink with him.

C. 因为他想赢贝克先生的钱.
yīn wèi tā xiǎng yíng bèi kè xiān shēng de qián.
he wanted to win some money from him.

3. 贝克先生为何还要与老人打十美元的赌？
bèi kè xiān shēng wèi hé hái yào yǔ lǎo rén dǎ shí měi yuán de dǔ?
Mr. Baker bet the old man ten dollars because _______.

A. 因为他不认为老人两只眼睛都是假的.
yīn wèi tā bú rèn wéi lǎo rén liǎng zhī yǎn jīng dōu shì jiǎ de.
he didn't think he would be blind in both eyes.

B. 因为他想帮助老人.
yīn wèi tā xiǎng bāng zhù lǎo rén.
he wanted to help him.

C. 因为他想和老人交朋友.
yīn wèi tā xiǎng hé lǎo rén jiāo péng yǒu.

he wanted to make friends with him.

4. 贝克先生一共输掉了多少美元？

bèi kè xiān shēng yí gòng shū diào le duō shǎo měi yuán?

How much money did Mr. Baker lose in total?

A. 十五美元.

shí wǔ měi yuán

Fifteen dollars.

B. 二十美元.

èr shí měi yuán.

Twenty dollars.

C. 十美元.

shí měi yuán.

Ten dollars.

5. 老人身上有哪些地方是假的？

lǎo rén shēn shàng yǒu nǎ xiē dì fāng shì jiǎ de?

What places of the old man were fake?

6. 贝克先生为什么要去度假？

bèi kè xiān shēng wèi shén me yào qù dù jià?

Why did Mr. Baker go on holiday?

7. 老人为什么要问贝克先生是否来过这里？

lǎo rén wèi shén me yào wèn bèi kè xiān shēng shì fǒu lái guò zhè lǐ?

Why did the old man ask Mr. Baker if he's been here before?

1. C
2. C
3. A
4. A
5. 他的左眼睛和牙齿.

tā de zuǒ yǎn jīng hé yá chǐ.

His left eye and his teeth.

6. 因为他一直很忙，几乎没有时间休息.

yīn wèi tā yì zhí hěn máng, jī hū méi yǒu shí jiān xiū xi.

Because he was busy all the time and had little rest.

7. 因为他想确定贝克先生不认识他.
yīn wèi tā xiǎng què dìng bèi kè xiān shēng bú rèn shí tā.
Because he wanted to make sure that Mr. Baker didn't know him.

Chapter 7: 猫和小鸟 (māo hé xiǎo niǎo) – The Cat and the Birds

有一天，一只**鸭子**和一只猫下到水里，它们看到了一只小鸟."它是谁啊?"猫问鸭子.

yǒu yì tiān, yì zhī yā zi hé yì zhī māo xià dào shuǐ lǐ, tā men kàn dào le yī zhī xiǎo niǎo. "tā shì shuí a?" māo wèn yā zi.

One day a duck and a cat went down to the water where they saw a little bird. "Who is it?" asked the cat.

"哦，它可是一只最好的**母鸟**."鸭子说.

"o, tā kě shì yì zhī zuì hǎo de mǔ niǎo." yā zǐ shuō.

"Well, it's the best of all the mother birds," said the duck.

"它很有钱吗?"猫又问.

"tā hěn yǒu qián ma?" māo yòu wèn.

"Is she very rich?" the cat asked.

"是的，它的巢里有很多**耳环**，还有你能想象到的所有好东西," 鸭子回答说. 虽然这并不是真的，可鸭子却这样说就是想**戏弄**一下猫.

"shì de, tā de cháo lǐ yǒu hěn duō ěr huán, hái yǒu nǐ néng xiǎng xiàng dào de suǒ yǒu hǎo dōng xi." yā zi huí dá shuō. suī rán zhè

bìng bú shì zhēn de, kě yā zi què zhè yàng shuō jiù shì xiǎng xì nòng yí xià māo.
"She is. Her nest is filled with earrings, and every good thing you can think of," the duck said to him. This was not so, but the duck wished to play a trick on the cat.
过了一会儿，母鸟外出**觅食**去了. 猫趁机奔向**鸟巢**，探头往里面看. 它发现这个巢竟跟其他的巢没有什么两样，里面仅仅只有三只**幼鸟**而已.
guò le yì huì ér, mǔ niǎo wài chū mì shí qù le. māo chèn jī bēn xiàng niǎo cháo, tàn tóu wǎng lǐ miàn kàn. tā fā xiàn zhè gè cháo jìng gēn qí tā de cháo méi yǒu shén me liǎng yàng; lǐ miàn jǐn jǐn zhī yǒu sān zhī yòu niǎo ér yǐ!
After a while, the mother bird went out to look for food. The cat ran as fast as it could to the nest and looked in. What he saw there surprised him; it was just a nest like any other. All that was in the nest were three baby birds!
"怎么回事?"猫问."那些耳环到哪里去了呢？哦，这里根本就不**富有**. 而且这里根本就没有一样我想要的东西."猫对被戏弄这件事感到很生气，它打了那几只幼鸟一顿.
"zěn me huí shì?" māo wèn. "nà xiē ěr huán dào nǎ lǐ qù le ne? o, zhè lǐ gēn běn jiù bú fù yǒu. ér qiě zhè lǐ gēn běn jiù méi yǒu yí yàng wǒ xiǎng yào de dōng xi." māo duì bèi xì nòng zhè jiàn shì gǎn dào hěn shēng qì, tā dǎ le nà jǐ zhī yòu niǎo yí dùn.
"What's going on?" asked the cat. "Where are all the rings? You're not rich at all. There is not a thing here for me to take." The cat was mad that he had been tricked; he smacked and punched the baby birds.
当母鸟回来后发现自己的巢被猫弄坏了，而且孩子们都在哭. 它把这件事告诉了**蚂蚁**、**蝴蝶**和**蜜蜂**."我知道该怎么做,"蜜蜂说完就飞走了.
dāng mǔ niǎo huí lái hòu fā xiàn zì jǐ de cháo bèi māo nòng huài le, ér qiě hái zi men dōu zài kū. tā bǎ zhè jiàn shì gào sù le mǎ yǐ、hú

dié hé mì fēng. "wǒ zhī dào gāi zěn me zuò," mì fēng shuō wán jiù fēi zǒu le.
When the mother bird came home, she saw that the cat had crushed her nest and made the children cry. She went to tell the ant, butterfly and the bee. "I think I know what to do," said the bee, and away it went.
当蜜蜂看到这只猫正弓着背时，它便冲下来朝它背上蛰了一下，猫的背立即缩了下去！当猫又将自己的背弓起来的时候，蜜蜂又蛰了它一下. 它疼得受不了，飞快地逃走了.
dāng mì fēng kàn dào zhè zhī māo zhèng gōng zhe bèi shí, tā biàn chōng xià lái cháo tā bèi shàng zhé le yí xià, māo de bèi lì jí suō le xià qù! dāng māo yòu jiāng zì jǐ de bèi gōng qǐ lái de shí hòu, mì fēng yòu zhé le tā yí xià. tā téng dé shòu bù le, fēi kuài de táo zǒu le.
When the bee saw the cat, the cat was bending its back. The bee swooped down and stung the cat. Down went the cat's back! Once more, the cat put its back up in the air, and once more, the bee stung it. It could stand no more! Away the cat ran as fast as it could.
现在这只猫仍要时不时地经过这些鸟的家，但它再也不敢在这里多做停留了，每次都飞快地从旁边溜过去.
xiàn zài zhè zhī māo réng yào shí bú shí de jīng guò zhè xiē niǎo de jiā, dàn tā zài yě bù gǎn zài zhè lǐ duō zuò tíng liú le, měi cì dōu fēi kuài de cóng páng biān liū guò qù.
Now the cat still must pass the home of the birds from time to time. But he doesn't stop. He just runs by as fast as he can.

总结（zǒng jié）— Summary

多嘴的鸭子想戏弄一下好奇的猫，说它看见鸟窝里有很多好东西. 一心想占便宜的猫满心欢喜，一溜小跑地来到鸟巢，盼望自己能碰上好运气. 但结果却并不如意，它没能如愿以偿还被蜜蜂蛰的痛苦不堪.
duō zuǐ de yā zi xiǎng xì nòng yí xià hǎo qí de māo, shuō tā kàn jiàn niǎo wō lǐ yǒu hěn duō hǎo dōng xi. yì xīn xiǎng zhàn pián yi de māo mǎn xīn huān xǐ, yì liū xiǎo pǎo de lái dào niǎo cháo, pàn wàng

zì jǐ néng pèng shàng hǎo yùn qi. dàn jié guǒ què bìng bù rú yì, tā méi néng rú yuàn yǐ cháng hái bèi mì fēng zhé de tòng kǔ bù kān.

The mouthy duck wanted to tease the curious cat, so it said that it saw a lot of good things in the nest. The cat who wanted to take advantage of it was very happy. It sprinted towards the bird's nest and hoped that he would have good luck. But the result was terrible: he didn't get what he wanted and was stung by the bee.

词汇（cí huì）— Vocabulary

鸭子（yā zi）duck

母鸟（mǔ niǎo）mother bird

耳环（ěr huán）earring

戏弄（xì nòng）to play a trick on

觅食（mì shí）to look for food

鸟巢（niǎo cháo）nest

幼鸟（yòu niǎo）baby bird

富有（fù yǒu）rich

蚂蚁（mǎ yǐ）ant

蝴蝶（hú dié）butterfly

蜜蜂（mì fēng）bee

蜇（zhē）to sting

练习与答案（liàn xí yǔ dá àn）— Questions and Answers

1. 当猫去鸟巢的时候 _______ .

dāng māo qù niǎo cháo de shí hòu _______.

When the cat went to the bird's nest _______.

A. 猫看到了好多好东西

māo kàn dào le hǎo duō hǎo dōng xi.

the cat saw many good things.

B. 母鸟出去了

mǔ niǎo chū qù le.

the mother bird was out.

C. 猫看到了很多蜜蜂

māo kàn dào le hěn duō mì fēng.

the cat saw some bees.

2. 母鸟看到孩子们在哭后做了什么？

mǔ niǎo kàn dào hái zi men zài kū hòu zuò le shén me?

What did the mother bird do to the cat when she saw her children were crying?

A. 它与猫打了一架.

tā yǔ māo dǎ le yí jià.

She fought the cat.

B. 它向蚂蚁、蝴蝶和蜜蜂求助.

tā xiàng mǎ yǐ 、hú dié hé mì fēng qiú zhù.

It asked the ants, butterflies, and bees for help.

C. 它也哭了.

tā yě kū le.

She cried too.

3. 猫看到鸟巢时是什么感觉？

māo kàn dào niǎo cháo shí shì shén me gǎn jué?

How did the cat feel after it saw the bird's nest?

A. 猫很高兴.

māo hěn gāo xìng.

The cat was happy.

B. 猫很兴奋.

māo hěn xīng fèn.

The cat was excited.

C. 猫很不高兴.

māo hěn bù gāo xìng.

The cat was unhappy.

4. 为什么幼鸟哭了？

wèi shén me yòu niǎo kū le?

Why did the little birds cry?

A. 因为它们的妈妈不在.

yīn wèi tā men de mā ma bú zài.

Because their mother wasn't in.

B． 因为猫想吃掉它们.

yīn wèi māo xiǎng chī diào tā men.

Because the cat wanted to eat them.

C． 因为猫毁了它们的巢还打了它们.

yīn wèi māo huǐ le tā men de cháo hái dǎ le tā men.

Because the cat crushed their nest and hit them.

5. 鸭子为什么要骗猫？

yā zǐ wèi shén me yào piàn māo?

Why did the duck lie to the cat?

6. 蜜蜂得知猫做的事情后做了什么？

mì fēng dé zhī māo zuò de shì qíng hòu zuò le shén me?

What did the bee do after learning of the cat's behavior?

7. 猫现在还敢惹鸟吗？

māo xiàn zài hái gǎn rě niǎo ma?

Does the cat dare to mess with birds now?

1. B
2. B
3. C
4. C
5. 因为鸭子想要戏弄猫.

yīn wèi yā zi xiǎng yào xì nòng māo.

Because the duck wanted to play a trick on the cat.

6. 它蛰了猫.

tā zhé le māo.

It stung the cat.

7. 不敢了.

bù gǎn le.

It dares not.

Chapter 8: 乞丐的爱好 (qǐ gài de ài hào) – The Beggar's Hobby

爱丽丝住在乡下，但是有一年她决定去首都买一些东西，同时也游览一下这个城市.

ài lì sī zhù zài xiāng xià, dàn shì yǒu yì nián tā jué dìng qù shǒu dū mǎi yì xiē dōng xi, tóng shí yě yóu lǎn yí xià zhè gè chéng shì.

Alice lived in the country, but one year she decided to visit the capital to do some shopping and to go sight-seeing.

她住在中央广场旁边的一间旅馆里. 以前她很少来这个城市，所以她非常兴奋地期待着能有新的发现.

tā zhù zài zhōng yāng guǎng chǎng páng biān de yì jiān lǚ guǎn lǐ. yǐ qián tā hěn shǎo lái zhè gè chéng shì, suǒ yǐ tā fēi cháng xīng fèn de qī dài zhe néng yǒu xīn de fā xiàn.

She stayed at a hotel beside the central market. She had seldom been to the city before and was very excited about what she would find.

住城里的第一个早上，当她从旅馆步行到市场的时候，她从一个乞丐身旁走过.

zhù chéng lǐ de dì yī gè zǎo shàng, dāng tā cóng lǚ guǎn bù xíng dào shì chǎng de shí hòu, tā cóng yí gè qǐ gài shēn páng zǒu guò.
On the first morning in the city, as she walked from the hotel to the market, she passed a beggar.
在地面上有一个告示，上面写着,"天生失明，请慷慨施舍."
zài dì miàn shàng yǒu yí gè gào shi, shàng miàn xiě zhe, " tiān shēng shī míng, qǐng kāng kǎi shī shě."
On the ground was a notice which said, "Blind since birth, please give generously."
爱丽丝非常同情失明的乞丐，就将一美元硬币放入了他的碗里.
ài lì sī fēi cháng tóng qíng shī míng de qǐ gài, jiù jiāng yì měi yuán yìng bì fàng rù le tā de wǎn lǐ.
Alice felt sorry for the blind beggar and put a dollar coin into his bowl.
"谢谢你,"乞丐说.
"xiè xie nǐ," qǐ gài shuō.
"Thank you," he said.
然而，第三天爱丽丝没有一元的硬币了，她就把仅有的五十美分放进了乞丐的碗内. 乞丐发现她给他的钱少于最初的两次.
rán ér, dì sān tiān ài lì sī méi yǒu yī yuán de yìng bì le, tā jiù bǎ jǐn yǒu de wǔ shí měi fèn fàng jìn le qǐ gài de wǎn nèi. qǐ gài fā xiàn tā gěi tā de qián shǎo yú zuì chū de liǎng cì.
On the third day, however, Alice did not have a dollar coin. She had only fifty cents, so she dropped this into the beggar's bowl instead. The beggar noticed that she gave him less money than the first two times.
"今天你为什么这么小气?"
"jīn tiān nǐ wéi shén me zhè me xiǎo qì?"
"Why are you so stingy today?"
爱丽丝听了乞丐的话感到非常惊讶.
ài lì sī tīng le qǐ gài de huà gǎn dào fēi cháng jīng yà.
Alice was very surprised by what the beggar said.

“你如何知道我给你的不是一元呢?”她说.“除非你不是失明的人，否则你不可能知道我放进你碗内是什么硬币.”

“nǐ rú hé zhī dào wǒ gěi nǐ de bú shì yī yuán ne?” tā shuō. “chú fēi nǐ bú shì shī míng de rén, fǒu zé nǐ bù kě néng zhī dào wǒ fàng jìn nǐ wǎn nèi shì shén me yìng bì.”

“How did you know I haven’t given you a dollar?” she said. “If you’re blind, you couldn’t have known which coin I put into your bowl.”

“哦,”乞丐说.“告诉你实情吧，我并不是失明. 因为乞丐在度假，所以我只是在为他照看这个地方.”

“ò,” qǐ gài shuō. “gào sù nǐ shí qíng ba, wǒ bìng bú shì shī míng. yīn wéi qǐ gài zài dù jià, suǒ yǐ wǒ zhī shì zài wéi tā zhào kàn zhè gè dì fāng.”

“Ah,” said the beggar. “To tell you the truth, I’m not blind. I’m just looking after this place for the beggar because he’s on holiday.”

“哦，度假!”爱丽丝感叹道.“你的盲朋友在假日里具体做什么?”

“ò, dù jià!” ài lì sī gǎn tàn dào. “nǐ de máng péng yǒu zài jiǎ rì lǐ jù tǐ zuò shén me?”

“Oh, holiday!” Alice exclaimed. “And what exactly does your blind friend do on holiday?”

“他去了乡下,”那男子说,“他去照相了. 他是一个非常好的摄影师.”

“tā qù le xiāng xià,” nà nán zǐ shuō, “ tā qù zhào xiàng le. tā shì yī gè fēi cháng hǎo de shè yǐng shī.”

“He goes into the country,” the man said, “and takes photographs. He’s a very good photographer.”

总结（zǒng jié）— Summary

乞丐似乎也成为了一些人的固定职业，虽然经常要面对别人鄙视的眼光，但有更多的好心人会表示同情并慷慨施舍. 爱丽丝就是个好心女孩，她却遇到了一个与众不同的冒牌乞丐，是被雇来看守地盘的，而这个地盘上的乞丐竟然去乡下度假了！

qǐ gài sì hū yě chéng wéi le yì xiē rén de gù dìng zhí yè, suī rán jīng cháng yào miàn duì bié rén bǐ shì de yǎn guāng, dàn yǒu gèng duō de hǎo xīn rén huì biǎo shì tóng qíng bìng kāng kǎi shī shě. ài lì sī jiù shì gè hǎo xīn nǚ hái, tā què yù dào le yí gè yǔ zhòng bù tóng de mào pái qǐ gài, shì bèi gù lái kān shǒu dì pán de, ér zhè gè dì pán shàng de qǐ gài jìng rán qù xiāng xià dù jià le.

Being a beggar seems to have become a fixed occupation for some people. Although a beggar often has to face the contempt of others, there are more nice people who will show their sympathy and give alms. Alice was a nice girl. She met a fake beggar who was hired to look after the territory. The original beggar was going for a holiday in the countryside.

词汇（cí huì）— Vocabulary

乡下（xiāng xià）the countryside

首都（shǒu dū）the capital

游览（yóu lǎn）to go sight-seeing

兴奋（xīng fèn）to be excited

失明（shī míng）to be blind

慷慨（kāng kǎi）to be generous

小气（xiǎo qì）to be stingy

惊讶（jīng yà）to be surprised

照看（zhào kàn）to look after

感叹（gǎn tàn）to exclaim

摄影师（shè yǐng shī）the photographer

练习与答案（liàn xí yǔ dá àn）— Questions and Answers

1. 爱丽丝前两天每次给乞丐多少钱？

ài lì sī qián liǎng tiān měi cì gěi qǐ gài duō shǎo qián?

Alice gave the beggar _______ on the first two days.

A. 两美元.

liǎng měi yuán.

two dollars.

B． 一美元.

yì měi yuán.

one dollar.

C． 五十美分.

wǔ shí měi fēn.

fifty cents.

2. 原来的那个乞丐去哪里度假了？

yuán lái de nà gè qǐ gài qù nǎ lǐ dù jià le?

The original beggar went on holiday _______.

A． 去乡下.

qù xiāng xià.

to the countryside.

B． 去沙滩.

qù shā tān.

to the beach.

C． 去城市.

qù chéng shì.

to the city.

3. 原来的那个乞丐的爱好是什么？

yuán lái de nà gè qǐ gài de ài hào shì shén me?

The regular beggar's hobby is _______.

A． 乞讨.

qǐ tǎo.

begging.

B． 照相.

zhào xiàng.

taking photos.

C． 游泳.

yóu yǒng.

swimming.

4. 爱丽丝家住哪里，她现在去哪里了？

ài lì sī jiā zhù nǎ lǐ, tā xiàn zài qù nǎ lǐ le

Where is Alice's home, and where is she now?

A. 她住在乡下，她现在在乡下.

tā zhù zài xiāng xià, tā xiàn zài zài xiāng xià

She lives in the countryside, and she is in the countryside.

B. 她住在首都，她现在在首都.

tā zhù zài shǒu dū, tā xiàn zài zài shǒu dū.

She lives in the capital, and she is in the capital.

C. 她住在乡下，她现在在首都.

tā zhù zài xiāng xià, tā xiàn zài zài shǒu dū.

She lives in the countryside, and she is in the capital.

5. 原来的乞丐是盲人吗？

yuán lái de qǐ gài shì máng rén ma?

Is the regular beggar blind?

A. 是的.

shì de.

Yes, he is.

B. 不是.

bú shì.

No, he isn't.

C. 不知道.

bù zhī dào.

We don't know.

6. 爱丽丝来到首都的感觉是什么？

ài lì sī lái dào shǒu dū de gǎn jiào shì shén me?

How did Alice feel about coming to the capital?

7. 爱丽丝第一次看到乞丐时的心情是怎样的？

ài lì sī dì yī cì kàn dào qǐ gài shí de xīn qíng shì zěn yàng de?

How did Alice feel when she met the beggar for the first time?

8. 乞丐发现爱丽丝给的钱比之前少时的反应是什么？

qǐ gài fā xiàn ài lì sī gěi de qián bǐ zhī qián shǎo shí de fǎn yìng shì shén me?

How did the beggar react when he noticed that Alice gave him less money than before?

9. 原来的乞丐为什么有钱雇人来照看地盘？

yuán lái de qǐ gài wéi shén me yǒu qián gù rén lái zhào kàn dì pán?
How did the regular beggar have money to hire someone to look after his place?
10. 爱丽丝是一个怎样的女孩？
ài lì sī shì yí gè zěn yàng de nǚ hái?
What kind of girl is Alice?
1. B
2. A
3. B
4. C
5. B
6. 她非常兴奋地期待着能有新的发现.
tā fēi cháng xīng fèn de qī dài zhe néng yǒu xīn de fā xiàn.
She was excited about what she would find.
7. 她非常同情他.
tā fēi cháng tóng qíng tā.
She felt sorry for him.
8. 他抱怨爱丽丝小气.
tā bào yuàn ài lì sī xiǎo qì.
He complained that Alice was stingy.
9. 他通过乞讨赚了很多钱.
tā tōng guò qǐ tǎo zuàn le hěn duō qián.
He earned a lot of money by begging.
10. 爱丽丝是一个善良的女孩.
ài lì sī shì yí gè shàn liáng de nǚ hái.
Alice is a kind girl.

Chapter 9: 和女生跳舞 (hé nǚ shēng tiào wǔ) – Dancing with a Girl

你好，我是吉米！这是我的关于**跳舞**的故事. 在上**中学**以前我总认为我很勇敢，但在新学校，我发现跳舞时我并没有那么**勇敢**. 我们每个月都有一个**舞会**，这意味着要和女生一起跳舞！

nǐ hǎo, wǒ shì jí mǐ! zhè shì wǒ de guān yú tiào wǔ de gù shì. zài shàng zhōng xué yǐ qián wǒ zǒng rèn wéi wǒ hěn yǒng gǎn, dàn zài xīn xué xiào, wǒ fā xiàn tiào wǔ shí wǒ bìng méi yǒu nà me yǒng gǎn. wǒ men měi gè yuè dōu yǒu yí gè wǔ huì, zhè yì wèi zhe yào hé nǚ shēng yì qǐ tiào wǔ!

Hi! I'm Jimmy. Here is my story about dance. I always thought that I was brave before I went to middle school. At my new school, I find that I'm not brave enough when I'm at dances. We have a dance party every month. That means dancing with girls!

第一次跳舞时，我只是和其他的男生一起跳. 而第二次就不一样了，一部分男生开始和**漂亮**的女孩跳舞.

dì yī cì tiào wǔ shí, wǒ zhī shì hé qí tā de nán shēng yì qǐ tiào. ér dì èr cì jiù bù yí yàng le, yí bù fèn nán shēng kāi shǐ hé piào liàng de nǚ hái tiào wǔ.

At the first dance, I just danced with the other boys. But the next time, it was different: a few of the boys started dancing with beautiful girls.

我怎么知道女孩是否愿意和我跳舞呢？我该怎么开口呢？我应该对她说什么呢？在接下来的几星期里，我开始注意我们班上的女孩：一些太高了，而另一些又太**恬静**了，但正好有一个适合我，她有一头长发.

wǒ zěn me zhī dào nǚ hái shì fǒu yuàn yì hé wǒ tiào wǔ ne? wǒ gāi zěn me kāi kǒu ne? wǒ yīng gāi duì tā shuō shén me ne? zài jiē xià lái de jǐ xīng qī lǐ, wǒ kāi shǐ zhù yì wǒ men bān shàng de nǚ hái: yì xiē tài gāo le, ér lìng yì xiē yòu tài tián jìng le, dàn zhèng hǎo yǒu yí gè shì hé wǒ, tā yǒu yì tóu cháng fà.

How can I know if a girl wants to dance with me? How can I ask? What should I say to her? During the next few weeks, I began thinking about the girls in my class. Some were too tall; some were too quiet. But one girl was just right for me. She had long hair.

我的朋友想尽力帮我，一个说："如果你**害怕**，我们就站在你后面，别**担心**."

wǒ de péng yǒu xiǎng jìn lì bāng wǒ, yí gè shuō, "rú guǒ nǐ hài pà, wǒ men jiù zhàn zài nǐ hòu miàn, bié dān xīn."

My friends tried to help me. One said, "If you're afraid, we'll stand behind you. Don't worry."

该准备跳舞了，我理了发，穿上了最喜欢的衬衫和裤子. 在路上，父亲对我说："看着她的眼睛，**友好**一点."

gāi zhǔn bèi tiào wǔ le, wǒ lǐ le fà, chuān shàng le zuì xǐ huān de chèn shān hé kù zi. zài lù shàng, fù qīn duì wǒ shuō, "kàn zhe tā de yǎn jīng, yǒu hǎo yì diǎn."

It was time to get ready. I got a haircut. I picked out my favorite shirt and trousers. On the way there, my dad said, "Look her in the eye, and be friendly."

但当我去跳舞时，我对自己并不**自信**. 我和朋友悄悄地四处寻找她. 当我们最终找到她时，我的心跳开始加速，她真美！

dàn dāng wǒ qù tiào wǔ shí, wǒ duì zì jǐ bìng bú zì xìn. wǒ hé péng yǒu qiāo qiāo de sì chù xún zhǎo tā. dāng wǒ men zuì zhōng zhǎo dào tā shí, wǒ de xīn tiào kāi shǐ jiā sù, tā zhēn měi!
But when I got to the dance, I didn't feel very confident about myself. I walked around quietly with my friends and looked for her. When I finally found her, my heart began to beat fast. I thought she was very beautiful.
最后一首慢节拍的歌响了起来，我朝她走去. 我的脚步很沉重，我能听到音乐已经响起. 当我来到她面前时，我望着她的蓝眼睛."可以和我跳支舞吗？"我问道. 她说可以. 我搂着她，她的双手搂着我的脖子. 当我们跳起来的时候，一个朋友朝我**挤眼睛**. 还可以，我觉得很爽.
zuì hòu yì shǒu màn jié pāi de gē xiǎng le qǐ lái, wǒ cháo tā zǒu qù. wǒ de jiǎo bù hěn chén zhòng, wǒ néng tīng dào yīn yuè yǐ jīng xiǎng qǐ. dāng wǒ lái dào tā miàn qián shí, wǒ wàng zhe tā de lán yǎn jīng. "kě yǐ hé wǒ tiào zhī wǔ ma?" wǒ wèn dào. tā shuō kě yǐ . wǒ lǒu zhe tā, tā de shuāng shǒu lǒu zhe wǒ de bó zi. dāng wǒ men tiào qǐ lái de shí hòu, yí gè péng yǒu cháo wǒ jǐ yǎn jīng. hái kě yǐ, wǒ jué de hěn shuǎng.
When the last slow song came on, I began to walk over to her. My feet felt so heavy; I could hear the music starting. When I finally got to her, I looked into her blue eyes. "Will you dance with me?" I asked. She said yes. I put my hands around her, and she put her arms around my neck. When we danced, one of my friends winked at me. This isn't too bad, I thought. This is fun.
舞会结束了，回家的路上我一直在笑，和那个女孩子跳舞的感觉真棒！
wǔ huì jié shù le, huí jiā de lù shàng wǒ yì zhí zài xiào, hé nà gè nǚ hái zi tiào wǔ de gǎn jué zhēn bàng!
The dance was over; I smiled all the way home. Dancing with that girl was really great!

总结（zǒng jié）— Summary

这是一次令吉米难忘的跳舞经历，那个音乐缭绕、彩灯变换的夜晚真是太美妙了！可是在此之前，吉米竟然不敢和女生牵手跳舞，直到有了自己这次难忘的经历之后，才发现这枯燥的学校生活原来也可以洒满阳光，同学之间的友谊也可以升华为生活的激情与学习的动力.

zhè shì yí cì lìng jí mǐ nán wàng de tiào wǔ jīng lì, nà gè yīn yuè liáo rào, cǎi dēng biàn huàn de yè wǎn zhēn shì tài měi miào le! kě shì zài cǐ zhī qián, jí mǐjìng rán bù gǎn hé nǚ shēng qiān shǒu tiào wǔ, zhí dào yǒu le zì jǐ zhè cì nán wàng de jīng lì zhī hòu, cái fā xiàn zhè kū zào de xué xiào shēng huó yuán lái yě kě yǐ sǎ mǎn yáng guāng, tóng xué zhī jiān de yǒu yì yě kě yǐ shēng huá wéi shēng huó de jī qíng yǔ xué xí de dòng lì.

This was an unforgettable dance experience for Jimmy. It was a wonderful night of music and colorful lights. But before the night, Jimmy didn't dare to dance with girls. It was not until Jimmy had this unforgettable experience that he discovered that this boring school life could have been filled with sunshine. The friendship between classmates could also be sublimated into the passion of life and the motivation of learning.

词汇（cí huì）— Vocabulary

跳舞（tiào wǔ）to dance

中学（zhōng xué）middle school

勇敢（yǒng gǎn）to be brave

舞会（wǔ huì）the dance party

漂亮（piāo liàng）to be beautiful

恬静（tián jìng）to be quiet

害怕（hài pà）to be afraid

担心（dān xīn）to be worried

友好（yǒu hǎo）to be friendly

自信（zì xìn）to be confident

挤眼睛（jǐ yǎn jīng）to wink

练习与答案（liàn xí yǔ dá àn）— Questions and Answers

1. 吉米认为他在中学并不勇敢的原因是什么？
jí mǐ rèn wéi tā zài zhōng xué bìng bù yǒng gǎn de yuán yīn shì shén me?
Jimmy thought he was not brave in middle school because _______.

A. 他不敢和女孩跳舞.
tā bù gǎn hé nǚ hái tiào wǔ.
he was afraid of dancing with girls.

B. 他害怕其他男孩.
tā hài pà qí tā nán hái.
he was afraid of other boys.

C. 他害怕老师.
tā hài pà lǎo shī.
he was afraid of the teachers.

2. 吉米想与那个女孩跳舞的原因是什么？
jí mǐ xiǎng yǔ nà gè nǚ hái tiào wǔ de yuán yīn shì shén me?
Jimmy wanted to dance with the girl because _______.

A. 那个女孩非常高挑.
nà gè nǚ hái fēi cháng gāo tiāo.
she was very tall.

B. 那个女孩很漂亮.
nà gè nǚ hái hěn piào liàng.
she was beautiful.

C. 那个女孩十分恬静.
nà gè nǚ hái shí fēn tián jìng.
she was really quiet.

3. 吉米在舞会结束后做什么？
jí mǐ zài wǔ huì jié shù hòu zuò shén me?
When the dance was over, Jimmy _______.

A. 他和女孩一起回家了.
tā hé nǚ hái yì qǐ huí jiā le.
went home with the girl.

B. 他和女孩一起去吃晚餐.

tā hé nǚ hái yì qǐ qù chī wǎn cān.
had dinner with the girl.

C. 他高兴地回家了.
tā gāo xìng de huí jiā le.
went home happily.

4. 父亲给吉米的建议是什么？
fù qīn gěi jí mǐ de jiàn yì shì shén me?
What did Jimmy's dad suggest he do?

A. 友好一点.
yǒu hǎo yì diǎn.
be friendly.

B. 热情一点.
rè qíng yì diǎn.
be enthusiastic.

C. 酷一点.
kù yì diǎn.
be cool.

5. 朋友对吉米约女孩跳舞是什么态度？
péng yǒu duì jí mǐ yuē nǚ hái tiào wǔ shì shén me tài dù?
What was the attitude of Jimmy's friends?

A. 反对.
fǎn duì.
They were opposed.

B. 冷漠.
lěng mò.
They were indifferent.

C. 支持.
zhī chí.
They were supportive.

6. 女孩接受吉米的邀请了吗？
nǚ hái jiē shòu jí mǐ de yāo qǐng le ma?
Did the girl accept Jimmy's invitation?

7. 吉米在舞会上找到女孩时是什么反应？

jí mǐ zài wǔ huì shàng zhǎo dào nǚ hái shí shì shén me fǎn yìng?
How did Jimmy feel when he found the girl at the dance party?
8. 为什么吉米在舞会结束后回家的路上一直笑？
wéi shén me jí mǐ zài wǔ huì jié shù hòu huí jiā de lù shàng yì zhí xiào?
Why did Jimmy smile all the way home after the dance party?
9. 吉米不想与班上其他女孩跳舞的原因是什么？
jí mǐ bù xiǎng yǔ bān shàng qí tā nǚ hái tiào wǔ de yuán yīn shì shén me?
Jimmy didn't want to dance with other girls in his class. Why?
10. 吉米以后会很享受舞会吗？
jí mǐ yǐ hòu huì hěn xiǎng shòu wǔ huì ma?
Will Jimmy enjoy dance parties in the future?

1. A
2. B
3. C
4. A
5. C
6. 是的.
shì de.
Yes, she did.
7. 他开始心跳加速.
tā kāi shǐ xīn tiào jiā sù.
His heart began to beat fast.
8. 他感觉跟那个女孩跳舞真棒.
tā gǎn jué gēn nà gè nǚ hái tiào wǔ zhēn bàng.
He thought dancing with that girl was really great.
9. 因为一些太高，另一些又太恬静.
yīn wéi yì xiē tài gāo, lìng yì xiē yòu tài tián jìng.
Because some girls were too tall, and others were too quiet.
10. 是的.
shì de.
Yes, he will.

Chapter 10: 你孤独吗 (nǐ gū dú ma) – Are You Lonely?

可以肯定地说，在许多国家，大量的年轻人都单独生活. 他们因为工作或上学而离开家庭和朋友，有一些人由于缺少足够的时间交友而感到**孤独**.
kě yǐ kěn dìng de shuō, zài xǔ duō guó jiā, dà liàng de nián qīng rén dōu dān dú shēng huó. tā men yīn wéi gōng zuò huò shàng xué ér lí kāi jiā tíng hé péng yǒu. yǒu yì xiē rén yóu yú quē shǎo zú gòu de shí jiān jiāo yǒu ér gǎn dào gū dú.
It is certainly true that in many countries, most young people live alone, often away from family or friends because of work or school. Some people feel lonely because they may not have enough time to make friends.
不仅只有不爱说话和**害羞**的人才会感到孤独，有些爱**开玩笑**、爱笑和爱出行的人有时也会害怕与他人交谈或交朋友. 他们总是与别人保持距离. 这些人似乎有很多朋友，但他们内心却感到很受伤.
bù jǐn zhǐ yǒu bú ài shuō huà hé hài xiū de rén cái huì gǎn dào gū dú, yǒu xiē ài kāi wán xiào、ài xiào hé ài chū xíng de rén yǒu shí yě huì

hài pà yǔ tā rén jiāo tán huò jiāo péng yǒu. tā men zǒng shì yǔ bié rén bǎo chí jù lí. zhè xiē rén sì hū yǒu hěn duō péng yǒu, dàn tā men nèi xīn què gǎn dào hěn shòu shāng.
It's not only quiet and shy people who feel loneliness. Some people are always joking, laughing, and outgoing, but they are sometimes afraid to talk to and make friends with others. They always try to keep other people away from them. They may seem to have lots of friends, but inside they are hurting.
有解决这个问题的办法吗？有！
yǒu jiě jué zhè gè wèn tí de bàn fǎ ma? yǒu!
Are there solutions? Yes!
你也许要**下点力气**才行呢！下面这些方法可**供参考**：
nǐ yě xǔ yào xià diǎn lì qì cái xíng ne! xià miàn zhè xiē fāng fǎ kě gōng cān kǎo:
You may need to work hard! Here are some ideas for reference:
要记住，不仅仅只有你才有孤独的感受——你周围大约有 25%的人都有同感.
yào jì zhù, bù jǐn jǐn zhǐ yǒu nǐ cái yǒu gū dú de gǎn shòu—nǐ zhōu wéi dà yuē yǒu bǎi fēn zhī èr shí wǔ de rén dōu yǒu tóng gǎn.
Remember, you are not the only one to feel this way—maybe 25% of the people around you feel the same.
你有爱好或嗜好吗？寻找一些趣味相投的人并加入他们.
nǐ yǒu ài hǎo huò shì hǎo ma? xún zhǎo yì xiē qù wèi xiāng tóu de rén bìng jiā rù tā men.
Do you have an interest or hobby? Find a group of people with this interest and join them.
你不应该要求你的伙伴来满足你的一切需要，尽管作为你最好的朋友，他们理所当然地应该满足你. 但是你也应该交一些别的朋友，你们之间要能够互相帮助.
nǐ bù yīng gāi yào qiú nǐ de huǒ bàn lái mǎn zú nǐ de yí qiè xū yào, jìn guǎn zuò wéi nǐ zuì hǎo de péng yǒu, tā men lǐ suǒ dāng rán de yīng gāi mǎn zú nǐ. dàn shì nǐ yě yīng gāi jiāo yì xiē bié de péng yǒu, nǐ men zhī jiān yào néng gòu hù xiāng bāng zhù.

You should not ask your partner to meet all your needs. They should certainly meet many of your needs because your partner should be your best friend. But you should also have many other friends; they can give and take help.

要生活在**真实**的世界里！脱离现实的生活固然是轻松的，但电影、电视、书本以及网上的事情并非真实的生活！影视里的人物和现实中的人们所做所说是不一样的，因特网里的天地也和真实的世界截然不同.

yào shēng huó zài zhēn shí de shì jiè lǐ! tuō lí xiàn shí de shēng huó gù rán shì qīng sōng de, dàn diàn yǐng、diàn shì、shū běn yǐ jí wǎng shàng de shì qing bìng fēi zhēn shí de shēng huó! yǐng shì lǐ de rén wù hé xiàn shí zhōng de rén men suǒ zuò suǒ shuō shì bù yí yàng de, yīn tè wǎng lǐ de tiān dì yě hé zhēn shí de shì jiè jié rán bù tóng .

Live in the real world! It can be easy to live out our lives in fantasy, but things in movies, TV, books, or on the Internet are not real. People on the TV and in movies do not act and talk like real people! The world on the Internet is not the real world, and it's very different from real life.

被别人需要是解决孤独问题的一个良策. 你有帮助别人的途径吗？你能帮别人做点什么吗？你可以通过走访**医院**、看望老人等来表达你的爱心，或者仅仅学会倾听别人，尽力理解别人的感受并帮助他们. 通过帮助别人，我们可以找到朋友，丢弃孤独！

bèi bié rén xū yào shì jiě jué gū dú wèn tí de yí gè liáng cè. nǐ yǒu bāng zhù bié rén de tú jìng ma? nǐ néng bāng bié rén zuò diǎn shén me ma? nǐ kě yǐ tōng guò zǒu fǎng yī yuàn、kàn wàng lǎo rén děng lái biǎo dá nǐ de ài xīn, huò zhě jǐn jǐn xué huì qīng tīng bié rén, jìn lì lǐ jiě bié rén de gǎn shòu bìng bāng zhù tā men. tōng guò bāng zhù bié rén, wǒ men kě yǐ zhǎo dào péng yǒu, diū qì gū dú!

To be wanted and needed is a big answer to loneliness. Is there any way you can help other people? Can you do something for others? You may visit hospitals, elders, and others to show your love to them. Or just learn to be a listening person. Try to understand how other

people feel and help them. In helping other people, we find friends and lose loneliness!
不要老是等别人给你打电话、发消息或邮件—，你要主动联系他们. 如果他们显得太忙，那也并不意味着你不受**欢迎**. 下次再联系他们！
bú yào lǎo shì děng bié rén gěi nǐ dǎ diàn huà、fā xiāo xi huò yóu jiàn, nǐ yào zhǔ dòng lián xì tā men. rú guǒ tā men xiǎn dé tài máng, nà yě bìng bú yì wèi zhe nǐ bú shòu huān yíng. xià cì zài lián xì tā men!
Don't wait for someone to call; send a message or e-mail—you call them. And if they seem too busy, it doesn't mean you are not welcome. Try another time!
不要过多饮酒——这样虽然会短时间里消除你的孤独感，但不解决根本问题.
bú yào guò duō yǐn jiǔ—zhè yàng suī rán huì duǎn shí jiān lǐ xiāo chú nǐ de gū dú gǎn, dàn bù jiě jué gēn běn wèn tí.
Don't drink too much—it may take away loneliness for a few hours but doesn't answer the real problem.
你也许会不搭理别人，因为你们之间互相做过错事或说过坏话. 这样在你们之间就像是堆起了一堵墙，要想办法重归于好. 不要太高傲了，即使你感到错误主要在对方，也要说一声抱歉.
nǐ yě xǔ huì bù dā lǐ bié rén, yīn wéi nǐ men zhī jiān hù xiàng zuò guò cuò shì huò shuō guò huài huà. zhè yàng zài nǐ men zhī jiān jiù xiàng shì duī qǐ le yì dǔ qiáng, yào xiǎng bàn fǎ chóng guī yú hǎo. bú yào tài gāo ào le, jí shǐ nǐ gǎn dào cuò wù zhǔ yào zài duì fāng, yě yào shuō yì shēng bào qiàn.
You may not want to talk with other people because of things they have done or said to you, or things you have done or said to others. These things build a wall between us. Look for a way to become friends again. Don't be too proud to say sorry, even if you feel it was mostly the other person's fault!
如果受了别人的伤害，你不要**忍气吞声**，要告诉他们你的感受.

rú guǒ shōu le bié rén de shāng hài, nǐ bú yào rěn qì tūn shēng, yào gào sù tā men nǐ de gǎn shòu.
If other people hurt you, don't hide your feelings. Tell them what you think about it.

总结（zǒng jié）— Summary

孤独就像一个幽灵，常常在人们独处的时候悄然来袭，有时甚至会造成压抑感和精神疾病. 孤独袭扰的对象不分男女和老幼，相信你也曾经感受过它的存在. 本文就是为了告诉你人们感到孤独的原因，以及提出摆脱孤独感的方法.
gū dú jiù xiàng yí gè yōu líng, cháng cháng zài rén men dú chǔ de shí hòu qiāo rán lái xí, yǒu shí shèn zhì huì zào chéng yā yì gǎn hé jīng shén jí bìng. gū dú xí rǎo de duì xiàng bù fèn nán nǚ hé lǎo yòu, xiàng xìn nǐ yě céng jīng gǎn shòu guò tā de cún zài. běn wén jiù shì wèi le gào sù nǐ rén men gǎn dào gū dú de yuán yīn, yǐ jí tí chū bǎi tuō gū dú gǎn de fāng fǎ.

Loneliness is like a ghost. It often creeps in when people are alone. It sometimes causes depression and mental illness. People feel lonely, regardless of gender or age; you must have felt the existence of it as well. This story is meant to tell you why people feel lonely and how to get rid of loneliness.

词汇（cí huì）— Vocabulary

孤独（gū dú）lonely
害羞（hài xiū）shy
开玩笑（kāi wán xiào）joke
下点力气（xià diǎn lì qi）work hard
供参考（gòng cān kǎo）for reference
真实（zhēn shí）real
医院（yī yuàn）hospital
欢迎（huān yíng）welcome

忍气吞声（rěn qì tūn shēng）hide one's feelings

练习与答案（liàn xí yǔ dá àn）— Questions and Answers

1. 以下哪一项不是人们感到孤独的原因？
yǐ xià nǎ yí xiàng bú shì rén men gǎn dào gū dú de yuán yīn?
Which is NOT a reason why people feel lonely?

A. 他们独居.
tā men dú jū.
They live alone.

B. 他们没有足够的时间交朋友.
tā men méi yǒu zú gòu de shí jiān jiāo péng yǒu.
They have not enough time to make friends.

C. 他们害羞.
tā men hài xiū.
They are shy.

2. 以下哪一项不是丢弃孤独的良策？
yǐ xià nǎ yí xiàng bú shì diū qì gū dú de liáng cè?
Which is NOT the right way to deal with loneliness?

A. 有一个爱好或嗜好.
yǒu yí gè ài hǎo huò shì hǎo.
Having an interest or hobby.

B. 让你的伙伴满足你的全部需要.
ràng nǐ de huǒ bàn mǎn zú nǐ de quán bù xū yào.
Asking your partner to meet all your needs.

C. 学会关心别人.
xué huì guān xīn bié rén.
Learning to care for others.

3. 有很多朋友的人不会感到孤独，对吗？
yǒu hěn duō péng yǒu de rén bú huì gǎn dào gū dú, duì ma?
People with many friends won't feel lonely, right?

A. 对.
duì.
Right.

B. 不对.
bú duì.
Wrong.

C．未提及.

wèi tí jí.

Not mentioned.

4. 你周围大约有多少的人感到孤独？

nǐ zhōu wéi dà yuē yǒu duō shǎo de rén gǎn dào gū dú?

How many people around you feel lonely?

D．10%.

bǎi fēn zhī shí.

10%.

E．15%.

bǎi fēn zhī shí wǔ.

15%.

F．25%.

bǎi fēn zhī èr shí wǔ.

25%.

5. 如果受了别人的伤害，你应该怎么做？

rú guǒ shòu le bié rén de shāng hài, nǐ yīng gāi zěn me zuò?

If other people hurt you, what should you do?

A．忍气吞声.

rěn qì tūn shēng.

Tolerate it.

B．跟他们打一架.

gēn tā men dǎ yí jià.

Fight them.

C．告诉他们你的感受.

gào sù tā men nǐ de gǎn shòu.

Tell them what you think about it.

6. 等别人先给你打电话、发消息或写邮件很好，对吗？

děng bié rén xiān gěi nǐ dǎ diàn huà、fā xiāo xi huò xiě yóu jiàn hěn hǎo, duì ma?

Waiting for someone to call, send messages or e-mail you first is good, right?

7. 过多饮酒能解决根本问题，对吗？

guò duō yǐn jiǔ néng gòu jiě jué gēn běn wèn tí, duì ma?
Excessive drinking can solve the fundamental problem, right?
8. 当你联系别人却发现他们很忙时应该怎么做？
dāng nǐ lián xi bié rén què fā xiàn tā men hěn máng shí yīng gāi zěn me zuò?
What should you do when you contact others and find that they are busy?
9. 我们可以通过帮助别人获得什么？
wǒ men kě yǐ tōng guò bāng zhù bié rén huò dé shén me?
How can we benefit by helping others?
10. 朋友间怎么忘记过去，重归于好？
péng yǒu jiān zěn me wàng jì guò qù, zhòng guī yú hǎo?
How can we look for a way to become friends again?

1. C
2. B
3. B
4. C
5. C
6. 不对.
bú duì.
Wrong.
7. 不对. 它也许能暂时消除孤独.
bú duì. tā yě xǔ néng zàn shí xiāo chú gū dú.
Wrong. It may only take away loneliness for a few hours.
8. 下次再联系.
xià cì zài lián xi.
Try another time.
9. 我们可以找到朋友并丢弃孤独.
wǒ men kě yǐ zhǎo dào péng yǒu bìng diū qì gū dú.
We can find friends and lose loneliness.
10. 主动道歉.
zhǔ dòng dào qiàn.
Don't be too proud to say sorry.

Chapter 11: 吉米与大红鱼 (jí mǐ yǔ dà hóng yú) – Jimmy and the Big Red Fish

吉米是个小孩子，他正在外面捕捉大红鱼. 一周前，他爸爸给他讲了一个故事，说他在河里看见了一条大红鱼. 吉米决定到河边把红鱼捉回来，他一直都想做一件事情，好让爸爸为他感到**骄傲**.

jí mǐ shì gè xiǎo hái zi, tā zhèng zài wài miàn bǔ zhuō dà hóng yú. yì zhōu qián, tā bà ba gěi tā jiǎng le yí gè gù shì, shuō tā zài hé lǐ kàn jiàn le yì tiáo dà hóng yú. jì mǐ jué dìng dào hé biān bǎ hóng yú zhuō huí lái, tā yì zhí dōu xiǎng zuò yí jiàn shì qíng, hǎo ràng bà ba wèi tā gǎn dào jiāo ào.

Jimmy was a little boy and was out to catch a big red fish. A week ago, his daddy told him a story about a big red fish he saw in the river. Jimmy decided he was going to go down to the river and catch the big red fish. There was one thing Jimmy always wanted, and that was to make Daddy proud.

吉米醒来时天还没有亮. 他看看**钟表**，才早上四点. 吉米知道爸爸早起**上班**之前常去河边**钓鱼**，于是他悄悄地坐了起来，下床穿上最旧的**牛仔裤**和那条幸运衬衫. 他下楼来到饭桌前，但是上面没有**早饭**，爸爸也不在. 吉米想，他肯定上班去了.
jí mǐ xǐng lái shí tiān hái méi yǒu liàng. tā kàn kan zhōng biǎo, cái zǎo shàng sì diǎn. jí mǐ zhī dào bà ba zǎo qǐ shàng bān zhī qián cháng qù hé biān diào yú, yú shì tā qiāo qiāo de zuò le qǐ lái, xià chuáng chuān shàng zuì jiù de niú zǎi kù hé nà tiáo xìng yùn chèn shān. tā xià lóu lái dào fàn zhuō qián, dàn shì shàng miàn méi yǒu zǎo fàn, bà ba yě bú zài. jí mǐ xiǎng, tā kěn dìng shàng bān qù le.
It was dark when Jimmy woke. He looked at his clock, and it was 4:00 a.m. Jimmy knew his daddy would often go out to the river to catch some fish before going to work. He sat up quietly and got out of bed, putting on his oldest blue jeans and lucky shirt. He came down to the breakfast table, but there was no breakfast; his daddy was not there. Jimmy thought his daddy must be at work.
哇塞！他想起了一个好主意. 如果能下河把那条大红鱼捉回来，自己肯定会成为全镇人谈论的焦点.
wà sāi! tā xiǎng qǐ le yí gè hǎo zhǔ yì. rú guǒ néng xià hé bǎ nà tiáo dà hóng yú zhuō huí lái, zì jǐ kěn dìng huì chéng wéi quán zhèn rén tán lùn de jiāo diǎn.
Well, he had a great idea! If he could go down to the river and catch the big red fish, he would be the talk of the town.
他上了楼，拿下来爷爷送他的小船和**鱼竿**. 然后他为妈妈留了一张纸条，告诉她自己要去河边. 接着，他以最快的速度向河边跑去.
tā shàng le lóu, ná xià lái yé ye sòng tā de xiǎo chuán hé yú gān. rán hòu tā wèi mā ma liú le yì zhāng zhǐ tiáo, gào sù tā zì jǐ yào qù hé biān. jiē zhe, tā yǐ zuì kuài de sù dù xiàng hé biān pǎo qù.
He ran upstairs and took his boat and the fishing pole that his grandpa gave him. He then left a note for his mom that he was going to be at the river, and then, he ran as fast as he could.
这些年来，很多钓手都在那条河里钓大红鱼，但很少有人幸运地钓出大个头的. 吉米的爷爷和爸爸一个上午接一个上午地钓，为的是能钓出一条大个头的红鱼来. 他们钓出过各种各样的鱼，甚至有小**鲨鱼**，但就是没有捉到过大红鱼.

zhè xiē nián lái, hěn duō diào shǒu dōu zài nà tiáo hé lǐ diào dà hóng yú, dàn hěn shǎo yǒu rén xìng yùn de diào chū dà gè tóu de. jí mǐ de yé ye hé bà ba yí gè shàng wǔ jiē yí gè shàng wǔ de diào, wéi de shì néng diào chū yì tiáo dà gè tóu de hóng yú lái. tā men diào chū guò gè zhǒng gè yàng de yú, shèn zhì yǒu xiǎo shā yú, dàn jiù shì méi yǒu zhuō dào guò dà hóng yú.

Over the years, many fishermen had fished there for big red fishes. However, only a few were lucky enough to catch a really big fish. Jimmy's daddy and grandpa had spent morning after morning trying to catch a big red fish. They had caught all kinds of fish in the past, even small sharks, but they never got a big red fish.

吉米把鱼钩抛到清清的河水里. 他等啊等，但什么也没有发生. 过了快一个小时，他决定再换一个新鲜的**虾**作鱼饵. 过了片刻，钓线绷紧了，吉米起钩钓出了一条鱼，他知道这鱼不大. 他收起钓线，看到线端上有一条小鱼."嗨，这下好了"他说,"至少今天开张了."

jí mǐ bǎ yú gōu pāo dào qīng qīng de hé shuǐ lǐ. tā děng a děng, dàn shén me yě méi yǒu fā shēng. guò le kuài yí gè xiǎo shí, tā jué dìng zài huàn yí gè xīn xiān de xiā zuò yú ěr. guò le piàn kè, diào xiàn bēng jǐn le, jí mǐ qǐ gōu diào chū le yì tiáo yú, tā zhī dào zhè yú bú dà. tā shōu qǐ diào xiàn, kàn dào xiàn duān shàng yǒu yì tiáo xiǎo yú. "hai, zhè xià hǎo le," tā shuō, "zhì shǎo jīn tiān kāi zhāng le."

Jimmy put the hook into the clear water and waited and waited and waited... nothing. Nearly an hour later, he decided to put a fresh shrimp on his hook. A few seconds later, the line became tight, and Jimmy hooked the fish. He knew it wasn't a big fish. He reeled in and saw at the end of the line that it was just a little fish. "Oh, well," he said, "at least I caught something."

快到早上五点半了，吉米清楚自己必须马上去赶**校车**了."再试一次,"他心里说."再是最后一次."

kuài dào zǎo shàng wǔ diǎn bàn le, jí mǐ qīng chǔ zì jǐ bì xū mǎ shàng qù gǎn xiào chē le. “zài shì yí cì,” tā xīn lǐ shuō, “ zài shì zuì hòu yí cì.”
It was almost 5:30 a.m. and Jimmy knew he would have to catch the school bus soon. “One more try,” he thought. “Just one more.”
这次吉米和前一次一样细心. 他移动了一下，使自己的船位于河的中心位置. 他等啊等啊……“哎呀，真该死!”他知道自己该走了，他感到**伤心**. 这么长时间以来，他一直都在想着捉一条大红鱼来**证明**自己是一个真正的垂钓手！
zhè cì jí mǐ hé qián yí cì yí yàng xì xīn. tā yí dòng le yí xià, shǐ zì jǐ de chuán wèi yú hé de zhōng xīn wèi zhǐ. tā děng a děng a… “ai ya，zhēn gāi sǐ! ” tā zhī dào zì jǐ gāi zǒu le, tā gǎn dào shāng xīn. zhè me cháng shí jiān yǐ lái, tā yì zhí dōu zài xiǎng zhe zhuō yì tiáo dà hóng yú lái zhèng míng zì jǐ shì yí gè zhēn zhèng de chuí diào shǒu!
Jimmy was just as careful this time as he was before putting the shrimp on his hook. He moved a little further so he could be in the middle of the river. He waited and waited and waited... “Oh no!” He knew it was time to go, and Jimmy was very sad. He had wanted to catch a big red fish for so long to prove that he was a real fisherman!
接着，就在吉米收钓线时，他感到了轻轻的响动……“哦，天哪，这就是那条鱼,”他心想. 又有了一次响动！吉米瞪大了双眼.
jiē zhe, jiù zài jí mǐ shōu diào xiàn shí, tā gǎn dào le qīng qīng de xiǎng dòng… “o, tiān na, zhè jiù shì nà tiáo yú,” tā xīn xiǎng. yòu yǒu le yí cì xiǎng dòng! jí mǐ dèng dà le shuāng yǎn .
Then as he was reeling in, he felt a little tap... “Oh my... here it is,” he thought. Again, a little tap. Jimmy’s eyes widened.
吉米开始收线……这条鱼可真棒耶！吉米一收线，那鱼儿就更加用力地往后使劲，离吉米也就更远了. 再后来……后来吉米就看见了他在**杂志**上看到过的那种鱼——一条水下大红鱼. 这条鱼体积硕大，一直都在**挣扎**、蹦跳和拉拽！
jí mǐ kāi shǐ shōu xiàn… zhè tiáo yú kě zhēn bàng ye! jí mǐ yì shōu xiàn， nà yú ér jiù gèng jiā yòng lì de wǎng hòu shǐ jìn, lí jí mǐ yě

jiù gèng yuǎn le. zài hòu lái… hòu lái jí mǐ jiù kàn jiàn le tā zài zá zhì shàng kàn dào guò de nà zhǒng yú —— yì tiáo shuǐ xià dà hóng yú. zhè tiáo yú tǐ jī shuò dà, yì zhí dōu zài zhèng zhā、bèng tiào hé lā zhuài!

Jimmy started to reel. It was a great fish! Every time Jimmy reeled, the fish would pull harder and go further. And then... and then... he saw only what he had seen in magazines... a big red fish under the water! This fish was huge! It kept fighting and jumping and pulling!

吉米太**兴奋**了，他浑身**颤抖**得厉害，几乎连鱼竿也抓不住了. 半个小时后，鱼终于靠近了. 当然这是一条大红鱼！

jí mǐ tài xīng fèn le, tā hún shēn chàn dǒu dé lì hai, jī hū lián yú gān yě zhuā bú zhù le. bàn gè xiǎo shí hòu, yú zhōng yú kào jìn le.dāng rán zhè shì yì tiáo dà hóng yú!

Jimmy was so excited and shaking so hard that he could hardly hold on to the pole. After nearly 30 minutes the fish was close enough to Jimmy. It was certainly a big red fish!

总结（zǒng jié）— Summary

一条大红鱼的故事，在吉米的脑海里留下了美好的记忆. 为了一睹大红鱼的风采，吉米策划了一次至今仍令他激动不已的垂钓之旅. 大个头的红鱼也是那些钓鱼高手们梦寐以求的尤物，但从来没有人能够钓上岸来，现在它却成为了一个小毛孩子的囊中之物！

yì tiáo dà hóng yú de gù shì, zài jí mǐ de nǎo hǎi lǐ liú xià le měi hǎo de jì yì. wèi le yì dǔ dà hóng yú de fēng cǎi, jí mǐ cè huá le yí cì zhì jīn réng lìng tā jī dòng bù yǐ de chuí diào zhī lǚ. dà gè tóu de hóng yú yě shì nà xiē diào yú gāo shǒu men mèng mèi yǐ qiú de yóu wù, dàn cóng lái méi yǒu rén néng gòu diào shàng àn lái, xiàn zài tā què chéng wéi le yí gè xiǎo máo hái zi de náng zhōng zhī wù!

The story of the big red fish left a wonderful memory in Jimmy's mind. In order to see the style of the red fish, Jimmy planned a fishing trip that still excites him. The big red fish was also the stunner of excellent fishermen, but no one could catch it. This time, it was in a small child's back pocket!

词汇（cí huì）— Vocabulary

骄傲（jiāo ào）proud

钟表（zhōng biǎo）clock

上班（shàng bān）to go to work

钓鱼（diào yú）to go fishing

牛仔裤（niú zǎi kù）jeans

早饭（zǎo fàn）breakfast

鱼竿（yú gān）fishing pole

鲨鱼（shā yú）shark

虾（xiā）shrimp

校车（xiào chē）school bus

伤心（shāng xīn）sad

证明（zhèng míng）to prove

杂志（zá zhì）magazine

挣扎（zhēng zhā）to fight

颤抖（chàn dǒu）to shake

兴奋（xīng fèn）excited

练习与答案（liàn xí yǔ dá àn）— Questions and Answers

1. 吉米放学后去抓大红鱼.
jí mǐ fàng xué hòu qù zhuā dà hóng yú.
Jimmy went to catch the big red fish after school.

A. 假的.
jiǎ de.
False.

B. 真的.
Zhēn de.
True.

C. 不清楚.
bù qīng chǔ.
Not clear.

2. 钓鱼那天吉米穿着他最旧的牛仔裤和最新的衬衫.

diào yú nà tiān jí mǐ chuān zhe tā zuì jiù de niú zǎi kù hé zuì xīn de chèn shān.

Jimmy was wearing his oldest jeans and a new shirt that day.

A. 假的.

jiǎ de.

False.

B. 真的.

Zhēn de.

True.

C. 不清楚.

bù qīng chǔ.

Not clear.

3. 镇上的人们经常能抓到大红鱼.

zhèn shàng de rén men jīng cháng néng zhuā dào dà hóng yú

People in the town often caught big red fish.

A. 假的.

jiǎ de.

False.

B. 真的.

Zhēn de.

True.

C. 不清楚.

bù qīng chǔ.

Not clear.

4. 钓鱼那天吉米抓到的第一条鱼很大.

diào yú nà tiān jí mǐ zhuā dào de dì yī tiáo yú hěn dà.

The first fish Jimmy caught that day was a big one.

A. 假的.

jiǎ de.

False.

B. 真的.

Zhēn de.

True.

C． 不清楚.

bù qīng chǔ.

Not clear.

5. 吉米最后终于在他上学之前抓到了大红鱼.

jí mǐ zuì hòu zhōng yú zài tā shàng xué zhī qián zhuā dào le dà hóng yú.

Jimmy caught a big red fish before he had to go to school.

A． 假的.

jiǎ de.

False.

B． 真的.

Zhēn de.

True.

C． 不清楚.

bù qīng chǔ.

Not clear.

6. 吉米为什么想抓大红鱼？

jí mǐ wèi shén me xiǎng zhuā dà hóng yú?

Why did Jimmy want to catch a big red fish?

7. 吉米的爸爸通常在上班前做什么？

jí mǐ de bà ba tōng cháng zài shàng bān qián zuò shén me?

What did Jimmy's daddy usually do before going to work?

8. 吉米的爷爷曾经给过他什么东西？

jí mǐ de yé ye céng jīng gěi guò tā shén me dōng xi?

What did Jimmy's grandpa give him?

9. 吉米在去钓鱼之前有没有把计划告诉别人？

jí mǐ zài qù diào yú zhī qián yǒu méi yǒu bǎ jì huá gào sù bié rén?

Did Jimmy tell anyone about his plan before going fishing?

10. 吉米最后上学迟到了吗？

jí mǐzuì hòu shàng xué chí dào le ma?

Was Jimmy late for school?

1. A
2. A
3. A
4. A
5. B
6. 他想让爸爸骄傲并证明自己是真正的垂钓高手.
tā xiǎng ràng bà ba jiāo ào bìng zhèng míng zì jǐ shì zhēn zhèng de chuí diào gāo shǒu.
He wanted to make his daddy proud and prove that he was a real fisherman.
7. 他常去河边钓鱼.
tā cháng qù hé biān diào yú.
He often went out to the river to catch some fish.
8. 一艘小船和一根鱼竿.
yì sōu xiǎo chuán hé yì gēn yú gān.
A boat and a fishing pole.
9. 没有，但他为妈妈留了一张纸条.
méi yǒu, dàn tā wéi mā ma liú le yì zhāng zhǐ tiáo
No, he didn't. But he left a note for his mom.
10. 未提及.
wèi tí jí.
Not mentioned.

Conclusion

When was the last time you read a book or a magazine? Is your daily reading just updates on Twitter and Facebook? Or looking at the text on your package of oatmeal? Develop a good reading habit, and you will benefit a lot. In addition, by reading books, you will understand the Chinese language better. Do you feel the progress you've made during reading this book?

Reading is the key to learning a new language. Students can increase their vocabulary by reading, which will improve their ability to speak and write. The more Chinese material you read, the more words you encounter, and these words will become part of your daily vocabulary unconsciously. Clear and precise Chinese is very advantageous for any occasion you want to use your Chinese, and knowing that you are speaking well will bring a strong sense of self-esteem.

It is important also to remember that we learn our own language by hearing people speak, not by seeing what they write. We copy what we hear. Though you learn to read and write as well as to hear and speak, it is best to learn to read and write as to hear and speak. It is best to learn all new words through the ear. You can read them, spell them, and write them later.

Congratulations on making it through to the end of this book. It should have been informative and enjoyable with interesting stories. Although you have finished this journey, never stop reading because reading will benefit you a lot. Good luck with your further study on the Chinese language.

Part 3: Chinese Phrase Book

Over 1000 Essential Mandarin Phrases You Don't Want to Be Without on Your Trip to China

Introduction: Why Choose this Chinese Phrase Book?

Many Chinese language textbooks are intended mainly for people who study Chinese in formal classes and are based on assumptions that are appropriate primarily for such learners. The words and phrases such textbooks introduce in early lessons are often those that help students function in a classroom setting. Such textbooks also assume that the learners' need to learn to read and write Chinese is as pressing as their need to speak it, so they introduce oral and written skills at the same rate. Underlying many such textbooks is also the assumption that they will be taught by a teacher, someone who will manage and guide the students' learning process.

However, what of people who live or work in China but do not have the opportunity to study Chinese in a formal classroom setting? Such people usually need to become "street functional" in Chinese relatively quickly, so their most pressing need is for the words and phrases that will help them deal with daily life in China. Also, during their first few trips to China, such people often have a much greater need to learn to speak and understand basic Chinese than to learn Chinese characters. Finally, such learners usually need to take charge of their language learning process, either by studying with a tutor or on their own and then going out to practice with whatever Chinese speakers they encounter.

This Chinese phrasebook is intended for this special category of Chinese learners, those people who are going to work, live or sightsee in China for an extended period but who do not have the opportunity to study in a formal Chinese language program. This book aims to meet the special needs of these learners in several ways:

1. It introduces the words, phrases, sentence patterns, and skills that are needed most often in daily life in China. The topics and content of lessons have been selected and organized to make learners functional in daily Chinese life as quickly as possible. Rather than learning how to interact socially with classmates and talk about a classroom, students learn how to buy things, ask for directions, order food in a restaurant, get assistance when something goes wrong, take buses and taxis, and so forth. Obviously, only the most basic elements of Chinese are introduced here, and learners will need to move onto other textbooks if they hope to progress beyond the initial stage, but the language tools (vocabulary, phrases, and sentence patterns) presented here are sufficient to get learners through some of the most commonly encountered situations—and also to prepare them for further Chinese study.

2. It encourages learners to make their own choices as to where to focus their efforts; especially in regards to the question of how much time and attention to devote initially to learning to read and write Chinese. Some learners will initially want to ignore Chinese characters and focus all their attention on speaking and listening. Others will want to dabble a little in characters but still invest most of their time in oral skills. Yet others will want to work on both written and spoken skills right from the start. Each unit has a core

lesson for those interested mainly in oral skills but also contains options for those who wish to begin with characters.

3. It recognizes that learners might be studying individually, with tutors, or with teachers who may have little experience teaching Chinese to foreigners (or whose ideas about teaching Chinese don't coincide with the learner's needs), and that an important part of Chinese study in such situations is learning how to work effectively with tutors who know Chinese but do not know how to teach it. In other words, learners need to learn how to gently turn well-meaning native speakers of Chinese into effective language teachers.

Underlying this book are several important assumptions:

1. It assumes that learners have different needs, interests, and learning strategies, and it is thus designed to accommodate a variety of different approaches to Chinese, especially individual decisions as to how much attention learners initially wish to devote to Chinese characters.

2. It assumes that people learn any language by first mastering that which is simple and only gradually moving into that which is more complex. As such, in the initial stages of Chinese language study, it is less important that explanations be thorough than that they are clear and easy to understand. It keeps explanations brief and relies heavily on examples to illustrate points of sentence construction and word order.

3. Finally, and most importantly, it operates under the assumption that as a language learner, you are most likely to succeed if you take charge of your learning program. In practice, this means that you need to choose the goals that are appropriate to your needs, the study methods that fit your situation and learning style, actively seek out and take advantage of opportunities to practice your Chinese, and learn how to give direction to your teachers and tutors.

Underlying each scenario in the book is a set of daily life communication problems—such as how to introduce yourself or get something to eat at a noodle stand—that you will face from your very first day traveling to China. The goal of each scenario is to provide you with the basic language tools (vocabulary, phrases, sentence patterns, and strategies) that will enable you to cope with these daily life situations using rudimentary (but ever-improving) Chinese.

Each scenario is divided into several basic sections:

Dialogue: Each piece of dialogue portrays a common daily life situation and the basic language tools and strategies you need for coping with the situation. The dialogue is presented in Pinyin and Chinese characters, and an English translation is provided for each Chinese sentence. Take note that the English translations are very literal—even to the point of being pidgin English. The danger in this is that the English translations may appear to caricature or even mock the Chinese. Please be assured that this is not at all the writer's intent; the writer has used such literal translations because their word-by-word nature preserves Chinese sentence structure and wording as much as possible, and previous learners have found that this helps them more quickly develop a feel for Chinese word order. For your reference, a more natural translation of the dialogue appears at the end of each scenario.

Vocabulary: This is a listing of all new Chinese words that are used in the dialogue and that appear elsewhere in the scenario as well as additional words that are pertinent to the topic. As much as possible, words closely related to the same topic or situation are grouped in one scenario so that they are easier to find and refer to. Occasionally, words are introduced in more than one scenario, mainly for the benefit of learners who choose to use the scenarios in an order different from the one in which they are presented in the book.

Phrases: This section presents useful short phrases relevant to the topic. Each phrase is followed by a literal English translation as well as a more natural English translation. Because of the book's title, this is the most important for you to master. You can always directly refer to this section for something you want to express in Chinese.

Notes: In each scenario, the section contains comments on new words and points of usage, which require elaboration. Here you will also find suggested strategies for dealing with daily life situations and tips on language learning.

Different Methods of Using This Chinese Phrase Book

The intent of this book is not that you work through it from beginning to end, studying all the material and doing all the exercises. Think of this book more as a menu of language material and learning methods from which you choose whatever suits your purposes. As much as possible, the material in this book has been designed and organized in such a way that it is flexible and learner-friendly, allowing you to study in a way that suits your needs and interests.

There is no end to the variety of different ways in which you could use the material in this book, but to help you get started thinking, a few basic plans are suggested:

Plan A: First Trip to China

What many people want and need during their first few trips to China are basic speaking and listening skills. Focusing your efforts on speaking and listening enables you to quickly learn how to get around China and meet your basic needs. This approach to the first stages of Chinese study also generates a lot of positive reinforcement daily because you can use what you learn and see your skills improve; also, as you speak to Chinese people, you will generally find that they are generous with praise and encouragement for foreigners who make the effort to try to learn to read and write Chinese. It might make sense to narrow your efforts to speaking and listening for a few weeks until you feel comfortable dealing with the most common daily situations.

If this sounds like the plan for you, a good strategy for using this book might be to:

1. Study the dialogue in each scenario, learning phrases, and sentence patterns. As you study the first few scenarios, you may also want to look at the sections of this book that introduce Chinese Pinyin, spelling, pronunciation, and tone.

2. Ignore the Vocabulary and Notes sections in the scenario.

3. Devote a lot of time to practicing speaking and listening.

Plan B: Speaking and Basic Reading

Some people want to begin studying selected Chinese characters right from the beginning of their study program, but do not want to slow down their progress in speaking and listening by investing the time it would take to learn the Chinese character for each new word they learn. Even during your first trip to China, it can be very useful to learn the most common Chinese characters found on street signs, maps, menus, and so forth in your environment. While it may be some time before you know enough characters to read all of a sign, even being able to read one or two of the characters often provides you with enough clues to determine whether or not this is the right bus, the place you are looking for, the proper bathroom door, or whatever. The other advantage of studying some Chinese characters right from the start is that as you learn to recognize a few characters, they will soon come to seem less intimidating and foreign to you; in fact, many people come to be fascinated by Chinese characters and find that learning how to read and write them becomes one of the most appealing aspects of learning Chinese.

If this plan sounds good, a suggested approach would be:

1. Follow Plan A above for speaking and listening skills.

2. Also, study the vocabulary section in each scenario. At first, you may only want to learn to recognize them, but you could also have your tutor (if you have one) point out the radicals from which most characters are constructed and perhaps show you how to write them.

3. When walking on the streets, get into the habit of looking at signs and so forth for Chinese characters that you know. This effort is not only a good way to review and memorize the characters you study in the book, but also gets you in the habit of paying attention and trying to make sense of the written Chinese in your environment; otherwise, you will probably get into the habit of simply ignoring it. You might even carry a little notebook with you for writing down new characters that look interesting or appear frequently enough to be worth learning.

Plan C: Total Mastery

If you are sure that your eventual goal is mastery of both written and spoken Chinese, you might choose to invest significant effort in developing oral and written skills right from the beginning. Making a broad frontal attack on Chinese requires a fair investment of time if you are to progress at a rate that makes you feel satisfied; for Westerners, it takes longer to learn Chinese than it does many other foreign languages—mainly because of the time investment required to learn to read and write. However, the benefit of this plan is that it will give you a good foundation for future efforts to learn to read, write, and speak Chinese.

If this plan sounds good, a suggested approach would be:

1. To study all of the material in each scenario. In particular, learn to read and write the Chinese characters in the

Dialogues and Vocabulary instead of just learning how to say them.

2. An alternative approach would be to quickly skim through this book to get your basic skills, following one of the two plans above, before starting to study with another textbook series that devotes more attention to reading. This would give you a jump-start to your study of Chinese, getting you out practicing on the streets sooner than most textbook series and programs would.

Clearly, none of these plans is the "right" plan in any universal sense, and there are endless variations on each. The right plan for you is the one that provides the best match between your goals, learning style, and the amount of time and effort you are willing to invest. Also, none of these plans are set in stone, and as you move along in your studies, you will no doubt want to set new goals and experiment with new approaches as you not only gain greater command of Chinese but also a better knowledge of what approaches to language learning work best for you.

Learning Chinese Pronunciation, Pinyin, and Tones

Westerners first learning Chinese often have the impression that it is very foreign and exotic-sounding, therefore presumably difficult to pronounce. In reality, most of the sounds used in Chinese are similar to sounds used in English and other Western languages, and most of those sounds, which are not familiar, are not very difficult to learn. There are, of course, a few exceptions to this generalization, but not many.

Chinese language books and study programs often begin with a rather long and detailed set of pronunciation exercises. Some learners find this to be a useful way to establish a foundation for later Chinese study; others find this phase of the learning process boring and not useful. The short introduction to Chinese Pinyin and pronunciation below is primarily to get you started, so the introduction below strives less for thoroughness than brevity and clarity. Little has been mentioned about sounds that are very easy or similar to English, saving effort for more challenging sounds. Ultimately, however, the best way for you to learn pronunciation is to listen to and mimic your tutor and other Chinese people. Deciding how much pronunciation drilling you need is up to you.

Chinese is a syllabic language, each word consisting of one or more short syllables. Traditionally, the Chinese consider each syllable as consisting of two parts, the initial and the final, and for the sake of convenience, the introduction below will make use of this handy division.

Initials:

b-: Pronounced like “b” in “boy”

p-: Pronounced like “p” in “pair”

m-: Pronounced like “m” in “mouse”

f-: Pronounced like “f” in “four”

d-: Pronounced like “d” in “duck”

t-: Pronounced like “t” in “tomorrow”

n-: Pronounced like “n” in “no”

l-: Pronounced like “l” in “let”

g-: Pronounced like “g” in “go”

k-: Pronounced like “k” in “king”

h-: Pronounced like “h” in “hug”, but a little more guttural

y-: Pronounced like “y” in “yes”

w-: Pronounced like “w” in “we”

s-: Pronounced like “s” in “sorry”

c-: A “ts” sound, pronounced like the end of “pants”

z-: A “dz” sound, pronounced like the end of “boys”

j-: Pronounced like “j” in “jeep”, but with the tongue just a little further forward

q-: Pronounced like "ch" in "chair", but with the tongue just a little further forward

x-: Pronounced like "sh" in "sheep", but with the tongue just a little further forward

zh-: Pronounced like "j" in "junk", but with the tongue just a little further back

ch-: Pronounced like "ch" in "cheap", but with the tongue just a little further back

sh-: Pronounced like "sh" in "ship", but with the tongue just a little further back

r-: Pronounced like "r" in "ring", but with the tongue a little higher so it buzzes ever so slightly

Finals:

-a: Pronounced like "a" in "father"

-ai: Pronounced like "y" in "why"

-ao: Pronounced like "ow" in "how"

-an: Pronounced like "an" in "fan"

-ang: Pronounced like "ung" in "hung"

-e: Pronounced like "e" in "her"

-ei: Pronounced like "ay" in "day"

-en: Pronounced like "en" in "hen"

-eng: Pronounced like "en" + "ng", no corresponding sound in English, but not difficult to make

-i: Pronounced like "ee" in "sweet" or "i" in "it" after c/z/s/ch/sh/zh/r

-ia: Pronounced like "ya" in "yard"

-ie: Pronounced like "ye" in "yes"

-iu: Pronounced like "you"

-iao: Pronounced like "y'all"

-in: Pronounced like "in"

-ing: Pronounced like "ing" in "wing"

-ian: Pronounced like "yearn" (British pronunciation)

-iang: Pronounced like "young"

-iong: Pronounced like "ong" below, but preceded by a "y"

-o: Pronounced like "wha" in "what" (British pronunciation)

-ou: Pronounced like "o" in "go" (American pronunciation)

-ong: Pronounced like "ou" + "ng", no corresponding sound in English, but not difficult to make

-u: Pronounced like "oo" in "book"

-ua: Pronounced like "oir" in "reservoir " (British pronunciation)

-ui: Pronounced like "way"

-uo: Pronounced like "woe"

-uai: Pronounced like "why"

-uan: Pronounced like "won"

-uang: Pronounced like the combination of "w" in "what" and "ung" in "hung"

-ü: Pronounced like "ew", hard to make

-ue: Pronounced like "ew" + "e" in "her", hard to make

-un: Pronounce like "ew" + "n", hard to make

er: Similar to "er" in American English, but the mouth opened a little more

wu: Pronounced like "oo" in "book"

yi: Pronounced like the letter "e"

yu: Similar to "ü"

In Chinese, the intonation of a word is an important part of its pronunciation. Generally speaking, one Chinese character corresponds to one syllable. A Chinese syllable can have no initials but must have a final and a tone. Thus, a syllable pronounced with a high intonation is a different word from the same syllable pronounced with a rising intonation, a falling-rising intonation, or a falling intonation. The classic example used to intimidate beginning learners in Chinese is the syllable "ma", which means "mother" when pronounced with a high intonation and "horse" when pronounced with a falling-rising intonation.

Westerners sometimes feel that they cannot hear tones, but this is not what the problem is. After all, speakers of English listen to and use intonation all the time. Consider the difference between a rising tone, "Yes?" (as someone answers the door) or a falling tone, "Yes!" (as an enthusiastic response to an invitation). The differences between Chinese and English is that the English intonation functions at the sentence level instead of the word level, with the rises and falls of tones, conveying the emotional impact of the sentence's message. The problem for Westerners learning Chinese is not hearing intonation per se, but hearing intonation as part of the pronunciation of a word.

The Tones of Mandarin

In Mandarin, most words are pronounced with one of four tones. Tones 1, 2, and 4 are relatively straightforward. Tone 3 changes according to the tone that follows, so will require greater elaboration:

-Tone 1:

The main vocal characteristic if the first tone is high and flat. When it is articulated, the vocal cords are tightened, and the pitch is kept at a relatively higher level for a while, like singing a long high note.

-Tone 2:

The second tone is a rising tone. It rises from the middle to a higher level while the vocal cords are gradually tightened, like the word "yes" used as a question in answering the door: "Yes?"

-Tone 3:

Usually described as a "falling-rising" tone, and this is what it sounds like when a word is pronounced in isolation or at the end of a sentence. However, you will find that if another word follows a Tone 3 word, it becomes a little cumbersome to do a complete fall + rise. Thus, one of two things will happen.

Usually, if another word follows a Tone 3 word, the rising part drops off and becomes just a low-falling tone. A good example phrase is 很快 (hěn kuài, very fast).

When one Tone 3 word is followed by another Tone 3 word, the tone of the first word changes to a rising tone just like Tone 2. Essentially, it is the initial falling part of the tone, which is now omitted. A good example phrase for this is 很好 (hěn hǎo, very good).

-Tone 4:

When it is pronounced, the vocal cords are first tightened and then relaxed. The voice hence rapidly falls from the higher to the lower level. It is relatively easy to pronounce for most people just like an enthusiastic affirmation: "Yes!"

How to Learn Tones

The natural assumption when first confronted with all these tones is that you need to memorize which tone category each new Chinese word belongs to, i.e., which word is Tone 1, Tone 2, and so forth. However, as you will quickly discover, trying to recall information in this format when you are trying to say a sentence is not very efficient; when talking, you don't have time to be constantly asking yourself "Is this word pronounced with the first or fourth tone?" It needs to come out naturally and quickly. So, what should you do?

One bit of advice is to start with your ears. When Chinese children learn to speak, nobody teaches them which words are Tone 3 and so forth. Rather, they listen and learn to say what sounds right. Likewise, to get your tones right without stopping to think before every word, you need to go with what sounds right. However, before you can do this, you need to train yourself to listen carefully to the pronunciation of new words, including their tones. For example, if you have a tutor, as your tutor pronounces new Chinese words, try to fix the intonation in your mind along with the pronunciation. Perhaps even ask your tutor to exaggerate the tone a little when pronouncing new words for you—making it funny may help you remember it better.

A second suggestion is practice, lots of it. The first few times you say anything new, it requires conscious thought, and you may well need to pause to remember which words are pronounced with which tones. However, after you have said a certain word, word combination, or phrase a few times, it starts to become automatic, and you do not need to think about it so much. Don't practice things just to the point where you can scrape your way through them once; practice until you can do them without thinking.

Finally, do not become overly concerned about tones. Yes, you should try to get them right, but you shouldn't become so worried that you are reluctant to speak. Remember: Chinese people will often understand you quite well even if your tones are wrong, especially if you speak in phrases rather than single words. For your information, if you speak in single word utterances and get the tone wrong, it may be more difficult for Chinese people to understand you, especially if the situation or context doesn't make it easy for the listener to guess what you might be trying to say. Therefore, do avoid speaking in single words! Also remember: it is much better to get a sentence out with the tones wrong than not to open your mouth at all. So long as you keep speaking—and keep paying attention to how things sound when Chinese people say them—, the accuracy of your tones and naturalness of your pronunciation will continue to improve.

Scenario 1: Exchanging Money

Dialogue

Foreigner A needs to exchange money and asks Chinese person B on the street to find out what the best place to exchange money is.

A: 请问，哪里可以换钱?

qǐng wèn, nǎ lǐ kě yǐ huàn qián?

May I ask, where possible to change money?

B: 机场、酒店和银行都可以

jī chǎng、jiǔ diàn hé yín háng dōu kě yǐ

Airport, hotel and bank, all possible

A: 哪个比较好?

nǎ gè bǐ jiào hǎo?

Which one relatively better?

B: 酒店和机场比较方便，他们肯定能讲英语。银行不太方便，但兑换率可能好一点。我也不太清楚

jiǔ diàn hé jī chǎng bǐ jiào fāng biàn, tā men kěn dìng néng jiǎng yīng yǔ. yín háng bú tài fāng biàn, dàn duì huàn lǜ kě néng hǎo yì diǎn. wǒ yě bú tài qīng chǔ

Hotel and airport relatively convenient, and they're able to speak English. Bank is not convenient, but their exchange rate is better a little. I'm not too sure

Vocabulary

换（huàn），to exchange / change

酒店（jiǔ diàn），hotel

银行（yín háng），bank

都（dōu），both / all

比较（bǐ jiào），comparatively / relatively

比（bǐ），compared to

但是（dàn shì），but

可能（kě néng），possible / possibly

方便（fāng biàn）, convenient

肯定（kěn dìng），definitely

能（néng），able to

讲（jiǎng），to speak (This word is interchangeable with " 说 ")

兑换率（duì huàn lǜ），exchange rate

高（gāo），high / tall

太（tài），too (as in "too much")

清楚（qīng chǔ），clear / sure about

写（xiě），to write

贵（guì），expensive

数（shǔ），to count

Phrases

我不太清楚（wǒ bú tài qīng chǔ）

I'm not too sure

兑换率多少（duì huàn lǜ duō shǎo）？

What is the exchange rate?

请你写一下（qǐng nǐ xiě yí xià）

Please write it down

If you don't trust your ears in getting an exchange rate, this request is very useful

请你数一下（qǐng nǐ shù yí xià）

Please count it

Bank clerks may ask you to do this when handing you your money.

银行比酒店近（yín háng bǐ jiǔ diàn jìn）

The bank is closer than the hotel

他比我高（tā bǐ wǒ gāo）

He's taller than me

她比我有钱（tā bǐ wǒ yǒu qián）

She has more money than I do

哪里可以吃饭（nǎ lǐ kě yǐ chī fàn）

Where can we get something to eat?

这个西瓜贵一点（zhè gè xī guā guì yì diǎn）

This watermelon is a little more expensive

Notes

Not all banks in China exchange foreign currency. Usually, your best bet is 中国银行(zhōng guó yín háng), but sometimes you can exchange money in other banks or at the airport. You may also encounter people on the street who want to exchange money, but this is both risky and illegal.

Colloquial Translation of Dialogue

A: Excuse me, where can I exchange money?

B: Airport, hotel, and bank. All work.

A: Which is better.?

B: The hotel and airport may be more convenient, and they can surely speak English. The bank is not as convenient as the others, but their exchange rate may be a little higher, but I'm not too sure.

Scenario 2: Buying (I)

Dialogue

An important task most foreigners need to accomplish in Chinese is making a purchase. Below, A is a hesitant foreigner pointing to something in a store. B is a Chinese store clerk.

A: 这个多少钱?

zhè gè duō shao qián?

This how much money?

B: 十元

shí *yuán*

Ten Yuan

A: 那么那个多少钱?

nà me nà gè duō shao qián?

Well that how much money?

B: 五块钱

wǔ kuài qián

Five pieces of money

B: 你要不要?

nǐ yào bú yào?

You want not want?

A: 不要，谢谢

bú yào, xiè xie

Not want. Thanks

Vocabulary

钱（qián），money

你（nǐ），you

要（yào），to want

块（kuài），Chinese dollar / *yuan*

请（qǐng），please

问（wèn），to ask

这（zhè），this

再见（zài jiàn），goodbye

谢谢（xiè xie），thank you

对（duì），correct

个（gè），measure word

好（hǎo），good

早（zǎo），early / good morning

很（hěn），very

贵（guì），expensive

便宜（pián yi），cheap

多少（duō shao），how much / how many

“duō” means “many” and “shǎo” means “few”. When these two are combined, “shǎo” loses its tone and become a “light tone” syllable.

不（bù），not / no

Is normally pronounced with a falling tone, but you may notice that the dialogue shows “bú”, the “不” in the middle doesn’t fall; rather it is pronounced with a rising tone or only a light tone. The rule is that if another fourth tone word follows “不”, it becomes a rising tone.

Numbers

一（yī），one

二（èr），two

三（sān），three

四（sì），four

五（wǔ），five

六（liù），six

七（qī），seven

八（bā），eight

九（jiǔ），nine

十（shí），ten

百（bǎi），hundred

千（qiān），thousand

万（wàn），ten thousand

亿（yì），a hundred million

Phrases

你好（nǐ hǎo）？

How are you?

This is the most common Chinese greeting. To respond, simply say it back

早上/下午/晚上好（zǎo shàng / xià wǔ / wǎn shàng hǎo）

Good morning / afternoon / evening

再见（zài jiàn）

Goodbye

谢谢（xiè xie）

Thanks

这个八块钱（zhè gè bā kuài qián）

Eight *yuan* for this

In daily speech, the word "钱" is often omitted, but the measure word will normally not be omitted. Thus, for "eight *yuan*", you will often hear "bā kuài," but never "bā qián." "块" is the colloquial measure word for "元"

我要到商店买些零碎的东西（wǒ yào dào shāng diàn mǎi xiē líng suì de dōng xi）

I'll go to pick up some odds and ends at the store

你跟我去买东西吗（nǐ gēn wǒ qù mǎi dōng xi ma）？

Will you go shopping with me?

这是找你的钱（zhè shì zhǎo nǐ de qián）

Here's your change

Notes

Measure Words

In Chinese, between a number and a noun, you always need to add a measure word. A measure word is like the word "bottles" in the English phrase "four bottles of water," a word that indicates the general kind or quantity of whatever object is being discussed. The difference between English and Chinese is that whereas English only requires measure words for mass nouns, Chinese always requires a measure word between numbers and nouns. In this scenario is the measure word "kuài"; above you also see the measure word "gè" in the phrases "zhè gè" and "nà gè." You will encounter more measure words in the scenarios to come.

Tip: Listening to Chinese in real life

Listening comprehension in a foreign language involves a lot of guessing, as you will no doubt discover when you try the material in today's scenario in a real Chinese store. People don't talk like scripts in a Chinese textbook. Instead, they speak in incomplete sentences, don't always enunciate slowly and clearly, and frequently use words you haven't learned yet. Also, not everyone in China speaks standard Mandarin of the kind taught in classrooms and spoken on TV; in fact, many Chinese learn Mandarin as a second language, and their first language is some Chinese dialect that is only more or less distantly related to Mandarin.

Mandarin is the name of the Chinese dialect used as the official national language in China. It is also known as "Putonghua" because for centuries it was the language used by China's officials. "Putonghua" literally means "common language". Most Chinese speak some variant of Mandarin as their first language, and all over China, it is the language generally used in schools, the media, and most interaction between people of different regions.

The first step toward success in Chinese listening comprehension is accepting this situation as normal rather than wasting emotional energy agonizing over it. The second is developing the habit of just wading in and guessing, using any clues you have. Start by trying to hear the numbers as you ask for prices in nearby Chinese stores.

Colloquial Translation of Dialogue

A: How much does this cost?

B: Ten *yuan*

A: How about that one?

B: Five *yuan*.

B: Do you want it?

A: No thank you.

Scenario 3: Buying (II)

Dialogue:

Emboldened by the success of the visit in Scenario 2, A has returned to the Chinese store for another purchase. B is still the clerk.

A: 有没有啤酒?

yǒu méi yǒu pí jiǔ?

Have not have beer?

B: 有，要几瓶?

Yǒu, yào jǐ píng?

Have. Want how many bottles?

A: 三瓶。有没有雪茄?

sān píng. yǒu méi yǒu xuě jiā?

Three bottles. Have not have cigars?

B:对不起，没有

duì bù qǐ, méi yǒu

Sorry, not have

A: 好吧，三瓶啤酒多少钱?

hǎo ba, sān píng pí jiǔ duō shǎo qián?

Well, three bottles of beer how much money?

B: 五元一瓶，一共十五块

wǔ yuán yì píng, yí gòng shí wǔ kuài

Five *yuan* one bottle; fifteen *yuan* in total

Vocabulary

有（yǒu），have

没有（méi yǒu），not have

啤酒（pí jiǔ），beer

雪茄（xuě jiā），cigar

几（jǐ），several / how many

对不起（duì bù qǐ），sorry / excuse me

意思（yì sī），meaning

肥皂（féi zào），soap

牙膏（yá gāo），toothpaste

笔（bǐ），pen

卫生纸（wèi shēng zhǐ），toilet paper

洗发水（xǐ fà shuǐ），shampoo

饮料（yǐn liào），beverage

零食（líng shí），snack

Phrases

什么意思（shén me yì sī）？

What does it mean?

“ 雪茄 “ 是什么意思（“ xuě jiā ” shì shén me yì sī）？

What does “cigar” mean?

糖多少钱（táng duō shǎo qián）？

How much for the sugar?

有没有糖（yǒu méi yǒu táng）？

Do you have any sugar?

This “有没有” construction is used where in English you would say “Do you have any _____?” or “Are there any _____?” It also has other uses: “你有没有吃饭 (nǐ yǒu méi yǒu chī fàn)?” is one way to say, “Have you eaten?”

打扰一下，你能告诉我雪茄在哪儿卖吗（dǎ rǎo yí xià, nǐ néng gào sù wǒ xuě qié zài nǎ ér mài ma）？

Excuse me, could you tell me where I can get some cigars?

我能看看这块表吗（wǒ néng kàn kan zhè kuài biǎo ma）？

May I have a look at the watch?

Notes

Strategy: Reading Chinese on the street

Reading, like listening, is a guessing game in which you will need to use whatever clues you have to get the information you need. You won’t be reading Chinese novels anytime soon, but you can already start using the characters you know to unlock the secrets of Chinese maps, signs, menus, and so forth. If you get into the habit of looking at the written Chinese around you in daily life, you will not only review the characters you already know but also notice new ones that appear frequently and beg you to learn them. Carry a little notebook so you can copy down characters you want to learn.

Colloquial Translation of Dialogue

A: Do you have any beer?

B: Yes, how many bottles do you want?

A: Three. Do you have any cigars?

B: Sorry, we don’t.

A: Well, how much for three bottles of beer?

B: Five yuan each, fifteen in total.

Scenario 4: Buying (III)

Dialogue

In some Chinese shops, goods are behind a counter and you will need to ask a clerk to get the item for you. A is attempting to make a rather mundane purchase in such a shop.

A: 你们这儿有没有毛巾?

nǐ men zhè ér yǒu méi yǒu máo jīn?

You here have not have towels?

B: 有，你要什么颜色?

yǒu, nǐ yào shén me yán sè?

Have. You want what color?

A: 我要红色的

wǒ yào hóng sè de

I want a red-colored one

B: 我们有大的和小的。你要什么样的?

wǒ men yǒu dà de hé xiǎo de. nǐ yào shén me yàng de?

We have big ones and small ones. You want what kind?

A: 麻烦你给我看看那个大的

má fán nǐ gěi wǒ kàn kan nà gè dà de

Trouble you give me look at that big one

B: 哪个?

nǎ gè?

Which one?

A: 对!那个!

Duì! nà gè!

Right! That!

Vocabulary

这儿（zhè ér），here

毛巾（máo jīn），towel

颜色（yán sè），color

大（dà），big

小（xiǎo），small

什么样（shén me yàng），what kind

麻烦（má fan），trouble / to trouble

给（gěi），give

对（duì），right / correct

那个（nà gè），that

商场（shāng chǎng），mall

公司（gōng sī），company

大厦（dà shà），building

百货大楼（bǎi huò dà lóu），department store

超市（chāo shì），supermarket

购物广场（gòu wù guǎng chǎng），plaza

衬衫（chèn shān），shirt

裙子（qún zi），skirt

外套（wài tào），coat

鞋子（xié zi），shoes

毛衣（máo yī），sweater

裤子（kù zi），pants

内衣（nèi yī），underwear

袜子（wà zi），socks

新（xīn），new

长（cháng），long

宽（kuān），wide / broad

旧（jiù），old

短（duǎn），short

窄（zhǎi），narrow

浅（qiǎn），shallow

深（shēn），deep

红（hóng），red

橙（chéng），orange

黄（huáng），yellow

绿（lǜ），green

蓝（lán），blue

紫（zǐ），purple

黑（hēi），black

白（bái），white

灰（huī），grew

Phrases

麻烦你给我那条毛巾（má fan nǐ gěi wǒ nà tiáo máo jīn）？

May I bother you to give me that towel?

还有别的颜色吗（hái yǒu bié de yán sè ma）？

Do you have another color?

有没有更好的（yǒu méi yǒu gèng hǎo de）？

Do you have a better one?

这个太小了，有大点的吗（zhè gè tài xiǎo le, yǒu dà diǎn de ma）？

This is too small for me, do you have a bigger one?

你穿多大号的（nǐ chuān duō dà hào de）？

What's your size?

它特别适合你（tā tè bié shì hé nǐ）

It suits you very much

能换一个吗（néng huàn yí gè ma）？

Can you show me another one?

麻烦你开门（má fan nǐ kāi mén）？

Can I trouble you to open the door?

我要那件紫色的裙子（wǒ yào nà jiàn zǐ sè de qún zi）

I want that purple skirt

这件衬衫真好看（zhè jiàn chèn shān zhēn hǎo kàn）

This shirt looks nice

我喜欢这条裤子（wǒ xǐ huān zhè tiáo kù zi）

I like these pants

能试一试吗（néng shì yí shì ma）?

Can I try them on?

对我来说太贵了（duì wǒ lái shuō tài guì le）

It's too expensive for me

我要了（wǒ yào le）

I'll take it

我该付多少钱（wǒ gāi fù duō shǎo qián）?

How much do I owe you?

Notes

Plurals

Chinese makes no distinction between the singular and plural forms of most nouns. For example, "门 (mén)" means both "door" and "doors". Whether or not something is singular or plural is determined from context.

-er ending

In Northern China, an -er ending is added to many words. For example, while Southern Chinese would say, "这里 (zhè lǐ)," northerners would say, "这儿 (zhè ér)." Both mean "here". You need to decide if you want to follow Northern or Southern custom or learn to switch depending on your audience, but for now, focus on not getting too confused by these reginal variations when you listen.

Tip: Tones

At the early stages of Chinese study and use you may make quite a few tonal mistakes when you speak. Generally, a tonal mistake in the context of a sentence won't confuse a Chinese speaker too much, but if you speak in isolated words and get the tones wrong, speakers may not understand you. One strategy for minimizing tones as a communication problem is to create context by using complete phrases or sentences—or lots of body language.

Colloquial Translation of Dialogue

A: Do you have any towels here?

B: Yes, what color would you like?

A: Red.

B: We have big ones and little ones, what kind do you want?

A: Could you let me have a look at that big one?

B: Which one?

A: Yeah, that one!

Scenario 5: Drinks and Snacks

Dialogue

A and B are hungry / thirsty foreigners passing a local general store. C is the store clerk.

A: 我饿了。你呢?

wǒ è le, nǐ ne

I hungry. You?

B: 我不饿，但是有一点渴

wǒ bú è, dàn shì yǒu yì diǎn kě

I not hungry, but a little thirsty

A: 你有没有饼干?

nǐ yǒu méi yǒu bǐng gān?

You have not have cookies?

C: 有。你要哪种?

Yǒu. nǐ yào nǎ zhǒng?

Have. You want which kind?

A: 那种是甜的还是咸的?

nà zhǒng shì tián de hái shì xián de?

That kind is sweet or salty?

C: 这种是巧克力的

zhè zhǒng shì qiǎo kè lì de

This kind is chocolate

B: 我要一个可乐

wǒ yào yí gè kě lè

I want a cola

C: 大瓶还是小瓶?

dà píng hái shì xiǎo píng?

Big bottle or small bottle?

B: 我要罐装的

wǒ yào guàn zhuāng de

I want can filled

Vocabulary

饿（è），hungry

渴（kě），thirsty

巧克力（qiǎo kè lì），chocolate

饼干（bǐng gān），crackers / cookies

可乐（kě lè），cola / coke

瓶（píng），bottle

种（zhǒng），kind / type

罐（guàn），can

还是（hái shì），or

甜（tián），sweet

咸（xián），salty

装（zhuāng），to fill / to install

酸（suān），sour

辣（là），hot / spicy

喝（hē），to drink

面包（miàn bāo），bread

冰淇淋（bīng qí lín），ice cream

杯子（bēi zi），cup

罐头（guàn tou），can food

干（gān），dry

汽水（qì shuǐ），soda

咖啡（kā fēi），coffee

茶（chá），tea

水（shuǐ），water

开水（kāi shuǐ），boiled water

冰水（bīng shuǐ），ice water

白酒（bái jiǔ），Chinese liquor

果汁（guǒ zhī），juice

牛奶（niú nǎi），milk

葡萄酒（pú táo jiǔ），wine

矿泉水（kuàng quán shuǐ），mineral water

Phrases

我有点饿（wǒ yǒu diǎn è）

I'm a little hungry

这儿有点儿冷（zhè ér yǒu diǎn ér lěng）

It's a little cold here

我要那个大的（wǒ yào nà gè dà de）

I want that big one

她想买酸的（tā xiǎng mǎi suān de）

She wants to buy the sour kind

你想吃面包还是饼干（nǐ xiǎng chī miàn bāo hái shì bǐng gān）？

Do want to eat bread or crackers?

这是甜的还是咸的（zhè shì tián de hái shì xián de）？

Is this sweet or salty?

你要大的还是小的（nǐ yào dà de hái shì xiǎo de）？

Do you want a big one or a small one?

Notes

Tip: Finding time

One of the greatest problems that learners outside formal language study programs face is a shortage of time, and usually, an abundance of other things need to be done. Usually, to sustain even a modest study program, you need to regularly block out a portion of prime time in your daily schedule (i.e., time when you are reasonably alert) to devote to study, and generally, this means making sacrifices in some other area of your life. Attempts to learn a language without allocating adequate time to the task typically result in more frustration than progress. In contrast, even if you can only find half an hour of quality time each day for Chinese study, you will be able to make gradual but genuine progress.

Colloquial Translation of Dialogue

A: I'm hungry. How about you?

B: I'm not hungry, but I'm a little thirsty.

A: Do you have any cookies?

C: Yes, what kind do you want?

A: Is that kind sweet or salty?

C: This kind is chocolate.

B: I want a cola.

C: Big or small bottle?

B: I want a can.

Scenario 6: In the Cafeteria

Dialogue

A is a curious and hungry foreigner looking at food in a Chinese cafeteria. B, the Chinese server, patiently answers questions.

A: 这是什么?

zhè shì shén me?

This is what?

B: 这是炸鸡

zhè shì zhá jī

This is fried chicken

A: 那个呢?

nà gè ne?

Then that?

B: 炸鱼。要来一份吗?

zhá yú. yào lái yí fèn ma?

Fried fish. Want one?

A: 可以

kě yǐ

Sure

B: 你的汉语还不错

nǐ de hàn yǔ hái bú cuò

Your Chinese not bad

A: 哪里哪里

nǎ lǐ nǎ lǐ

Where, where

Vocabulary

这（zhè），this

是（shì），is

什么（shén me），what

The “n” in this word is silent. This is one of the very few Chinese words not pronounced exactly as the Pinyin spelling would indicate.

鸡（jī），chicken

鸡肉（jī ròu），chicken meat

鱼（yú），fish

吃（chī），to eat

的（de），possessive marker

吗（ma），question marker

汉语（hàn yǔ），Chinese language

哪里（nǎ lǐ），where

听（tīng），to listen

懂（dǒng），to understand

肉（ròu），meat

猪（zhū），pig

猪肉（zhū ròu），pork

羊（yáng），sheep / goat

羊肉（yáng ròu），mutton

牛（niú），cow / bull

牛肉（niú ròu），beef

Phrases

这是什么?（zhè shì shén me）

What is this?

Notice that the word order for this question is the opposite of the order in English, and that the same word order is used for both question and answer

这是猪肉吗?（zhè shì zhū ròu ma）

Is this pork?

你要点菜了吗?（nǐ yào diǎn cài le ma）

Are you ready to order?

你要什么甜点?（nǐ yào shén me tián diǎn）

What would you like for dessert?

这是你的吗?（zhè shì nǐ de ma）

Is this yours?

咸不咸?（xián bú xián）

Salty or not?

甜不甜?（tián bú tián）

Sweet or not?

辣不辣?（là bú là）

Spicy or not?

我听不懂（wǒ tīng bù dǒng）

I don't understand

好吃（hǎo chī）

Tastes good

不好吃（bù hǎo chī）

Tastes bad

我能用支票或信用卡吗?（wǒ néng yòng zhī piào huò xìn yòng kǎ ma）

Can I pay by check or credit card?

对不起，我们只收现金（duì bù qǐ, wǒ men zhī shōu xiàn jīn）

Sorry, we only accept cash

Notes

In the previous scenario, you saw that a measure word is required between numbers and nouns. In the dialogue above, you see that a measure word is also usually required after "这".

个 (gè)

This is the most common measure word in Chinese, and when you are in doubt as to what measure word to use, you can simply use "gè".

呢 (ne)

A question marker, but it is only used for brief follow-up questions in situations where context already makes the question clear. So, for example, instead of asking the whole question "这是什么(zhè shì shén me)?" several times in a row as you point to different items in a store or restaurant, for the follow-up questions you could ask, "这个呢 (zhè gè ne)?" and "那个呢 (nà gè ne)?"

的 (de)

Can mark possession, like so:

-我的 (wǒ de), my/mine

-你的 (nǐ de), your/yours

-他/她的 (tā de), his/hers

哪里哪里 (nǎ lǐ nǎ lǐ)

The normal polite Chinese response to a compliment is to deny it, and this is often done with this phrase, which literally means "where, where?" but would better be translated something like "Not at all".

Strategy: Controlling conversations with questions

In early stages of Chinese practice in real life, a good way to give yourself a fighting chance to understand what Chinese speakers say is by controlling the conversation with questions that help you predict what you might hear in response. "这是什么 (zhè shì shén me)?" is a very useful question because it both generates predictable responses and new vocabulary. Yes/no questions are also good because they limit the possible responses.

Tip: Grammar

Learning Chinese grammar is largely a question of remembering word order. This is the main reason why Chinese word order is preserved as much as possible in the English translation of the dialogue sentences, even when the result is pidgin English. For example, note that the word order in “这是什么 (zhè shì shén me)?” is the opposite of the English “What is this?”

Colloquial Translation of Dialogue

A: What is this?

B: Fried chicken.

A: What about that?

B: Fried fish, do you want some?

A: Sure.

B: Your Chinese isn’t bad.

A: Thank you.

Scenario 7: The Noodle Stand

Dialogue

Foreigner B is ordering a meal at a small Chinese noodle stand. A is the Chinese owner.

A: 你想吃什么?

nǐ xiǎng chī shén me?

You want to eat what?

B: 等一下，我看一下菜单。好，我来一碗面条

děng yí xià, wǒ kàn yí xià cài dān. hǎo, wǒ lái yì wǎn miàn tiáo

Wait a minute, I look a moment menu. Okay, I take one bowl noodles

A: 好的，你还要吃什么?喜欢吃水饺吗?

hǎo de, nǐ hái yào chī shén me? xǐ huān chī shuǐ jiǎo ma?

Okay. You also want to eat what? Like to eat dumpling?

B: 很喜欢，那再要一盘水饺吧

hěn xǐ huān, nà zài yào yì pán shuǐ jiǎo ba

Very much, then also want a plate dumpling

Vocabulary

等（děng），to wait

一下（yí xià），a moment

菜单（cài dān），menu

来（lái），to come / to take

碗（wǎn），bowl / a bowl of

面条（miàn tiáo），noodles

喜欢（xǐ huān），to like

也（yě），also

水饺（shuǐ jiǎo），dumpling

碟（dié），plate / a plate of

用（yòng），to use

菜（cài），dishes / food

筷子（kuài zi），chopsticks

结账（jié zhàng），to count up a bill

走（zǒu），to walk / to leave

炒饭（chǎo fàn），fried rice

馒头（mán tou），steamed bread

包子（bāo zi），steamed bread with filling

煎饼（jiān bing），fried flatbread

烧饼（shāo bing），baked flatbread

油条（yóu tiáo），deep fried breadsticks

Phrases

我要结账（wǒ yào jié zhàng）

Please get me the bill

来一碗面条怎么样（lái yì wǎn miàn tiáo zěn me yàng）？

How about having a bowl of noodles?

很喜欢（hěn xǐ huān）

Note the word order in this phrase. The “很” comes before “喜欢”, unlike word order in English

Very like

Questions you will often hear in a restaurant:

你会不会用筷子（nǐ huì bú huì yòng kuài zi）？

Can you use chopsticks?

你喜欢中国菜吗（nǐ xǐ huān zhōng guó cài ma）？

Do you like Chinese food?

需要给你一套刀叉吗（xū yào gěi nǐ yí tào dāo chā ma）？

Do you need a knife and a fork?

你快一点（nǐ kuài yì diǎn）！

Hurry up!

请等一下（qǐng děng yí xià）

Please wait a moment

我们来两碗面和三个包子（wǒ men lái liǎng wǎn miàn hé sān gè bāo zi）

We'll take two bowls of noodles and three steamed buns

Notes

Tip: Accents and dialects

One frustration of learning Chinese for average people instead of language teachers is that not all people use standard Chinese pronunciation. In fact, there are only a few places in China where the average person pronounces things the way textbooks say they should. Furthermore, in many provinces, Chinese people speak a dialect and only learn Mandarin as a second language.

First, accept this as reality rather than burning a lot of emotional energy getting frustrated by it. Perhaps even revel in it as a reflection of China's rich regional diversity. Second, get used to guessing; the sentence that sounded vaguely like "你好" might actually have been "你好" , albeit with a heavy local accent. Third, learn a few words in the local dialect. You will probably get all kinds of brownie points with local people for knowing a few of their words.

Colloquial Translation of Dialogue

A: What do you want to eat?

B: Wait a minute. I'll take a look at the menu. Okay. I'll have a bowl of noodles.

A: Okay. What else do you want to have? Do you like dumplings?

B: Yes, I like dumplings a lot. I'd also like a plate of dumplings.

Scenario 8: In the Restaurant

Dialogue

Foreigner B and their friend have been emboldened by earlier success with noodles and try ordering a more sophisticated meal at a local restaurant. A is the eager waitress.

A: 你们吃什么菜?

nǐ men chī shén me cài?

You eat what dishes?

B: 有什么好吃的?

yǒu shén me hǎo chī de?

Have what good to eat?

A: 烤虾，行不行?

kǎo xiā, xíng bú xíng?

Baked shrimp, okay not okay?

B: 请给我看看菜单。烤虾太贵了，还有别的吗?

qǐng gěi wǒ kàn kan cài dān. kǎo xiā tài guì le, hái yǒu bié de ma?

Please give me look at menu. Baked shrimp too expensive. Also have other?

A: 青椒肉片，怎么样?

qīng jiāo ròu piàn, zěn me yàng?

Green pepper with pork slices, what about it?

B: 好。我们再来一个青菜、一碗酸辣汤和两碗米饭

hǎo. wǒ men zài lái yí gè qīng cài, yì wǎn suān là tāng hé liǎng wǎn mǐ fàn

Alright. We also want a green vegetable dish, a bowl of hot-sour soup, and two bowls of rice

Vocabulary

虾（xiā），shrimp

烤（kǎo），bake

酸辣（suān là），sour-hot

米饭（mǐ fàn），cooked rice

行（xíng），okay

别的（bié de），other

肉片（ròu piàn），meet slices

青椒（qīng jiāo），green pepper

青菜（qīng cài），greens

汤（tāng），soup

怎么样（zěn me yàng），how about

味精（wèi jīng），MSG

饱（bǎo），full

蔬菜（shū cài），vegetables

海鲜（hǎi xiān），seafood

汤匙（tāng chí），spoon

勺子（sháo zi），ladle

酱油（jiàng yóu），soy sauce

油（yóu），oil

醋（cù），vinegar

盐（yán），salt

糖（táng），sugar

蒜（suàn），garlic

辣椒酱（là jiāo jiàng），hot sauce

Some Chinese dishes beloved by foreigners:

蛋花汤（dàn huā tāng），egg flower soup

酸辣汤（suān là tāng），sour-hot soup

麻婆豆腐（má pó dòu fu），spicy bean curd

鱼香肉丝（yú xiāng ròu sī），spicy pork threads

鱼香茄子（yú xiāng qié zi），spicy eggplant

糖醋里脊（táng cù lǐ jǐ），sweet sour pork

家常豆腐（jiā cháng dòu fu），home-style tofu

宫保鸡丁（gōng bǎo jī dīng），Kong Bao chicken

腰果鸡丁（yāo guǒ jī dīng），cashew chicken

红烧牛肉（hóng shāo niú ròu），braised beef

西红柿炒蛋（xī hóng shì chǎo dàn），tomato scrambled eggs

苦瓜炒蛋（kǔ guā chǎo dàn），bitter melon scrambled eggs

炒青菜（chǎo qīng cài），fried green vegetables

干煸四季豆（gān biān sì jì dòu），fried full season beans

炒空心菜（chǎo kōng xīn cài），fried leafy vegetable

油炸土豆条（yóu zhà tǔ dòu tiáo），fried potato threads

拔丝地瓜（bá sī dì guā），candied sweet potato

Phrases

不要放味精（bú yào fàng wèi jīng）

No MSG

干杯!（gān bēi）

Bottoms up!

我吃饱了（wǒ chī bǎo le）

I'm full

我自己来（wǒ zì jǐ lái）

I can do it by myself

Useful when a host insists on putting food in your bowl for you—perhaps things you don't want. You may feel uncomfortable with this kind of behavior, especially if someone is doing this with their own chopsticks, but this is indeed a Chinese way of showing hospitality

够了（gòu le）

It's enough

This is useful when a zealous host heaps too much food into your bowl

你想吃什么？（nǐ xiǎng chī shén me）

What do you want to eat?

有沙拉吗?（yǒu shā lā ma）

Is there any salad?

这里面是什么?（zhè lǐ miàn shì shén me）

What's in this dish?

我要这个（ wǒ yào zhè gè）

I want this

给我两碗米饭（ gěi wǒ liǎng wǎn mǐ fàn）

Two bowls of rice, please

米饭和菜一起上（ mǐ fàn hé cài yì qǐ shàng）

Please bring the rice and dish together

还要些什么?（hái yào xiē shén me）

What else do you want?

就要这些（ jiù yào zhè xiē）

These will be enough

不要了（bú yào le）

Nothing else

我们不吃螃蟹（ wǒ men bù chī páng xiè）

We don't like to eat crab

再来一瓶果汁（zài lái yì píng guǒ zhī）

A cup of juice, please

我要买单（wǒ yào mǎi dān）

I'll pay the bill

我们要发票和收据（wǒ men yào fā piào hé shōu jù）

We want the receipt and invoice

可以打包吗?（kě yǐ dǎ bāo ma）

Can we pack the remaining food?

Notes

Strategy: Ordering in a restaurant

If you know what you want and how to say what you want, there will not be a problem. However, this is often not the case, so the dialogue above models a coping strategy. Ask the waiter/waitress to recommend something, but most places will recommend their best and most expensive dishes. Therefore, check what they recommend on the menu to ensure that it isn't beyond your means. Remember: ask before ordering a dish that has no price listed next to it—they are usually the expensive delicacies.

Tip: Memorizing vocabulary

Learning a new language requires memorizing lots of vocabulary, so you need to develop good strategies for embedding many new words in your memory. Some suggestions:

- *Repetition*: The more times you see, hear, say, write a word, the more likely you are to remember it.

- *Concentration*: Staying alert when you memorize is vitally important.

- *Application*: A word that you find a chance to use in a conversation is more likely to stay with you than one you only study in a book.

- *Movement*: Physical movement combined with memorization helps you remember words better. Sway your arms, rock your head, pace the room, do whatever you need to.

- *Associations*: Associate a word with something memorable, funny, shocking, etc. It may help to associate the Chinese word with some word in your own language that the Chinese word sounds like—the more absurd, the better.

Colloquial Translation of Dialogue

A: What would you like to eat?

B: What's good?

A: How about baked shrimp?

B: Please let me look at the menu. Shrimp is too expensive, do you have anything else?

A: How about green pepper with pork slices?

B: Okay. We'll also take a dish of greens, a bowl of hot-sour soup, and two bowls of rice.

Scenario 9: In the Market

Dialogue

Foreigner A is in a market. B is a well-supplied fruit vendor.

A: 这水果新鲜吗?

zhè shuǐ guǒ xīn xiān ma?

This fruit fresh?

B: 很新鲜。要买多少?

hěn xīn xiān. yào mǎi duō shǎo?

Very fresh. Want buy how much?

A: 西瓜多少钱一斤?

xī guā duō shǎo qián yì jīn?

Watermelon per catty how much?

B: 五块六一斤。要几斤?

wǔ kuài liù yì jīn. yào jǐ jīn?

One catty 5.6 yuan. Want how many catties?

A: 十块钱两斤，好不好?

shí kuài qián liǎng jīn, hǎo bú hǎo?

Two catties 10 yuan. Okay not okay?

B: 行，行

xíng, xíng

Okay, okay

Vocabulary

水果（shuǐ guǒ），fruit

西瓜（xī guā），watermelon

新鲜（xīn xian），fresh

斤（jīn），catty / half-kilo

两（liǎng），tenth of a catty

公斤（gōng jīn），kilogram

半（bàn），half

苹果（píng guǒ），apple

香蕉（xiāng jiāo），banana

梨（lí），pear

桃子（táo zi），peach

橙子（chéng zi），orange

胡萝卜（hú luó bo），carrot

白萝卜（bái luó bo），turnip

葱（cōng），green onion

洋葱（yáng cōng），onion

菜花（cài huā），cauliflower

白菜（bái cài），cabbage

Phrases

便宜一点，行不行?（pián yi yì diǎn, xíng bù xíng）

Can it be cheaper?

太贵了!（tài guì le）

Too expensive!

有点贵（yǒu diǎn guì）

A bit expensive

五块钱，卖不卖?（wǔ kuài qián, mài bú mài）

How about five *yuan*?

这个水果坏了（zhè gè shuǐ guǒ huài le）

This fruit has gone bad

香蕉三斤多少钱?（xiāng jiāo sān jīn duō shǎo qián）

How much for 3 catty banana?

西瓜多少钱一斤?（xī guā duō shǎo qián yì jīn）

How much is watermelon per catty?

两块六一斤（liǎng kuài liù yì jīn）

2.6 *yuan* per catty

Notes

The main traditional weight measurement used in Chinese markets is the "斤(jīn)" . This is about half a kilogram or a little more than a pound. A "两 (liǎng)" is a tenth of a " 斤" . These are the measurements most often used in markets for buying food. Metric weights, however, are also commonly used in Chinese markets. The word for kilogram in Chinese is "公斤(gōng jīn)" .

Strategy: Bargaining in markets

Foreigners sometimes avoid Chinese markets because sentences fly around too fast, and they might worry about being cheated. However, there are several good reasons to become "market literate". First, there is a lot of good food in markets. Second, markets are a great free language class where you can practice much of your most basic language tools. Third, bargaining is fun once you have done it a few times and learned the ropes. Finally, having a few vendors at the market who recognize you is a wonderful boost to your sense that you are becoming a part of "life" when you are in China.

You can often bargain at markets or with street vendors, although usually, the price won't go down too far. Here are some suggestions:

- Try to find out roughly what price something should be before you go to the market so that you know if the quoted price is outrageous. Remember: the quoted prices vary by the season and even by the day, so to get good information you need to ask someone who shops in the market often.

- Basic bargaining moves include asking for a cheaper price or making a counter-offer.

- If you are buying more than one item, a good strategy is to offer the vendor a rounded price that is slightly lower than the original total amount.

- If the purchase is not vital to you, you can always try walking away. You may get called back with a better offer, but not always.

- Finally, become a regular customer, and you will probably get a good price right off the bat.

Colloquial Translation of Dialogue

A: Is this fruit fresh?

B: Very fresh. How much do you want to buy?

A: How much is watermelon per catty?

B: 5.6 *yuan* per catty.

A: How about two catties for 10 *yuan*?

B: Okay, okay.

Scenario 10: In the Bookstore

Dialogue

B wants to make a purchase in a bookstore. A is the Chinese clerk.

A: 你想买什么?

nǐ xiǎng mǎi shén me?

You want to buy what?

B: 我想买几本书

wǒ xiǎng mǎi jǐ běn shū

I want to buy several books

A: 什么样的书?

shén me yàng de shū?

What kind of books?

B: 有没有汉语课本?

yǒu méi yǒu hàn yǔ kè běn?

Have not have Chinese textbooks?

A: 没有。你还要什么?

méi yǒu. nǐ hái yào shén me

Not have. You still want what?

B: 汉英词典有没有?

hàn yīng cí diǎn yǒu méi yǒu?

Chinese-English dictionary have or not?

A: 有。还有吗?

yǒu. hái yǒu ma?

Have. What else?

B: 一本中国历史书

yì běn zhōng guó lì shǐ shū

A Chinese history book

Vocabulary

想（xiǎng），want to

本（běn），measure word for books

课本（kè běn），textbook

还（hái），still / else

汉英（hàn yīng），Chinese-English

词典（cí diǎn），dictionary

张（zhāng），measure word for photos / maps / papers

历史（lì shǐ），history

政治（zhèng zhì），politic

经济（jīng jì），economy

文化（wén huà），culture

数学（shù xué），math

物理（wù lǐ），physics

化学（huà xué），chemistry

生物（shēng wù），biology

地理（dì lǐ），geography

文学（wén xué），literature

中国文学（zhōng guó wén xué），Chinese literature

外国文学（wài guó wén xué），foreign literature

文具（wén jù），stationary, pen, etc

地图（dì tú），map

小说（xiǎo shuō），novel / fiction

Phrases

还有呢（hái yǒu ne）？

What else?

你想看书吗（nǐ xiǎng kàn shū ma）？

Do you want to read?

我想坐在这（wǒ xiǎng zuò zài zhè）

I want to sit here

有没有汉英词典（yǒu méi yǒu hàn yīng cí diǎn）？

Do you have any Chinese-English dictionaries?

地图有没有（dì tú yǒu méi yǒu）？

Do you have any maps?

Notes

Chinese word order:

Chinese word order is sometimes flexible, especially in spoken Chinese. Note that in the dialogue above, "有没有" can come before the subject or after. In your speaking, you might initially choose to stick with one pattern, but expect to hear Chinese people vary the pattern.

Chinese dictionaries:

When getting a dictionary for studying Chinese, choose one with many example phrases and sentences so you can learn word usage as well as meaning. Examples also give you good clues as to connotations, level of formality, and so forth.

Colloquial Translation of Dialogue

A: What do you want to buy?

B: I want to buy some books.

A: What kind of books?

B: Do you have any Chinese textbooks?

A: No, we don't. Was there anything else that you want?

B: Do you have any Chinese-English dictionaries?

A: We do, anything else?

B: One Chinese history book.

Scenario 11: Taking the Taxi

Dialogue

Foreigner A is headed to the museum and waves down a taxi; B is the taxi driver.

B: 去哪里?

qù nǎ lǐ?

Go to where?

A: 到博物馆。请打表

dào bó wù guǎn. qǐng dǎ biǎo

To museum. Please start meter

A: 请停车

qǐng tíng chē

Please stop the taxi

B: 这儿不可以停车。我在前面停吧

zhè ér bù kě yǐ tíng chē. wǒ zài qián miàn tíng ba

Here not permitted stop taxi. I at ahead stop car, how's that?

A: 好吧

hǎo ba

Okay

Vocabulary

博物馆（bó wù guǎn），museum

医院（yī yuàn），hospital

公安局（gōng ān jú），police office

汽车站（qì chē zhàn），bus stop

飞机场（fēi jī chǎng），airport

火车站（huǒ chē zhàn），train station

公园（gōng yuán），park

游乐园（yóu lè yuán），amusement part

海边（hǎi biān），seaside

停（tíng），to stop

打表（dǎ biǎo），to start a meter

抽烟（chōu yān），to smoke

拐弯（guǎi wān），to turn

路（lù），road

高速公路（gāo sù gōng lù），highway

走（zǒu），to walk / to go / to leave

出租车/的士/计程车（chū zū chē / dī shì / jì chéng chē），taxi

公交车（gōng jiāo chē），bus

自行车（zì xíng chē），bike

摩托车（mó tuō chē），motorcycle

Phrases

你要去哪里（nǐ yào qù nǎ lǐ）？

Where are you going?

打不打表 (dǎ bù dǎ biǎo)?

Do you have a meter?

This is a good question not only for checking to see if a vehicle has a meter—and is thus a legal taxi—but also for suggesting that the meter be used

请开一下后备箱 (qǐng kāi yí xià hòu bèi xiāng)

Please open the trunk

你知道怎么去超市吗 (nǐ zhī dào zěn me qù chāo shì ma）？

Do you know how to get to the supermarket?

看表吧 (kàn biǎo ba)?

Let's go according to the meter price, okay?

This is useful if a taxi driver starts trying to negotiate a price instead of using the meter

你能停一下吗 nǐ néng tíng yí xià ma）？

Can you stop for a minute?

你能等我十分钟吗 (nǐ néng děng wǒ shí fèn zhōng ma）？

Can you wait for me for like ten minutes?

到机场多少钱 (dào jī chǎng duō shǎo qián)?

How much to the airport?

This is used when you want to negotiate a price

我到了（wǒ dào le）！

I'm there!

这儿可以停车（zhè ér kě yǐ tíng chē）

It's permitted to stop the vehicle here

在图书馆不可以抽烟（zài tú shū guǎn bù kě yǐ chōu yān）

You are not allowed to smoke in the library

我们走吧（wǒ men zǒu ba）

Let's leave

我们明天去公园吧（wǒ men míng tiān qù gōng yuán ba）

Let's go to the park tomorrow

Notes

车（chē）

In Chinese, the word "车" is used much more often than the word "vehicle" is in English. In fact, whereas in English one usually says "car," "bus," or whatever, in Chinese, the more general word "车" is often used, with context clarifying what kind of vehicle is in question.

Strategy: Negotiating taxis

Your ability to get around Chinese cities expands dramatically once you become comfortable using Chinese taxis, so this is a skill worth developing as soon as possible. In general, you don't need to worry much about taxi drivers overcharging you in China, but there are always a few exceptions, and it would be too bad if concern for being overcharged were to cause you to avoid taxis. A few suggestions for minimizing problems:

- Taxis with meters are less likely to overcharge than those which lack meters.

- It is better to get a taxi at a regular taxi stand or to hail one on the street than it is to go with a taxi driver who hustles business at places like a train and bus station. These locations generally have a regular taxi stand, though you may need to look for it. If you can't find one, you might want to walk a little distance from the station before hailing a taxi.

- For more distant destinations, such as airports, taxis often don't charge according to the meter. For these destinations, it is especially important to find out in advance what would be a fair price according to local custom.

Colloquial Translation of Dialogue

B: Where are you going?

A: To the museum, please use the meter.

A: Please stop the taxi.

B: I can't stop here. I'll stop up ahead, okay?

A: Sure.

Scenario 12: On the Train

Dialogue

Foreigner A is at a train station trying to buy a ticket to Shanghai but isn't sure which is the right ticket window. B is the ticket seller.

A: 这儿有没有到上海的火车票?

zhè ér yǒu méi yǒu dào shàng hǎi de huǒ chē piào?

Here have not have to Shanghai's train tickets?

B: 有。你要几点钟的?

yǒu. nǐ yào jǐ diǎn zhōng de?

Have. You want what times?

A: 三点半的

sān diǎn bàn de

Three o'clock half's

B: 要几张?

yào jǐ zhāng?

What how many?

A: 一张。到上海要坐多久?

yì zhāng. dào shàng hǎi yào zuò duō jiǔ?

One. To Shanghai have to sit how long?

B: 一般来说，三个小时

yì bān lái shuō, sān gè xiǎo shí

In general, three hours

Vocabulary

卖（mài），to sell

票（piào），ticket

到（dào）, to

一般来说（yì bān lái shuō），in general / generally speaking

上（shàng），up / to get on

下（xià），down / to get off

面包车（miàn bāo chē），mini-van

迷你巴士（mí nǐ bā shì），mini-bus

卡车（kǎ chē），truck

码头（mǎ tóu），dock

长途车站（cháng tú chē zhàn），long distance bus station

铁路（tiě lù），railway

动车（dòng chē），EMU Train 高铁（gāo tiě），High-Speed Train

地铁（dì tiě），underground train

Phrases

车站在哪（chē zhàn zài nǎ）？

Where is the train station / bus stop?

上车（shàng chē）

Board the train / get on the bus / get in the taxi

下车（xià chē）

Get off the train / get off the bus / get out of the taxi

到北京的火车在哪里（dào běi jīng de huǒ chē zài nǎ lǐ）？

Where is the train to Beijing?

这辆公交车不是到书店的吗（zhè liàng gōng jiāo chē bú shì dào shū diàn de ma）？

Is this bus to the bookstore?

我在等九点到上海的火车（wǒ zài děng jiǔ diǎn dào shàng hǎi de huǒ chē）

I'm waiting for the train at 9 o'clock to Shanghai

你的座位是几号（nǐ de zuò wèi shì jǐ hào）？

What is your seat number?

你能帮我照看下行李吗（nǐ néng bāng wǒ zhào kàn xià xíng li ma）？

Could you please keep an eye on my luggage?

Notes

Buying train tickets

The price of a trip often varies according to distance, and the conductor may ask you where you are going, so knowing a place name helps. If you don't like to wait in lines, you can always go to the TVM. If you are not familiar with the TVM, don't be afraid to ask for help. Chinese people will be happy to help you out.

Tip: Mistakes and learning grammar

One of the best ways to learn grammar is through experimentation. The process by which people most naturally learn grammar is called successive approximation; in other words, at first, people use simple but flawed sentences and gradually refine them by trial and error until they become more accurate and complex.

It is not only okay to make many mistakes in conversation, but virtually necessary if you are to do the kind of grammar experimentation needed for learning, so one of the best ways to learn is by plunging in and speaking at every opportunity. It is less important that you get every sentence right than that you learn from your mistakes.

Colloquial Translation of Dialogue

A: Do you have train tickets to Shanghai here?

B: Yes, which train do you want?

A: The 3:30.

B: How many tickets?

A: One. How long does it take to get to Shanghai?

B: In general, three hours.

Scenario 13: Asking for Directions

Dialogue

A needs directions to the park and asks B.

A: 请问，公园在哪里?

qǐng wèn, gōng yuán zài nǎ lǐ?

May I ask, the park is where?

B: 就在前面

jiù zài qián miàn

Just up ahead

A: 远不远?

yuǎn bù yuǎn?

Far or not?

B: 不远，很近了，走路只要十分钟

bù yuǎn, hěn jìn le, zǒu lù zhī yào shí fēn zhōng

Not far, very near, by walk only ten minutes

A: 在左边吗?

zài zuǒ biān ma?

On left side?

B: 不是，在右边

bú shì, zài yòu biān

Not is. On right side

Vocabulary

远（yuǎn），far

近（jìn），near

左边（zuǒ biān），left side

右边（yòu biān），right side

左转（zuǒ zhuǎn），turn left

右转（yòu zhuǎn），turn right

直走（zhí zǒu），go straight

米（mǐ），meter

千米（qiān mǐ），kilometer

公里（gōng lǐ），kilometer

里（lǐ），half of kilometer

前面（qián miàn），ahead

后面（hòu miàn），behind

对面（duì miàn），in front of

里面（lǐ miàn），inside

外面（wài miàn），outside

洗手间（xǐ shǒu jiān），toilet / washroom

东（dōng），east

南（nán），south

西（xī），west

北（běi），north

Phrases

书店怎么走（shū diàn zěn me zǒu）？

Where is the bookstore?

洗手间在哪里（xǐ shǒu jiān zài nǎ lǐ）？

Where is the washroom?

书店就在前面（shū diàn jiù zài qián miàn）

The bookstore is ahead

洗手间在什么地方 (xǐ shǒu jiān zài shén me dì fāng）？

Can you show me the way to the toilet?

附近有饭店吗 (fù jìn yǒu fàn diàn ma）？

Are there any restaurants nearby?

前面有个公园（qián miàn yǒu gè gōng yuán）

There is a park ahead

直走五百米右转（zhí zǒu wǔ bǎi mǐ yòu zhuǎn）

Go straight for five hundred meters and turn right

这是什么地方 (zhè shì shén me dì fāng）？

What is this place?

我们现在在哪里 (wǒ men xiàn zài zài nǎ lǐ）？

Where are we?

走这边还是那边（zǒu zhè biān hái shì nà biān）？

Shall we go this way or that way?

Notes

在(zài)

In Chinese, one preposition of place, 在(zài), covers everything—in, on, at, etc.

Strategy: Asking directions

You won't be able to understand a complicated set of directions in Chinese anytime soon, but if you can ask where something is, people can always point you in the right direction. A yes/no question like "远不远? (yuǎn bù yuǎn)" also has a good chance of prompting a response that you can understand.

Colloquial Translation of Dialogue

A: Excuse me, where's the park?

B: Just up ahead.

A: Is it far?

B: No, it's very close; only ten minutes by foot.

A: Is it on the left?

B: No, it's on the right.

Scenario 14: Asking for the Time

Dialogue

A: 请问现在几点了?

qǐng wèn xiàn zài jǐ diǎn le?

May I ask, now what time?

B: 三点五十分

sān diǎn wǔ shí fēn

Three o'clock fifty minutes

A: 你是学生吗?

nǐ shì xué shēng ma?

You are student?

B: 不是，我是英语老师。但是，我也在学习汉语

bú shì, wǒ shì yīng yǔ lǎo shī. dàn shì, wǒ yě zài xué xí hàn yǔ

No, I am English teacher. But, I also am learning Chinese

A: 你已经学了多久?

nǐ yǐ jīng xué le duō jiǔ?

You already have studied how long?

B: 就几个月

jiù jǐ gè yuè

Just a few months

A: 你进步很快

nǐ jìn bù hěn kuài.

You progress very fast

B: 哪里哪里

nǎ lǐ nǎ lǐ

Where, where

Vocabulary

现在（xiàn zài），now

几点（jǐ diǎn），what time

点（diǎn），o'clock

分（fēn），minute

但是（dàn shì），but / however

已经（yǐ jīng），already

学习（xué xí），to study

多久（duō jiǔ），how long

月（yuè），month

进步（jìn bù），progress / to progress

天（tiān），day

年（nián），year

做（zuò），to do

钟（zhōng），clock

习惯（xí guàn），to be accustomed to / to get used to

今天（jīn tiān），today

昨天（zuó tiān），yesterday

明天（míng tiān），tomorrow

后天（hòu tiān），the day after tomorrow

前天（qián tiān），the day before yesterday

Days of the week:

周一/礼拜一/星期一（zhōu yī / lǐ bài yī / xīng qī yī），Monday

周二/礼拜二/星期二（zhōu èr / lǐ bài èr / xīng qī èr），Tuesday

周三/礼拜三/星期三（zhōu sān / lǐ bài sān / xīng qī sān），Wednesday

周四/礼拜四/星期四（zhōu sì / lǐ bài sì / xīng qī sì），Thursday

周五/礼拜五/星期五（zhōu wǔ / lǐ bài wǔ / xīng qī wǔ），Friday

周六/礼拜六/星期六（zhōu liù / lǐ bài liù / xīng qī liù），Saturday

周日/周末/礼拜天/星期天（zhōu rì / zhōu mò / lǐ bài tiān / xīng qī tiān），Sunday

Months:

一月（yī yuè）January

二月（èr yuè）February

三月（sān yuè）March

四月（sì yuè）April

五月（wǔ yuè）May

六月（liù yuè）June

七月（qī yuè）July

八月（bā yuè）August

九月（jiǔ yuè）September

十月（shí yuè）October

十一月（shí yī yuè）November

十二月（shí èr yuè）December

Phrases

你在中国习惯吗?（nǐ zài zhōng guó xí guàn ma）

Are you used to life in China?

现在几点了?（xiàn zài jǐ diǎn le）

What time is it now?

今天几号?（jīn tiān jǐ hào）

What day is today?

明天星期几?（míng tiān xīng qī jǐ）

What day is tomorrow?

现在四点整（xiàn zài sì diǎn zhěng）

It is four o'clock now

现在两点十五（xiàn zài liǎng diǎn shí wǔ）

It is 2:15

她正在做什么?（tā zhèng zài zuò shén me）

What is she doing right now?

她正在学习（tā zhèng zài xué xí）

She's studying

他已经来中国两年了（tā yǐ jīng lái zhōng guó liǎng nián le）

He has been in China for two years

Notice here, unlike "already" in English, "已经" can't be placed at the end of a sentence

我们在这学习一个月（wǒ men zài zhè xué xí yí gè yuè）

We will study here for a month

火车几点开（huǒ chē jǐ diǎn kāi）？

When will the train leave?

飞机什么时候起飞（fēi jī shén me shí hòu qǐ fēi）？

When will the plane depart?

明天几点到北京（míng tiān jǐ diǎn dào běi jīng）？

When will you arrive in Beijing tomorrow?

你们哪天回家（nǐ men nǎ tiān huí jiā）？

What day are you going back home?

你打算什么时候再来（nǐ dǎ suàn shén me shí hòu zài lái）？

When are you planning to come back?

你什么时候有空（nǐ shén me shí hòu yǒu kòng）？

When will you be free?

周末我没时间（zhōu mò wǒ méi shí jiān）

I'm busy on the weekend

你几点到几点上班（nǐ jǐ diǎn dào jǐ diǎn shàng bān）?

What time do you work?

我明天九点来找你（wǒ míng tiān jiǔ diǎn lái zhǎo nǐ）

I'll come to get you tomorrow at 9 o'clock

请晚上八点后打电话（qǐng wǎn shàng bā diǎn hòu dǎ diàn huà）

Please call me after 8 p.m.

你等多久了（nǐ děng duō jiǔ le）?

How long you have been waiting?

Notes

Tip: Morale in language learning

Sometimes learning Chinese can seem hopeless as there is so much to learn, and your progress seems so slow. This is less of a problem during the first few exciting days of Chinese study than later as studying becomes less fresh and new, but even early on, it can be a problem.

To keep yourself going, it helps to take things one step at a time rather than brooding over how far away the goal of total mastery is. Set a series of limited and reasonable goals for yourself, and then keep putting one foot in front of the other until you achieve them. Every time you reach a little goal, reward yourself with a pat on the back, a chocolate bar, and a satisfying look back at what you have already learned. Success in language learning has more to do with persistence in making small steps than it does with any magical talent for languages.

Colloquial Translation of Dialogue

A: Excuse me, what time is it now?

B: 3:50.

A: Are you a student?

B: No, I'm an English teacher. But I am also studying Chinese.

A: How long have you been studying?

B: Just a few months.

A: Your progress is fast.

B: Thank you.

Scenario 15: Making an Appointment

Dialogue

Foreigner A needs a haircut and hopes her Chinese acquaintance, Mr. Wang, will come along to provide assistance and moral support.

A: 王先生，你下午有没有空?

wáng xiān shēng, nǐ xià wǔ yǒu méi yǒu kòng?

Mr. Wang, you afternoon have free time?

B: 什么事?

shén me shì?

What matter?

A: 不好意思麻烦你，但是你可以陪我去剪头发吗?剪完头发以后，我请你喝咖啡

bù hǎo yì sī má fán nǐ, dàn shì nǐ kě yǐ péi wǒ qù jiǎn tóu fà ma? jiǎn wán tóu fà yǐ hòu, wǒ qǐng nǐ hē kā fēi

Embarrassed to trouble you, but you can accompany me go out cut hair? Cut hair after, I invite you to drink coffee

B: 你不用这么客气。我们几点在哪里见面?

nǐ bú yòng zhè me kè qì. wǒ men jǐ diǎn zài nǎ lǐ jiàn miàn?

You not necessary so polite. We what time at where meet?

A: 我们三点在理发店见面，好吗?

wǒ men sān diǎn zài lǐ fà diàn jiàn miàn, hǎo ma?

We 3:00 o'clock at barbershop meet, okay?

B: 好的，下午见

hǎo de, xià wǔ jiàn

Okay, afternoon see

Vocabulary

下午（xià wǔ），afternoon

请（qǐng），to treat

事（shì），business / matter

这么（zhè me），so

客气（kè qi），polite

不好意思（bù hǎo yì sī），embarrassed / excuse me

陪（péi），to accompany

见面（jiàn miàn），to meet together

剪（jiǎn），to cut

理发店（lǐ fà diàn），barbershop

头发（tóu fà），hair

以后（yǐ hòu），after

问题（wèn tí），question

早上（zǎo shàng），morning

晚上（wǎn shàng），evening

请教（qǐng jiào），to respectfully ask

以前（yǐ qián），before

Phrases

我想问你一个问题（wǒ xiǎng wèn nǐ yí gè wèn tí）

I want to ask you a question

我想请教你一个问题（wǒ xiǎng qǐng jiào nǐ yí gè wèn tí）

I want to ask you a question

Although the translations are the same, the second one is a very polite way to introduce a question to an older person or someone of higher status

我想请你吃饭（wǒ xiǎng qǐng nǐ chī fàn）

I want to treat you to a meal

下午/早上/晚上/明天/机场/门口/楼下见（xià wǔ / zǎo shàng / wǎn shàng / míng tiān / jī chǎng / mén kǒu / lóu xià jiàn）

See you in the afternoon / morning / evening / tomorrow at the airport / gate / downstairs 吃饭前我们做点什么?（chī fàn qián wǒ men zuò diǎn shén me

What shall we do before we eat?

到北京后我们去爬长城吧!（dào běi jīng hòu wǒ men qù pá cháng chéng ba）

Let's visit the Great Wall after we arrive in Beijing!

我们下午三点在图书馆见面吧（wǒ men xià wǔ sān diǎn zài tú shū guǎn jiàn miàn ba）

Let’s meet in the library at three o’clock in the afternoon

对不起，我有约了（duì bù qǐ, wǒ yǒu yuē le）

Sorry, I’ve got plans

那么就定下来了，如果来不了，请打电话给我（nà me jiù dìng xià lái le, rú guǒ lái bù liǎo, qǐng dǎ diàn huà gěi wǒ）

Then that’s settled. Please call me if you can’t make it

她打电话来取消约会（tā dǎ diàn huà lái qǔ xiāo yuē huì）

She phoned to cancel the appointment

我不得不把约会从周一改到周四（wǒ bù dé bù bǎ yuē huì cóng zhōu yī gǎi dào zhōu sì）

I've got to change my appointment from Monday to Thursday

他早晨在网上买了火车票（tā zǎo chén zài wǎng shàng mǎi le huǒ chē piào）

He bought a train ticket online this morning

你有预约吗?（nǐ yǒu yù yuē ma）

Do you have an appointment?

你能在这里等一下吗?（nǐ néng zài zhè lǐ děng yí xià ma）

Could you wait here for a minute?

你一点也没变（nǐ yì diǎn yě méi biàn）

You haven't changed at all

Notes

Strategy: Making Chinese friends

Often you need to take some initiative to make Chinese friends, and one good strategy is to approach Chinese people for help or with questions about working, sightseeing, and living in China. There is much, after all, that you need to learn, and your need for assistance plays to a deep-felt Chinese desire to be good hosts and help guests. Such an approach also puts you in a student role which "gives face" to whomever you ask for help. Sometimes little else grows out of such conversations, but sometimes, they serve to break the ice and start a friendship.

Colloquial Translation of Dialogue

A: Mr. Wang, do you have some free time this afternoon?

B: What's up?

A: I hate to bother you, but could you go with me to help me get a haircut? After the haircut, I'll treat you to a cup of coffee.

B: You don't need to be so polite; when should we meet and where?

A: How about meeting at 3:00 at the barber's?

B: Okay. See you this afternoon.

Scenario 16: Introducing Yourself

Dialogue

A is a curious Chinese student who has encountered foreigner B and B's two companions at a store. A strikes up a conversation.

A: 请问，你是从哪个国家来的?

qǐng wèn, nǐ shì cóng nǎ gè guó jiā lái de?

Please ask, you are from which country come?

B: 我从英国来的

wǒ cóng yīng guó lái de

I am from England come

A: 你在中国做什么?

nǐ zài zhōng guó zuò shén me?

You in China do what?

B: 我要去北京看长城

wǒ yào qù běi jīng kàn zhǎng cháng chéng

I want go to Beijing see the Great Wall

A: 他们呢?

tā men ne?

Them?

B: 他们是美国人，也要去北京

tā men shì měi guó rén, yě yào qù běi jīng

They are Americans, also want to go to Beijing

Vocabulary

从（cóng），from

哪（nǎ），which

来（lái），to come

国家（guó jiā），country

英国（yīng guó），England

中国（zhōng guó），China

美国（měi guó），America

工作（gōng zuò），work / job / to work

学生（xué shēng），student

小学（xiǎo xué），elementary school

中学（zhōng xué），middle school

大学（dà xué），university

姓（xìng），surname

名（míng），first name

老师（lǎo shī），teacher

警察（jǐng chá），police officer

工人（gōng rén），worker

司机（sī jī），driver

公务员（gōng wù yuán），government official

律师（lǜ shī），lawyer

科学家（kē xué jiā），scientist

服务员（fú wù yuán），waiter / waitress

接待员（jiē dài yuán），receptionist

厨师（chú shī），chef

Phrases

你是哪个国家的人?（nǐ shì nǎ gè guó jiā de rén）

What country are you from?

我是从英国来的（wǒ shì cóng yīng guó lái de）

I'm from England

你在哪里工作?（nǐ zài nǎ lǐ gōng zuò）

Where do you work?

我在美国工作（wǒ zài měi guó gōng zuò）

I work in America

In Chinese word order, the place must come before the predicate. In other words, while in English, you can say, "I work in America," in Chinese, you must say, "我在美国工作." It is incorrect to say, "我工作在美国."

你做什么工作（nǐ zuò shén me gōng zuò）?

What do you do?

我是老师（wǒ shì lǎo shī）

I'm a teacher

我是警察（wǒ shì jǐng chá）

I'm a police officer

请问您贵姓（qǐng wèn nín guì xìng）？

May I ask your honorable surname?

This is a polite, formal way to ask someone's name. It is appropriate especially for people whose social rank is higher or age is older than yours

你叫什么名字（nǐ jiào shén me míng zi）？

What is your name?

This is less formal and more appropriate for social equals or children

穿白衣服的那位女士是谁（chuān bái yī fú de nà wèi nǚ shì shì shuí）？

Who is the lady in white?

你能把我介绍给她吗（nǐ néng bǎ wǒ jiè shào gěi tā ma）？

Could you introduce me to her?

很高兴认识你（hěn gāo xìng rèn shí nǐ）

Nice to meet you

Notes

们 (men)

This suffix word is added to form the plural of "我， 你，他/她/它", and a few words relating to people.

Colloquial Translation of Dialogue

A: Excuse me, which country are you from?

B: I'm from England.

A: What do you do in China?

B: I want to go to Beijing to see the Great Wall.

A: And them?

B: They are Americans. They also want to go to Beijing.

Scenario 17: Talking About Family

Dialogue

A answers a knock at the door and is pleasantly surprised to find their Chinese colleague, Professor B.

A: 教授!请进来吧!

jiāo shòu! qǐng jìn lái ba!

Professor! Please enter!

B: 你好，现在忙吗?

nǐ hǎo, xiàn zài máng ma?

Hello, you now busy?

A: 不忙，不忙。进来坐

bù máng, bù máng. jìn lái zuò

Not busy, not busy. Enter come sit

B: 这张照片里的人是谁?

zhè zhāng zhào piàn lǐ de rén shì shuí?

This picture in is who?

A: 这是我父母和我妹妹

zhè shì wǒ fù mǔ hé wǒ mèi mei

There are my parents and younger sister

B: 你的爸爸做什么工作?

nǐ de bà ba zuò shén me gōng zuò?

Your father does what work?

A: 我的爸爸是司机

wǒ de bà ba shì sī jī

My father is driver

B: 你妈妈呢?

nǐ mā ma ne?

Your mother?

A: 我妈妈在医院工作

wǒ mā ma zài yī yuàn gōng zuò

My mother in hospital works

B: 你的妹妹呢?

nǐ de mèi mei ne?

Your sister?

A: 她还在上学。毕业以后她想当警察

tā hái zài shàng xué. bì yè yǐ hòu tā xiǎng dāng jǐng chá

She still is studying. Graduate after she wants to be police

Vocabulary

进（jìn），to enter

进来（jìn lái），to come in

坐（zuò），to sit / to have a seat

照片（zhào piàn），photo

父母（fù mǔ），parents

妹妹（mèi mei），younger sister

爸爸（bà ba），father

妈妈（mā ma），mother

哥哥（gē ge），older brother

姐姐（jiě jie），older sister

弟弟（dì di），younger brother

儿子（ér zi），son

女儿（nǚ ér），daughter

孩子（hái zi），child

毕业（bì yè），to graduate

家（jiā），home / family

老家（lǎo jiā），hometown

照相（zhào xiàng），to take a photo

读书/念书（dú shū / niàn shū）

Literally, this means “read books”. This means “ to study ” in two senses：

-他还在念书（tā hái zài niàn shū）。

He’s still a student.

-我们今天晚上一起读书吧（wǒ men jīn tiān wǎn shàng yì qǐ dú shū ba）。

Let’s study tonight.

玩（wán），to play

This word is used for adult’s recreational activities as well as children’s, so it is not exactly equivalent to the English word “play”.

Phrases

你家里有几口人?（nǐ jiā lǐ yǒu jǐ kǒu rén）

How many people are there in your family?

你有没有兄弟姐妹?（nǐ yǒu méi yǒu xiōng dì jiě mèi）

Do you have any brothers or sisters?

你结婚了吗?（nǐ jié hūn le ma）

Are you married?

你有孩子了吗?（nǐ yǒu hái zi le ma）

Do you have any children?

你的老家在哪里?（nǐ de lǎo jiā zài nǎ lǐ）

Where is your hometown?

我们照个相吧 wǒ men zhào gè xiàng ba）

Let’s take a picture

您慢走（nín màn zǒu）

This is a fixed phrase that means “Please take care .”

有空来玩（yǒu kōng lái wán）

When you have some time, come over and visit

一路顺风（yí lù shùn fēng）

Have a safe trip

你妹妹还在学校（nǐ mèi mei hái zài xué xiào）

Your younger sister is still in school

Notes

A few tips on politely hosting Chinese guests:

- Addressing someone by name and title when greeting your guests is considered polite and respectful in China.

- Chinese hosts will almost never turn away a guest unless strictly necessary and will apologize profusely if it is necessary to turn away a guest, even an unexpected one.

- Chinese hosts will normally offer drinks and perhaps light snacks. You may need to offer several times before a guest will take refreshments, but you should keep trying. Often it is best to simply provide refreshments rather than asking if the guest wants any—the guest will virtually always say no whether he/she wants something or not.

Strategy: Social conversation

Social conversation with new Chinese acquaintances often starts with questions about family members and what they do, and if you are in a Chinese home, there is a very good chance this conversation will be conducted over a photo album. Having a photo album is also a good strategy when you have Chinese visitors and aren't quite sure what to talk about, especially if there is no common language you both speak comfortably. You might keep a photo album of your own handy as a tool to help you conduct simple Chinese conversations with visitors or other Chinese people you meet.

Colloquial Translation of Dialogue

A: Professor! Come in!

B: How are you? Are you busy now?

A: No, no. Come in and have a seat.

B: Who are the people in this photo?

A: They are my parents, and this is my younger sister.

B: What does your father do?

A: My father is a driver.

B: Does your mother work?

A: My mother works in a hospital.

B: How about your younger sister?

A: She is still a student. But after she graduates, she wants to join the police.

Scenario 18: Personal Questions

Dialogue

Foreigner B is in the middle of her first conversation with inquisitive but helpful Chinese neighbor A.

A: 你成家了吗?

nǐ chéng jiā le ma?

You have formed family?

B: " 成家 " 是什么意思?

"chéng jiā" shì shén me yì sī?

"Formed family" is what meaning?

A: " 成家 " 就是结婚的意思

"chéng jiā" jiù shì jié hūn de yì sī

"Formed family" is to get marries meaning

B: 啊， 我没有结婚

ā, wǒ méi yǒu jié hūn

Ah, I haven't married

A: 那你多大了?

nà nǐ duō dà le?

Well, you how old?

B: 我二十七岁

wǒ èr shí qī suì

I twenty-seven years old

A: 你应该成家了。我给你介绍一个男朋友，好吗?

nǐ yīng gāi chéng jiā le. wǒ gěi nǐ jiè shào yí gè nán péng yǒu, hǎo ma?

You should form family. I for you introduce a boyfriend, okay?

B: 不用，谢谢。我觉得单身不错

bú yòng, xiè xie. wǒ jué dé dān shēn bú cuò.

Not necessary, thanks. I think single not bad

Vocabulary

成家（chéng jiā），to marry

结婚（jié hūn），to get married

老公 / 丈夫（lǎo gōng / zhàng fu），husband

老婆 / 妻子（lǎo po / qī zi），wife

爱人（ài rén），lover

岁（suì），years old

觉得（jué dé），to feel / to think that

单身（dān shēn），single

应该（yīng gāi），should

介绍（jiè shào），to introduce

男朋友（nán péng yǒu），boyfriend

女朋友（nǚ péng yǒu），girlfriend

礼貌（lǐ mào），polite

工资（gōng zī），salary

有意思（yǒu yì si），to be interesting

想（xiǎng），to miss

Phrases

你多大了?（nǐ duō dà le）?\

How old are you?

我二十二了（wǒ èr shí èr le）

I'm twenty-two years old

你结婚了吗?（nǐ jié hūn le ma）

Are you married?

我离婚了（wǒ lí hūn le）

I'm divorced

你想家吗? (nǐ xiǎng jiā ma)

Do you miss your home?

我很想家 (wǒ hěn xiǎng jiā)

I miss home very much

我一点儿也不想家 (wǒ yì diǎn ér yě bù xiǎng jiā)

I don't miss home at all

你在这里习惯吗? (nǐ zài zhè lǐ xí guàn ma)

Are you accustomed to life here?

还不太习惯 (hái bú tài xí guàn)

I'm still not very accustomed

你觉得中国怎么样? (nǐ jué dé zhōng guó zěn me yàng)

What do you think about China?

我很喜欢中国 (wǒ hěn xǐ huān zhōng guó)

I like China very much

我觉得中国很有意思 (wǒ jué dé zhōng guó hěn yǒu yì sī)

I feel China is very interesting

你一个月挣多少钱? (nǐ yí gè yuè zhèng duō shǎo qián)

How much do you make a month?

你的工资多少钱? (nǐ de gōng zī duō shǎo qián)

What is your salary?

These questions are not unusual in China. Possible answers include:

我一个月八千块钱 (wǒ yí gè yuè bā qiān kuài qián)

I make 8,000 *yuan* a month

对不起。外国人觉得这个问题让人不舒服 (duì bù qǐ. wài guó rén jué dé zhè gè wèn tí ràng rén bù shū fú)

Excuse me. Foreigners are a little uncomfortable with this question

我挣钱不多 (wǒ zhèng qián bù duō)

I don't make much

我工资不高 (wǒ gōng zī bù gāo)

My salary is not high

Notes

Many Chinese will be curious about you, and as you get into conversations, you will be asked some questions that would be considered overly personal in Western countries. Of course, it is up to you to decide how much or little to say when answering these questions, but try not to take offense to them. Such questions are generally not ill-intended, and a rude response on your part may only confuse and offend someone who has no idea why you suddenly became so testy.

Colloquial Translation of Dialogue

A: Have you formed a family?

B: What does "formed a family" mean?

A: "Formed a family" means to get married.

B: Ah, I'm not married.

A: Oh, how old are you?

B: I'm twenty-seven.

A: You should get married. Why don't I introduce you to someone?

B: That's not necessary, thanks. I think being single isn't too bad.

Scenario 19: Politely Refusing Requests

Dialogue

B: 你是美国人吗?

nǐ shì měi guó rén ma?

You are American?

A: 是的

shì de

Yes

B: 我在学英语，但是我没有机会练习。你愿意教我英语吗?

wǒ zài xué yīng yǔ, dàn shì wǒ méi yǒu jī huì liàn xí. nǐ yuàn yì jiāo wǒ yīng yǔ ma?

I am learning English, but I don't have opportunity to practice. You willing to teach me English?

A: 对不起，我在学校已经有很多学生了

duì bù qǐ, wǒ zài xué xiào yǐ jīng yǒu hěn duō xué shēng le

Sorry, I at school already have many students

B: 那我周天去找你好吗?

nà wǒ zhōu tiān qù zhǎo nǐ hǎo ma?

Then, I Sundays go look for you, okay?

A: 很抱歉，我实在太忙了

hěn bào qiàn， wǒ shí zài tài máng le

Very sorry. I really too busy

Vocabulary

机会（jī huì），opportunity

练习（liàn xí），to practice

愿意（yuàn yì），to be willing

那么（nà me），well / in that case

找（zhǎo），to look for / to visit

实在（shí zài），really / truly

忙（máng），busy

抱歉（bào qiàn），sorry

交换（jiāo huàn），to exchange

朋友（péng yǒu），friend

Phrases

Two requests foreigners often encounter in China are:

我想练习英语（wǒ xiǎng liàn xí yīng yǔ）

I want to practice English

我们做朋友吧（wǒ men zuò péng yǒu ba）

Let's become friends

我很忙（wǒ hěn máng）

I'm very busy

我的工作很忙（wǒ de gōng zuò hěn máng）

I have a lot of work to do

我没有时间（wǒ méi yǒu shí jiān）

I don't have time

我很乐意，但我恐怕没时间（wǒ hěn lè yì, dàn wǒ kǒng pà méi shí jiān）

I'm glad to, but I'm afraid I don't have time

我们做个交易，好吗?（wǒ men zuò gè jiāo yì, hǎo ma）

Let's make a deal, okay?

This sentence is useful if you want to do an exchange, for example, English lessons for Chinese.

Notes

Strategy: Refusing requests

One problem that foreigners who want to learn Chinese often have in China is that many eager people would love to practice English with a foreigner. Thus, there is a fairly good chance that you will get more offers to practice English than you care to accept, sometimes from total strangers. When you want to refuse, the most common strategy is generally to plead that you are too busy—this excuse is not offensive and is understandable. Suitors may not give up easily, but if you politely persist, you can usually prevail.

Tip: Focusing your efforts

As you move into your work, you will probably have less time for studying Chinese, and your progress in Chinese may well slow down. This is especially a problem if you maintain a full program of study, working simultaneously on speaking, listening, reading, and writing because the more spread out your efforts are, the less progress you will feed into any particular skill area, and the greater the chance that you will become discouraged and quit.

One solution is to devote enough time to studying Chinese that you still make satisfactory progress in all areas. However, an alternative, which is often more realistic, is to narrow the range of your efforts, for example, by just working on speaking and listening for a period, or by focusing heavily on characters for a while. Having a sense of progress is vitally important in maintaining the will to keep studying, and the narrower the range of your efforts is, the more progress you will see in that one area.

Colloquial Translation of Dialogue

B: Are you an American?

A: Yes.

B: I'm studying English, but I don't have a chance to practice. Can you teach me English?

A: Sorry. I already have many students at school.

B: In that case, how about I visit you on Sundays?

A: I'm sorry. I'm really too busy.

Scenario 20: Dealing with the Delivery Company (I)

Dialogue

A is handing two unstamped letters to B, a clerk in a delivery company.

B: 要寄到哪里?

yào jì dào nǎ lǐ?

Want to send to where?

A: 到加拿大。寄到加拿大多少钱?

dào jiā ná dà. jì dào jiā ná dà duō shǎo qián?

To Canada. Send to Canada how much money?

B: 到加拿大要五十元。几封信?

dào jiā ná dà yào wǔ shí yuán. jǐ fēng xìn?

To Canada fifty *yuan*. How many letters?

A: 两封。我再买几张邮票

liǎng fēng. wǒ zài mǎi jǐ zhāng yóu piào

Two letters. I also buy several stamps

Vocabulary

寄（jì），to mail

哪里（nǎ lǐ），where

加拿大（jiā ná dà），Canada

买（mǎi），to buy

再（zài），also / again

包裹（bāo guǒ），package

邮票（yóu piào），stamp

快递公司（kuài dì gōng sī），delivery company

收件人（shōu jiàn rén），receiver

寄件人（jì jiàn rén），sender

爱尔兰（ài ěr lán），Ireland

丹麦（dān mài），Denmark

澳大利亚（ào dà lì yà），Australia

俄罗斯（é luó sī），Russia

德国（dé guó），Germany

菲律宾（fēi lǜ bīn），Philippines

韩国（hán guó），Korea

挪威（nuó wēi），Norway

瑞典（ruì diǎn），Sweden

新西兰（xīn xī lán），New Zealand

意大利（yì dà lì），Italy

法国（fǎ guó），France

芬兰（fēn lán），Finland

荷兰（hé lán），Netherland

日本（rì běn），Japan

泰国（tài guó），Thailand

Phrases

我想寄个件（wǒ xiǎng jì gè jiàn）

I want to send a package

收件地址是美国（shōu jiàn dì zhǐ shì měi guó）

The receiver's address is in America

包裹从北京到美国要多久（bāo guǒ cóng běi jīng dào měi guó yào duō jiǔ）？

How long does it take for a package to get to America from Beijing?

要想快点的话就发个特快专递（yào xiǎng kuài diǎn de huà jiù fā gè tè kuài zhuān dì）

If you want it to be quick, you can send an express mail

Notes

Tip: Practice makes perfect

By now, you may be getting tired of practicing numbers and buying. However, in language studies, there is much to be said for practicing something until you can do it rapidly and almost automatically. One of the arts of language studies is finding variations on basic forms of practice so that you can get the repetition you need without becoming so bored that your mind switches off.

Colloquial Translation of Dialogue

B: Where do you want to send this?

A: Canada. How much does it cost?

B: Fifty yuan. How many letters?

A: Two. I'll also buy several stamps.

Scenario 21: Dealing with the Delivery Company (II)

Dialogue

Foreigner A arrives at the delivery company with a package notice clutched firmly in hand. B is a postal worker.

A: 我来取包裹

wǒ lái qǔ bāo guǒ

I come get package

B: 哪里寄来的?

nǎ lǐ jì lái de?

Where sent?

A: 美国

měi guó

America

B: 有没有带证件?

yǒu méi yǒu dài zhèng jiàn?

Have not have identification?

A: 有，这是我的护照

yǒu, zhè shì wǒ de hù zhào

Have. This is my passport

Vocabulary

排队（pái duì），to stand in line

护照（hù zhào），passport

东西（dōng xī），thing

证件（zhèng jiàn），identification

身份证（shēn fèn zhèng），ID card

工作证（gōng zuò zhèng），work permit

居留证（jū liú zhèng），residence permit

签证（qiān zhèng），visa

拿（ná），to get / to take / to carry

带（Dài），to take / to bring

Phrases

在哪里排队?（zài nǎ lǐ pái duì）

Where should I line up?

我忘记了（wǒ wàng jì le）

I forgot

你有没有带护照?（nǐ yǒu méi yǒu dài hù zhào）

Did you bring your passport?

我一分钱没带（wǒ yì fēn qián méi dài）

I didn't bring any money

Notes

带 (Dài) and 拿 (ná)

While the usage of these two words often overlaps, there are some differences:

带 usually means to carry on one's person, to bring/take with one. For example:

你带了多少钱?（nǐ dài le duō shǎo qián）

How much money did you bring?

我忘记带钱了（wǒ wàng jì dài qián le）

I forgot to bring money with me

拿 usually means to get/take something, and also refers to the physical act of carrying something, for example:

我要去拿包裹（wǒ yào qù ná bāo guǒ）

I'm going to get a package

他忘记拿钱了（tā wàng jì ná qián le）

He forgot to get money (from somewhere)

Colloquial Translation of Dialogue

A: I've come to get a package.

B: Where is it from?

A: America.

B: Do you have any identification?

A: Yes, here is my passport.

Scenario 22: Not Feeling Well

Dialogue

At the guesthouse where she is staying, foreigner A is not feeling well and is explaining to staff B that she wants to see a doctor.

A: 我想看医生

wǒ xiǎng kàn yī shēng

I want to see a doctor

B: 你哪里不舒服?

nǐ nǎ lǐ bù shū fu?

You where uncomfortable?

A: 我的胃很痛

wǒ de wèi hěn tòng

My stomach very painful

B: 你有没有吃药?

nǐ yǒu méi yǒu chī yào?

You have not have eaten medicine?

A: 我没带药

wǒ méi dài yào

I don't have medicine

B: 我带你去医院

wǒ dài nǐ qù yī yuàn

I take you to hospital

Vocabulary

医生（yī shēng），doctor

门诊（mén zhěn），clinic

护士（hù shì），nurse

舒服（shū fu），comfortable

痛（tòng），to hurt / to be painful

病（bìng），illness / to be sick

感冒（gǎn mào），a cold / have a cold

拉肚子（lā dù zǐ），diarrhea / to have diarrhea

发烧（fā shāo），fever / to have a fever

便秘（biàn mì），constipated / to have a constipated

头痛（tóu tòng），headache / to have a headache

咳嗽（ké sou），cough / to have a cough

肿（zhǒng），to swell

断（duàn），to break

怎么了?（zěn me le），what's wrong?

挂号（guà hào），to register at hospital

地方（dì fāng），place

酸（suān），sore

痒（yǎng），itch / itchy

药（yào），medicine

胃（wèi），stomach

头（tóu），head

眼睛（yǎn jīng），eye

耳朵（ěr duo），ear

嘴巴（zuǐ bā），mouth

鼻子（bí zi），nose

喉咙（hóu long），throat

手（shǒu），hand

脖子（bó zi），neck

背（bèi），back

胸口（xiōng kǒu），chest

肚子（dù zi），abdomen

脚（jiǎo），foot

腿（tuǐ），leg

皮肤（pí fū），skin

牙齿（yá chǐ），tooth

舌头（shé tou），tongue

Phrases

你怎么了?（nǐ zěn me le）

What's wrong with you?

Said sympathetically, this is the appropriate inquiry to a person who looks sick or upset. In a sharper tone of voice, it can also be an accusing question about someone's mental competence

你今天感觉怎么样?（nǐ jīn tiān gǎn jué zěn me yàng）

How are you feeling today?

我觉得不太舒服（wǒ jué dé bú tài shū fu）

I don't feel very well

你现在觉得好点了吗?（nǐ xiàn zài jué dé hǎo diǎn le ma）

Do you feel better now?

好多了（hǎo duō le）

Much better

我想看病（wǒ xiǎng kàn bìng）

I want to see a doctor

我病了（wǒ bìng le）

I'm sick

我感冒了（wǒ gǎn mào le）

I have a cold

我拉肚子（wǒ lā dù zi）

I have diarrhea

他头疼的厉害（tā tóu téng de lì hài）

He's got a bad headache

我退烧了（wǒ tuì shāo le）

My fever is gone

我背疼（wǒ bèi téng）

I’ve got a pain in my back

就这儿疼（jiù zhè ér téng）

It hurts right here

吃两片药，好好休息一下（chī liǎng piàn yào, hǎo hǎo xiū xī yí xià）

Take two pills and have a good rest

祝你早日康复（zhù nǐ zǎo rì kāng fù）

I hope you’ll be well soon

去哪里挂号?（qù nǎ lǐ guà hào）

Where do I register?

In a Chinese hospital or clinic, you need to register before seeing a doctor

Notes

Chinese Names of Common Medicines

考的松（kǎo dí sōng），Cortisone

抗真菌（kàng zhēn jūn），anti-fungal

红药水（hóng yào shuǐ），mercurochrome

肌肉止痛膏（jī ròu zhǐ tòng gāo），analgesic cream

止痛药（zhǐ tòng yào），pain relievers

泰诺林（tài nuò lín），Tylenol

必理通（bì lǐ tōng），Panadol

曲马多（qǔ mǎ duō），Tramal

百服宁（bǎi fú níng），Bufferin

阿司匹林（ā sī pǐ lín），aspirin

消炎药（xiāo yán yào）anti-inflammatory drugs

芬必得（fēn bì dé），Fenbid

布洛芬（bù luò fēn），Ibuprofen

感冒药（gǎn mào yào），cold medicines

抗组胺（kàng zǔ àn），antithistimines

抗生素（kàng shēng sù），antibiotics

红霉素（hóng méi sù），erythromycin

安必仙（ān bì xiān），ampicillin

阿莫灵（ā mò líng），amoxycillin

维生素片（wéi shēng sù piàn），vitamins

金施尔康（jīn shī ěr kāng），Gold Theragran

止泻药（zhǐ xiè yào），diarrhea Medicine

易蒙停（yì méng tíng），Imodium

抗恶心药（kàng è xīn yào），anti-nausea medicine

抗酸剂（kàng suān jì），antacids

Colloquial Translation of Dialogue

A: I want to see a doctor.

B: Where do you feel bad?

A: I have a terrible stomachache.

B: Have you taken any medicine?

A: I don't have any medicine.

B: I'll take you to the hospital.

Scenario 23: Getting Things Fixed

Dialogue

Foreigner A needs help from Chinese guesthouse staff B. A's ability to explain is limited, so the goal is just to get someone to come and look.

A: 请你来看看。卫生间有一点问题

qǐng nǐ lái kàn kan, wèi shēng jiān yǒu yì diǎn wèn tí

Please you come look look. Bathroom has a little problem

B: 什么问题?

shén me wèn tí?

What problem?

A: 马桶坏了，你看怎么处理

mǎ tǒng huài le, nǐ kàn zěn me chù lǐ

Toilet has broken, you look how to deal with

B: 我马上联系人来修

wǒ mǎ shàng lián xì rén lái xiū

I immediately contact people come fix

Vocabulary

看（kàn），to look

坏（huài），bad / to break

一点（yì diǎn），a little

帮忙（bāng máng），to help

热（rè），hot

冷（lěng），cold

快（kuài），fast

修理（xiū lǐ），to repair

空调（kōng tiáo），air conditioner

窗户（chuāng hu），window

电视（diàn shì），television

电灯（diàn dēng），light

电话（diàn huà），telephone

床（chuáng），bed

网络（wǎng luò），network

拖鞋（tuō xié），slippers

浴缸（yù gāng），bath tub

马桶（mǎ tǒng），toilet

Phrases

有问题（yǒu wèn tí）

Literally “问题” means problem or question, but in the phrase “有问题” it often means something wrong, for example:

他有问题（tā yǒu wèn tí）

There’s something wrong with him

你还有问题?（nǐ hái yǒu wèn tí）

Do you have any questions?

看看（kàn kan）

This means to take a look. In Chinese, repeated verbs often have the sense of “a little” or “a bit”. The following phrases have the same sense as “看看”:

看一看（kàn yí kàn）

看一下（kàn yí xià）

房间里太热/冷了（fáng jiān lǐ tài rè /lěng le）

The room is too hot/cold

请帮我开门（qǐng bāng wǒ kāi mén）

Please open the door for me

请快一点 （qǐng kuài yì diǎn）

Please hurry a little

请打扫下房间（qǐng dǎ sǎo xià fáng jiān）

Please clean the room

能帮忙移一下冰箱吗?（néng bāng máng yí yí xià bīng xiāng ma）

Would you help me remove the refrigerator?

请帮我拿下外套（qǐng bāng wǒ ná xià wài tào）

Please get me my coat

给我冲杯咖啡，好吗？（gěi wǒ chōng bēi kā fēi, hǎo ma）

Could you make me a cup of coffee?

我不懂（wǒ bù dǒng）

I don't understand

我不知道（wǒ bù zhī dào）

I don't know

请你再说一遍（qǐng nǐ zài shuō yí biàn）

Please say that again

请你说慢一点（qǐng nǐ shuō màn yì diǎn）

Please speak a little more slowly

Notes

了 (le)

Whole dissertations have been written on this little word, but the simple idea is that it indicates that an action has been completed. For example:

我吃了 (wǒ chī le)

I've eaten

我走了 (wǒ zǒu le)

I left

空调坏了 (kōng tiáo huài le)

The air conditioner has broken

她开了窗户 (tā kāi le chuāng hu)

She opened the window

帮（bāng）and 帮忙（bāng máng）

Both mean “ to help”, but “帮” is followed by an object and “帮忙” is not. For example:

请你帮我（qǐng nǐ bāng wǒ）

Please help me

请你帮忙（qǐng nǐ bāng máng）

Please help

Tip: The unfamiliarity of a new language

One of the main problems Westerners face in studying Chinese is the sheer unfamiliarity of the language—it simply sounds so different from a Western language that initially it all seems a blur of sound. Do not despair though—slowly but surely your ears will get used to the sounds and contours of Chinese if you persist and give yourself time.

Colloquial Translation of Dialogue

A: Could you come and take a look? There’s something wrong with the bathroom.

B: What’s the problem?

A: The toilet is broken. Could you help with this?

B: I’ll ask someone to fix it immediately.

Scenario 24: A Long-distance Phone Call

Dialogue

Foreigner A wants to make a long-distance phone call in a small hotel in China. B works at the front desk. C is the operator at the hotel A calls, and D is Mr. Wang.

A: 请问，长途电话怎么打?

qǐng wèn, cháng tú diàn huà zěn me dǎ?

May I ask, long-distance phone call, how to make?

B: 电话号码是什么?我帮你打

diàn huà hào mǎ shì shén me? wǒ bāng nǐ dǎ

Phone number is what? I help you call

A: 不用，我自己打

bú yòng, wǒ zì jǐ dǎ

Not necessary, I myself call

A: 金山酒店吗?

jīn shān jiǔ diàn ma?

Golden Mountain Hotel?

C: 请说大声一点，我听不见

qǐng shuō dà shēng yì diǎn, wǒ tīng bú jiàn

Please speak louder a little, I listen not hear

A: 金山酒店吗?

jīn shān jiǔ diàn ma?

Golden Mountain Hotel?

C: 是的，你找谁?

shì de, nǐ zhǎo shuí?

Is. You look for who?

A: 请转 306 房间

qǐng zhuǎn sān líng liù fáng jiān

Please forward 306 room

D: 喂?

wéi?

Hello?

A: 王先生在不在?

wáng xiān shēng zài bú zài?

Mr. Wang there not there?

D: 我就是

wǒ jiù shì

I am

Vocabulary

长途（cháng tú），long distance

不用（bú yòng），it's not necessary

自己（zì jǐ），self

大声（dà shēng），loud

怎么（zěn me），how

找（zhǎo），to look for

谁（shuí），who

打电话（dǎ diàn huà），make a phone call

房间（fáng jiān），room

转接（zhuǎn jiē），to forward

错（cuò），wrong

分机号（fēn jī hào），extension number

清楚（qīng chǔ），clear

国际（guó jì），international

直拨（zhí bō），direct dial

Phrases

你打错了（nǐ dǎ cuò le）

You called the wrong number

你会不会说英语?（nǐ huì bú huì shuō yīng yǔ）

Can you speak English?

This sentence is useful if a Chinese speaker answers the phone and you need to hint that you would like to speak to someone who knows English

请再说一遍（qǐng zài shuō yí biàn）

Please say that once again

我是外国人，我听不懂（wǒ shì wài guó rén, wǒ tīng bù dǒng）

I am a foreigner. I don't understand

This sentence is useful when you answer the phone and find yourself bombarded with more Chinese than you are ready to handle yet

请说大声一点（qǐng shuō dà shēng yì diǎn）

Please speak a little louder

请讲慢一点（qǐng jiǎng màn yì diǎn）

Please speak a little slower

请讲清楚一点（qǐng jiǎng qīng chǔ yì diǎn）

Please speak a little more clearly

他不在，我能替他捎个口信吗?（tā bú zài, wǒ néng tì tā shāo gè kǒu xìn ma）

He's not in, may I take a message for him?

我一定是拨错号了（wǒ yí dìng shì bō cuò hào le）

I must have dialed a wrong number

我打不通（wǒ dǎ bù tōng）

I couldn't get through

我得挂了（wǒ děi guà le）

I have to hang up

你能明天回个电话吗?（nǐ néng míng tiān huí gè diàn huà ma）

Can you call back tomorrow?

我试着给你打电话，但老占线（wǒ shì zhe gěi nǐ dǎ diàn huà, dàn lǎo zhàn xiàn）

I tried to call you, but the line was busy

Notes

Strategy: Using the phone in Chinese

Using a phone in a foreign language tends to be intimidating because the sound often isn't clear, and you can't see the expression and gestures of whomever you are talking to. However, when the phone rings, you have one great advantage—predictability. The first question the caller will ask 90 percent of the time is "Is so-and-so there?" so successfully answering the phone is largely a matter of having strategies to get the caller to slow down and let you clearly hear the name of the person they want to talk to. Likewise, making a phone call mainly involves getting to the right extension and then finding out if the person you want to talk to is there or not. Most of the time, the few basic sentences in this lesson will get you where you want to go.

Colloquial Translation of Dialogue

A: Excuse me, how do I make a long-distance phone call?

B: What is the phone number? I'll place the call for you.

A: That's not necessary. I'll call myself.

A: Is this the Golden Mountain Hotel?

C: Please speak a little louder; I can't hear you.

A: Is this the Golden Mountain Hotel?

C: Yes. Who do you wish to speak to?

A: Please forward me to Room 306.

D: Hello?

A: Is Mr. Wang there?

D: Speaking.

Epilogue: Making a Plan for Your Chinese Studies

Hopefully, you have enjoyed this book and learned something! You may use the book flexibly according to the actual situations. It has strived to make Chinese easier to learn so that readers can study the language happily, effortlessly, and efficiently.

As mentioned at the beginning of this book, there are different methods for using this book. Therefore, it is encouraged that you make plans for your long-term Chinese studies. As you go about making these plans, you need to be realistic about the fact that independent language study also poses some special problems, and a plan of study which doesn't take these problems into account has a relatively low chance of success. Here are a few of the issues you need to consider:

1- **Limits on your time and energy:** Presumably, most foreigners who can study Chinese full-time will be in formal language programs (both for academic and visa reasons), so those who take an independent study approach are often in China for work-related or travel-related reasons and generally have job, family or other obligations, which make it impossible to study Chinese full time. This means that finding time in your schedule for Chinese lessons, study, and practice may be difficult, and your other obligations which generally seem more immediately pressing, may encroach on—and even overwhelm—your Chinese study. Even if you have enough time in your schedule for a regular but limited study program, you will need to be on guard against discouragement because your progress under such circumstances may only be gradual.

2- **Absence of outside pressure:** One of the great advantages of formal language programs is that tests, grades, and the watchful eye of the teacher provide constant pressure to keep studying. Students in formal programs are often forced to keep studying, and when their will fails, there are external prods to ensure that their efforts don't decrease. On the contrary, as an independent learner, you will usually be under little or no outside pressure to keep studying Chinese. There are usually no tests to worry about, and even no tutor (if you don't find one) to pressure you. Also, foreigners who don't speak Chinese can generally get by in China using English (though the results often aren't very pretty), so pressure from the environment is much weaker than one might initially imagine. All of this means that you will probably be tempted from time to time by the knowledge that you can choose to put off studying Chinese—or even give it up completely—more or less at will. Much is therefore demanded of your will power and self-discipline, more than is the case for students in formal programs.

3- **Absence of structure:** While the goals and methods of a formal language program may not fully match the needs of a given learner, a structured program spares that learner the effort of creating a study program from scratch, and also provides the learner with a sense of direction and progress through the program. In contrast, as an independent learner, more is demanded of you because you need to design your own program. At the practical level, this means going through the effort of setting your own goals, choosing your own study materials and methods, finding a tutor (if necessary), and finding ways to evaluate and measure your progress. At the affective level, you may also be less certain about whether or not your approach to Chinese study is "right", especially if you have limited previous experience with language learning, and this sense of uncertainty may subtly corrode your confidence and resolution. This is especially likely if you adopt a very informal approach to Chinese study, doing a little of this and a little of that without much continuity or sense of a plan. Relatively unorganized study approaches often leave learners feeling that they are not learning much, either because they genuinely aren't or because the absence of structure in their approach denies them bench posts against which they can measure and see their progress, and this sets the stage for deciding that Chinese study isn't worth the effort.

As you have probably noticed, the underlying theme in the problems discussed above is not so much one of technique as it is of feelings, and this suggests one of the most basic truths of language learning: the key to success in language learning is generally sustained effort more than a special technique or language learning talents, so the most important issue is whether or not you can sustain the learning effort over a period of time. The main problem faced by most independent language learners is that it is relatively easy for them to opt out of the Chinese learning process if they become discouraged or feel they are not making enough progress to justify the effort. Designing a good study plan is thus, to a large degree, a question of how to carry out a program of study that you won't give up on. With this problem in mind, here are a few suggestions you may wish to consider as you begin setting out your Chinese study program:

1- **Be realistic about your time and energy:** The first step to successfully sustaining a program of Chinese study is realistically assessing how much time and energy you have to devote to the task, and then designing a study approach that fits within the time you have available. A common mistake that learners make, especially when just starting out with Chinese study, is making an overly optimistic assessment of their time and energy, and then setting goals that are far too high. The problem here is that when learners begin running out of steam, and especially if they fall far below the goals they set, they often get discouraged and quit, either putting off Chinese study until they have more time (a situation which often never materializes) or simply abandoning the effort altogether.

The first step to realistic planning is making a good assessment of how much time a day you can devote to studying Chinese, and also being realistic about how much energy you will have at those times of day when you are free to study. Obviously, you cannot expect to learn as much in an hour of study at a time of day when you are exhausted as you could in an hour when you are fresh and alert. Therefore, you don't need to be harsh on yourself. But remember, learners who stick with sustained study will continue to make progress, and even slow-but-steady study efforts can deliver impressive results if sustained.

2- **Setting limited goals and focusing your efforts:** As suggested above, overly ambitious goals often undermine learners' morale, so you must set reasonably limited goals that you can realistically achieve with the time and energy you have available. One implication of this idea is that it is often wise to focus on a relatively narrow set of goals, especially during the early stages of learning Chinese. For example, it might make more sense for busy people to focus their initial efforts on speaking and listening, only turning later to Chinese characters. The difficulty with trying to make a full-scale assault on Chinese, working on speaking, listening, reading, and writing simultaneously, is that dividing limited time among so many goals will probably result in slow progress toward each, and this tends to be discouraging. In contrast, a narrower focus allows you to make more visible progress in the skills of areas you focus on and encourages you to keep going.

3- **Reward:** Independent Chinese study places more demands on your self-discipline than formal Chinese classes do. As noted above, even if you work with a tutor, there will still be less outside pressure placed on you than would be the case in formal Chinese classes, and there may also be periods when you cannot find a suitable tutor—and when you therefore don't have a tutor to drive your study efforts. Thus, you need to supply the discipline for your learning process if you don't want the whole thing to dissolve into a puddle of good intentions.

When it comes to persuading yourself to study Chinese at the crack of dawn or after a long day at work, you are more likely to study properly if you are doing something you find enjoyable, rewarding, or at least useful. Thus, someone who loves to chat will probably have more motivation for sessions with a tutor, or perhaps for learning some new phrases to try out in a Chinese restaurant, while someone who is fascinated by Chinese characters may be willing to sit down and draw characters with a brush when he/she wouldn't have enough motivation to listen to audios. Know yourself, and as much as possible, design your study approach so that your interests pull you along.

4- **Structure:** Some people learn fairly well just doing whatever they feel like doing on any given day, but for most people, a casual, irregular approach to language learning is a recipe for failure. Perhaps the greatest problem with unstructured approaches to language learning is that they lack the visible indications of achievement that are present in more structured approaches, and learners who do not have the advantage of the encouragement provided by these measures of achievement are more prone to a sense that they aren't making progress.

There are a variety of ways that structure can be introduced into independent Chinese study. One of the most obvious is through the use of a textbook or other Chinese study materials—your progress through the materials provides a visible sense of satisfaction and accomplishment. Another is through setting and adhering to a regular schedule of study and practice. In this case, the amount of your time investment becomes a measure of achievement. A third, less obvious, approach involves establishing a cycle of activities that you carry out for each lesson in your book or topic that you study. For example, a cycle might consist of: Step 1 – Studying a certain lesson in your book; Step 2 – Practicing material from the lesson with a tutor; Step 3 – Trying the new material out in the community, for example, by chatting with the waitress at the nearby Chinese restaurant; and Step 4 – At the next lesson, asking your tutor about anything puzzling that occurred in your practical practice. In this approach, achievement is measured in the number of cycles you carry out. One advantage of this approach is that it not only provides structure for your program but also includes a healthy dose of live practice.

5- **Find a support group:** To a degree that might be surprising, your ability to sustain the study of Chinese will be affected by the company you keep. Unlike learners in formal Chinese programs, who have a ready-made support group of fellow learners, many of the people you live and work with—especially other Westerners—may not share your interest in learning Chinese. If this is the case, you will probably get only minimal encouragement in your efforts learning Chinese, and you may well face at least some social pressure not to devote too much time to Chinese. Keep in mind that many Westerners in China explain their failure to learn Chinese by arguing that it is simply too hard, and your progress in Chinese might make others look bad by comparison. It is thus important that you try to find at least one or two people—either other Westerners or Chinese—who will support and encourage you as you learn Chinese.

6- Making your own plan:

The strategy carried out by the suggestions above is that you need to take charge of your language learning by investing time in making your own plan for studying Chinese. Among the issues that you will need to consider are:

- *What are your initial study goals?* For example, do you wish initially to focus on speaking and listening skills, or do you want to work on Chinese characters right from the start?

- *What study materials will you use?* For example, if you are working with a textbook, you might consider also having your tutor (if you have one) make language audios for you to increase your amount of listening practice. If so, what kind of material would be best to put on the audios?

- *How are you going to spend your study time?* Again, assuming you are working with some kind of textbook, what is the best way for you to learn the material in any given lesson? Keep in mind that different people often have very different learning styles, so through trial and error, you need to find approaches that work well for you.

- *How do you wish to spend any time you have with a tutor if you finally hired one?*

- *How will you practice the material you learn outside language class?* You need to practice if you are to really master the material you study, so it is important to find ways to practice your Chinese in the community.

Obviously, it takes some time and effort to think about all of these things, and this list of questions may have left you longing for a teacher who would simply tell you what to do. However, by deciding these issues for yourself, you take advantage of the opportunity to tailor-make your own approach to studying Chinese, an approach that suits your goals, personality, learning style, and skill levels much better than any off-the-rack Chinese class could. Learners who take control of their Chinese learning this way generally wind up with a study program that gives them a high level of return for the effort they invest, and this provides excellent conditions for significant progress in learning Chinese.

Although you have finished this particular language journey, never stop learning because it will benefit you a lot. All in all, well done for studying and completing this book, and good luck with your further studies on the Chinese language!

CPSIA information can be obtained
at www.ICGtesting.com
Printed in the USA
LVHW081454070723
750156LV00057B/22